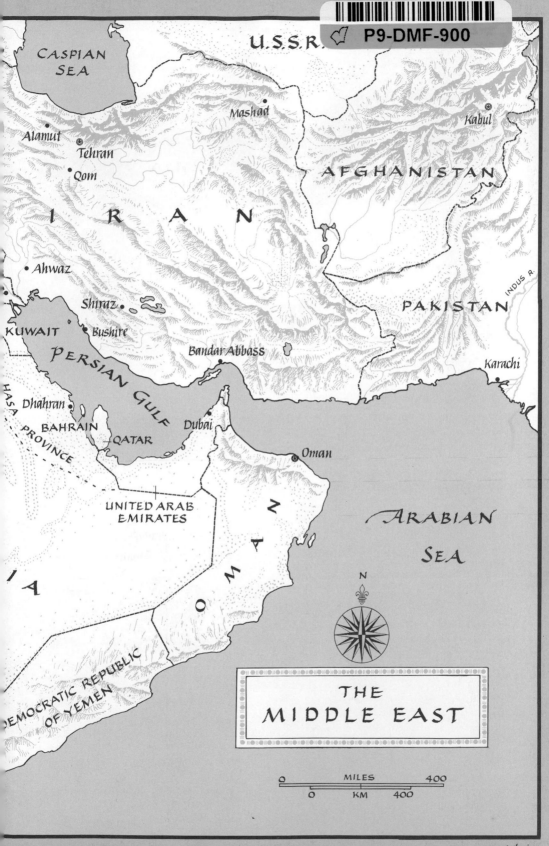

P9-DMF-900

CASPIAN SEA

U.S.S.R.

Mashad

Kabul

Alamut

Tehran

AFGHANISTAN

Qom

I R A N

Ahwaz

Shiraz

Bushire

Bandar Abbass

PAKISTAN

KUWAIT

PERSIAN GULF

INDUS R.

Karachi

HASA

Dhahran

BAHRAIN

PROVINCE

QATAR

Dubai

Oman

UNITED ARAB EMIRATES

O M A N

ARABIAN

SEA

IA

DEMOCRATIC REPUBLIC OF YEMEN

N

THE MIDDLE EAST

MILES
0   400

0   KM   400

palacios

SACRED RAGE

The Crusade of Modern Islam

ROBIN WRIGHT

LINDEN PRESS / SIMON & SCHUSTER
NEW YORK 1985

Simon & Schuster Building
Rockefeller Center
1230 Avenue of the Americas
New York, New York 10020
LINDEN PRESS/SIMON & SCHUSTER and colophon are trademarks of
    Simon & Schuster, Inc.
Designed by Levavi & Levavi
Manufactured in the United States of America

10 9 8 7 6 5 4 3 2

Library of Congress Cataloging in Publication Data
Wright, Robin B., date.
  Sacred rage.

  Includes index.
  1. Islam and politics—Near East.   2. Near East—

Politics and government—1945–   . 3. Lebanon—
History—1974–   . 4. Terrorism—Near East.
5. Violence—Religious aspects—Islam. 6. Islam—
20th century. I. Title.
DS63.1.W75   1985   956.04   85-18126
ISBN: 0-671-60113-X

To a woman whose only comment when I covered my ninth war was
"How marvelous to be in the middle of history" and who is so much
more than my mother

And to the memory of my father

One man with beliefs is equal to a thousand with only interests.
—JOHN STUART MILL

Contents

Acknowledgments

I owe thanks to so many for assisting in preparing or promoting this book. My first thanks must go to *The Sunday Times* of London, particularly to Stephen Milligan, James Adams and Cal McCrystal, who gave me the time, resources and encouragement to probe the Islamic movement throughout the Middle East. Duke University's Institute of Policy Sciences and Public Affairs offered me a semester break to collect my thoughts, for which I am deeply grateful to Professor James David Barber and Vice President William L. Green, Jr. Special note should also be given Professor Sheridan Baker of the University of Michigan, who tirelessly read through more than one version of the book, and was pivotal in all decisions about structure, organization and style.

The book could not have been written without several vital sources in the Middle East and in Western capitals who specifically asked not to be named. They include members of the diplomatic and intelligence communities, as well as Muslim moderates and fundamentalists. I appreciate their trust and openness in sharing information with me.

I have relied heavily on Middle East and Islamic specialists to check the historic and religious aspects of the manuscript. Many have generously shared their expertise with me. From the beginning, Professor Augustus Richard Norton of West Point, who did extensive field work in Lebanon and has an unusual knowledge of the Shi'ites, went to great trouble to point me in the right direction and provide solid background material.

Others who have offered helpful criticism or suggestions that were incorporated into the text include Professors Bruce Kuniholm and Bruce Lawrence at Duke, Professor James Bill at the University of Texas, Professor R. K. Ramazani at the University of Virginia, and Dr. Marvin Zonis at the University of Chicago. Brian Jenkins at the

Rand Corporation shared his expertise on terrorism with me, and Professor Tom Rowe at Duke University Law School offered useful advice. Colonel Alfred J. Baker, who served twice in Lebanon, with the United Nations and as chief of the U.S. Office of Military Cooperation, read through the manuscript thoughtfully to check particularly the military aspects. Timur Goksel of the United Nations provided endless clippings and sources of information throughout my stint in the Middle East.

I also owe an enormous debt to my colleagues, especially David Ottaway of *The Washington Post* and David Smith of Britain's ITN television. Both read the manuscript and provided useful insights and criticism. They and others provided solid reporting that helped me along the way, especially while I was out of the region finishing the book. Those who gave me crucial assistance, directly or indirectly, include Tom Friedman of *The New York Times,* John Borrell of *Time,* Jonathan Randal of *The Washington Post,* John and Penny Kifner of *The New York Times,* Robin Mannock of the Beirut *Daily Star,* Tewfik Mishlawi of *The Middle East Reporter,* Hirsh Goodman of *The Jerusalem Post,* Gerald Butt of the BBC, Agnetta Ramberg of Swedish Radio, Chris Drake of NBC and Allen Pizzey of CBS. There is no way of thanking each of them sufficiently.

A great deal of credit is also due two women. My mother spent many months helping with research, proofreading and the tedious aspects of writing a book. Marjorie Williams has been a friend as well as a thoughtful and thorough editor. Special thanks should also be given to Robben and Sally Fleming, who have been a major influence in my life for many years. Last but not least, I must acknowledge Jim Ginley, who, after months of agonizing by so many over an appropriate title, finally came up with "Sacred Rage."

1 The Crusade

THE GROWTH OF ISLAMIC FUNDAMENTALISM IS AN EARTH-QUAKE.

—*SAEB SALAM, FORMER LEBANESE PRIME MINISTER*

WE MUST SETTLE OUR ACCOUNTS WITH GREAT AND SUPERPOW-ERS, AND SHOW THEM THAT WE CAN TAKE ON THE WHOLE WORLD IDEOLOGICALLY, DESPITE ALL THE PAINFUL PROBLEMS THAT FACE US.

—*AYATOLLAH KHOMEINI*

URGENT

BEIRUT, Lebanon (AP)—A powerful explosion ripped through the U.S. Embassy compound in Beirut Monday, setting off a fire and causing an undetermined number of casualties, police said.

The American Embassy switchboard was not answering telephone calls shortly after the 1:05 P.M. blast at the seaside compound in West Beirut's mostly Moslem Ein Mreisseh neighborhood.

A towering cloud of brownish smoke was seen looming from the area of the embassy shortly after the explosion. . . .

Associated Press, Monday, April 18, 1983

Robert Ames, a former CIA station chief in Lebanon, had just begun a meeting with eight intelligence operatives on that brisk Monday afternoon. Ames, elevated to CIA Middle East analyst, had returned to Beirut from the U.S. for "consultations." The nine agents were meeting on a top floor of the U.S. Embassy's north wing, offices favored because they afforded a spectacular view over the Mediterranean.

Downstairs, Lebanese gendarmes manning the red-and-white striped security booth in the front driveway saw a dark delivery van approach. This was unusual, since the small parking space in front of the embassy was reserved for the ambassador's vehicles. But drivers with heavy goods often tried it. No one survived to tell how this driver managed to make the sharp left swing into the guarded cobblestone lane and ram straight into the front wall.

The deafening roar seemed to echo throughout Beirut. Behind the black smoke that enveloped the entire seven-story complex, Ames and the eight operatives were crushed to death, wiping out the top level of U.S. intelligence in Lebanon. The Lebanese guards were literally torn to pieces. In all, sixty-three corpses, or bits of bodies collected in blue plastic bags, were counted after a week of digging. More than a hundred others had been injured. This bombing by a daring suicide driver ranked as the bloodiest terrorist attack ever against a U.S. diplomatic mission.

But it was only the beginning.

BULLETIN

BEIRUT, Lebanon (AP)—Two car bomb explosions devastated the U.S. Marine command center at Beirut's International Airport and a command post of the French contingent of the Multi-National Peacekeeping Force early Sunday, according to the state radio. It reported heavy casualties in both sites. . . .

Associated Press, Sunday, October 23, 1983

Lieutenant Joe Golebiowski was making breakfast tea at his position on the Marine perimeter when the blast nearly shook him off his feet. He immediately cranked up the field telephone to headquarters to ask where the bomb had gone off. There was no answer. He grabbed his binoculars. Then he realized he was looking at a view he had never been able to see before. The headquarters had always stood in the way.

Blood caked on his Marine fatigues, Major Bob Jordan, a survivor, surveyed the pile of twisted steel and crumpled concrete that just minutes before had been the living and working center for an entire Marine battalion. Rescuers were now frantically digging for survivors of yet another suicide truck bombing. Jordan said with quiet fury, "I haven't seen carnage like that since Vietnam."

No wonder. It was in fact the worst disaster for the U.S. military since the Vietnam War: 241 Marines and Navy personnel were dead, dozens more left crippled for life. The suicide attack was no longer an isolated incident, but a trend, one that neither the massive intelligence apparatus nor the elite military wing of the free world's superpower could prevent.

Scapegoats within the military were found, blame was laid on them for inadequate security, their careers were ruined. But the internal reprimands served only to prove that the U.S. and its Western allies still did not understand the dimensions of this new phenomenon.

In anonymous telephone calls made after each attack to boast of responsibility, "the trend" called itself Islamic Jihad—or Islamic Holy War. Little was known about those responsible except that they were thought to be Shi'ite Muslims. The U.S. and others searched desperately for names and a structure behind the invisible force. It appeared they did not fathom the basic clue in the name itself, as well as abundant other evidence.

And that was to cost more lives.

URGENT

KUWAIT (AP)—A truck packed with explosives rammed through the gate of the U.S. Embassy compound Monday and blew up in one of six car bombings that rocked this tiny Persian Gulf state.

Other targets included the French Embassy, a power station, the control tower of Kuwait Airport, an oil depot and a U.S. residential compound. . . .

Associated Press, Monday, December 12, 1983

Ahmed Shama, a U.S. Embassy receptionist, was at his desk when "the ceiling fell on our heads . . . We heard screams outside, people asking for help, but we did not know what happened to them." William Miller, a Cleveland businessman staying at the Hilton across the street, said he saw fires at the compound and "people staggering around dazed. I told my wife last week that I was safe in Kuwait, unlike Beirut," he said. "But I don't know. I am thinking of leaving the country right now."

This time there were six bombs. This time the attacks were in the nation with oil reserves that, according to production levels, would last longer than anywhere else in the world. If the connections linking the explosives to gas cylinders had not been faulty, Kuwait might have been permanently crippled.

More frightening, as the Americans saw it, the threat had now expanded from chaotic Lebanon, where violence was almost endemic, to the Gulf. The region under threat was, economically and strategically, one of the most important in the world.

■   ■   ■

In 1983, more people were killed or injured by international terrorists "than in any year in which governments began keeping records," Deputy Secretary of State Kenneth Dam later disclosed. "It is a fact that the United States is the favorite target of terror," he said, noting that some two hundred of the five hundred terrorist attacks worldwide in 1983 were against U.S. facilities and personnel. In 1984 the number of terrorist attacks increased to 652, according to State Department figures. And in the first three months of 1985, there were 200 attacks around the world.

"Normally, wars are not won by dying for one's country. They are won by making the enemy die for his. Unfortunately, holy wars are not waged under this harsh but rational precept," wrote *Time* after the Kuwait blasts.

After the 1979 Iranian revolution, the Middle East had begun witnessing a virulent new strain of terrorism that spread like an infectious virus. The results, proportionate to the brief time span, were more deadly than any terrorist trend experienced since the Arab–Israeli conflict began in 1948.

The early targets were not Western. Many incidents were spectacular and well publicized: the 1981 plot to overthrow the government of Bahrain and install an Islamic republic; sabotage and assassination attempts over an extended period against the President of Iraq; the 1979 seizure of the Grand Mosque in Mecca, and uprisings that year and the next in the oil fields of Saudi Arabia; the assassination of Egyptian President Anwar Sadat in 1981. But scores of other incidents had passed and been forgotten: airplane hijackings, six alone in three years by one Lebanese who was never tried or jailed; kidnappings of Arab civilians and officials; assassinations or shootings of others; attacks on cultural centers and Arab businesses.

Only when Westerners came under attack did the United States begin to look deeper. By the end of 1983, the Reagan administration officially labeled the trend "state-sponsored terrorism" and charged that, in the Middle East, the Iran of Ayatollah Ruhollah Khomeini was chiefly responsible. Under the intense scrutiny of the media and the diplomatic and intelligence communities, Shi'ite Islam, the name of the so-called "second sect" after the mainstream Sunnis, became virtually synonymous with terrorism.

It is not quite so simple, or so one-sided.

The roots of the trend date back thirteen centuries, and have more to do with the fanatic adherents of religious groups than with the leadership of a single country. They are fundamentalists. They belong to more than one Muslim group, and more than one sect. Their movement amounts to a crusade.

So far, attempts to understand the crusade have led to suggestions that a wrathful Muslim world is rising up in a holy war against Christianity or Judaism, capitalism or communism. An extension of this view warns of the "domino" or regional menace—that one state after another will "fall" if militant Islam makes further headway. Paradoxically, this way of thinking both exaggerates the phenomenon in some ways, and underrates it in others.

First, it is unfair to attribute the entire phenomenon to Iran, for Islam throughout the seventy nations with significant Muslim populations that make up "Dar al Islam," or the House of Islam, was headed in a militant direction long before the Iranian revolution. Indeed, since the faith was founded thirteen hundred years ago, almost every century has witnessed sporadic outbursts of fundamentalism. Islamic fundamentalism in the 1980s is also far from being exclusive to Iran or the Shia. The impact of the crusade has been the most obvious in the twenty-one Arab League nations stretching from North

Africa through the Persian Gulf. And, although the dramatic tactics of the Shia have made them more visible, fundamentalist extremism has also grown among the mainstream Sunnis.

Second, Islam does not promote terrorism. Indeed, in its doctrines, Islam is the most tolerant of the world's monotheistic religions. It accepts Christians and Jews as "people of the book," and their leaders as men of the same God. Nor is there any quality inherent to the Shia, or any other sect of Islam, that promotes terrorism.

Third, the crusade is not a coordinated phenomenon. One writer has argued: "There is no single worldwide Islamic resurgence, but there has been a series of coincident upheavals in which Islam is the common expression of political dissent." Unlike other insurgents and terrorists, the Muslim commandos are not members of a single group or nation; their tactics and intensity are as diverse as their backgrounds. The various groups should not be interpreted or handled as one, even though the historic roots and current motives of the various groups often appear to be similar. There is no single worldview, Shi'ite or Sunni. In Beirut alone, the groups differ from neighborhood to neighborhood, and are often in disagreement with one another.

Yet it is true that the Islamic crusade is the greatest single threat to the status quo in the region, as well as to Western powers that rely on the strategic position and the mineral resources of moderate Muslim states. In varying forms, it has become widespread, stretching from Saudi Arabia on the Persian Gulf into Lebanon and Tunisia on the Mediterranean, and on through North Africa to Morocco on the Atlantic. No single trend has so threatened the interests of Arab, Israeli, Western and, to a lesser degree, Eastern governments. Nor has any movement sparked such visible fear.

The Islamic Republic of Iran has indeed played a major role. The fall of Shah Mohammed Reza Pahlavi inspired those who have seen themselves as underdogs and victims at the hands of other Muslims as well as of foreign ideologies. Most Shia, and many Sunni, have been affected—and their faith has been strengthened—including those who disagree with the practices of the theocracy in Tehran. Even the Soviet Union, which has the fifth-largest Muslim population in the world, and China, where there are three times as many Muslims as in Saudi Arabia, have felt some spillover from the Iranian experience.

Beyond acting as a model and a catalyst, Iran has also actively encouraged the crusade, providing resources, the means for those already willing to become martyrs in righting perceived injustices.

Ayatollah Khomeini has been open about his ambitious dreams. Six months after his triumphant return to Iran, ending fifteen years in exile, he declared, "The governments of the world should know that Islam cannot be defeated. Islam will be victorious in all the countries of the world, and Islam and the teachings of the Koran will prevail all over the world."

More specifically, he said: "We have in reality, then, no choice but to destroy those systems of government that are corrupt in themselves and also entail the corruption of others, and to overthrow all treacherous, corrupt, oppressive and criminal regimes. This is the duty that all Muslims must fulfill, in every one of the Muslim countries, in order to achieve the triumphant political revolution of Islam."

Much of what has happened would not have occurred without the Iranian revolution. In particular, Iran has played on the anger and frustration of one small group of Shi'ites who have launched a protest, a very vicious protest, against their regional rivals and the West. Emphasis must be placed on "small." Of the 832 million Muslims in seventy nations—accounting for almost one-fifth of mankind— roughly 10 percent are Shia, and the violent extremists are but a tiny percentage of that.*

It is a distortion to view Shi'ite Islam as the personification of terrorism. But the Shi'ite "soldiers of God," while only one part of a multi-faceted movement, are certainly symbolic of the Islamic crusade, not only because they have succeeded in the most extreme forms of violence, but because they are the most visible and vivid elements of the Islamic crusade.

Their actions are a protest against what they feel are injustices— first from other Muslims, beginning shortly after the faith was founded in the seventh century. That bitterness has built up over more than one millennium. It has been accentuated during confrontations with the West over the past two centuries, since Napoleon conquered Egypt, making France the first Western power to control a Muslim territory. Western dealings with and attitude toward the Islamic bloc since World War II have been the final straw.

* Thirty-two countries have Muslim majorities of 85 percent or higher.

But the Shia extremists are by no means alone. Sunni fundamentalists, most of whom do not have the same motive as the downtrodden
minority, have also responded to the Islamic reawakening symbolized by Iran. The accumulated reaction has been an explosion of
Muslim fervor in the 1980s.

■   ■   ■

THE TACTICS of the bombers and assassins and hijackers have rede-
fined the word "security." Embassies and government ministries
throughout the Gulf and the Arab heartland have become fortresses,
some complete with tank traps and machine gun emplacements at
their gates. The approach and the pace of business, education, diplomacy and government have been dogged by the proportionate dangers involved.

And still it has not been enough.

URGENT
    BEIRUT, Lebanon (AP)—Lebanese state and private radios re-
ported an explosion Thursday at the East Beirut annex of the U.S. Embassy. Lebanon's state radio said the explosion was in the building and
may have started a fire . . .
                        Associated Press, Thursday, September 20, 1984

Chief Warrant Officer Kenneth Welch had been in Lebanon less
than four months, working as an operations coordinator in the office
of the Defense Intelligence Agency. With the bulk of the embassy
staff, he had moved to the annex less than two months earlier—for
security reasons. Christian-controlled East Beirut was considered
safer than the Muslim west, where all the earlier attacks and kidnappings had taken place.

Welch was typing a report at his desk on the third floor shortly
before noon that Thursday when a cream-colored Chevrolet van
maneuvered past a concrete dragon's-teeth barricade and several
Lebanese guards at the cordoned entrance road leading to the annex.
Welch appears to have stood up after hearing guards fire shots at the
van. He was not fast enough. The force of the two-thousand-pound
load of explosives blew the tall, solidly built officer against the wall.
His neck snapped.

Thirteen others also died. More than thirty were injured.

"We are not against the American people," said a young member of the Shi'ite "Party of God" two weeks later. "We are against oppression and injustice. The fire of Islam will burn those who are responsible for these practices [against Islam]. We have been dominated by the U.S. government and others for too long." A leading Shi'ite academic put it another way: "The extreme expressions of fundamentalism are expressions of despair."

■   ■   ■

TWO GREENISH-BLACK STONE PLAQUES listing in gold letters the names and dates of 143 U.S. diplomats killed in the line of duty hang in the lobby of the State Department Building in Washington. The first plaque begins in 1780, with the name of a diplomat lost at sea, and ends in 1967. The second plaque has almost been filled in eighteen years, as diplomats have increasingly become victims of terrorism. As of the spring of 1985, when this book went through final revisions, four of the last five people whose names were added to the plaque had died at the hands of Shia extremists. The names of Ken Welch and another military attaché who died in the second embassy bombing in Beirut, and two U.S. Agency for International Development envoys killed in the hijacking of a Kuwaiti plane to Tehran, were added in a ceremony in May. A third plaque is already being planned.

Yet, for all the agonizing results of the Islamic crusade, it did not happen in a vacuum or without precedent. Religions besides Islam have also been vulnerable to extremist elements throughout history. The recent incidents include the murder of a U.S. congressman and the suicide deaths of 913 followers of the People's Temple Cult at Jonestown, Guyana, in November 1978. In 1984, Sikh religious militants assassinated Indian Prime Minister Indira Gandhi. A bomb planted by the Catholic Irish Republican Army narrowly missed British Prime Minister Margaret Thatcher during the 1984 Conservative Party convention, but four people were killed and thirty-two injured. Right-wing Jewish fanatics deeply embarrassed the Israeli government with attacks on moderate Jews as well as on Arabs.

In the past decade, a worldwide rebirth of religious fervor has touched many average Christians as well, often also spilling over into politics. In an interview about the extreme Muslim fundamentalists, a member of the National Security Council staff pointed out that the premier issues of 1984 in the United States were religion-oriented. He raised issues such as abortion and prayer in the schoolroom. Jerry Falwell's right-wing "Champions for Christ" had grown to such an extent by 1984 that they were courted as a power bloc during the U.S. elections. To say that is not, however, to equate the various movements.

Among the other indicators have been the popularity and the policies of Pope John Paul II, as well as the "liberation theology" of activist priests and nuns in Latin America and the Philippines. Poland's Solidarity unions grew out of a church base. Anti-apartheid champion Bishop Desmond Tutu, the black Anglican who has campaigned against South African racism, was awarded the 1984 Nobel Peace Prize. Ironically, he was fighting minority repression often justified with Biblical quotations by ministers of South Africa's Dutch Reformed Church.

"Religious intensity was thus ascribed solely to Islam even when religious feeling was spreading remarkably everywhere," wrote a leading Arab scholar at Columbia University.

■   ■   ■

BY SHEER COINCIDENCE, I first landed in the Middle East, Beirut specifically, on October 6, 1973—the day the fourth modern Arab–Israeli war broke out, an event that was to play a key role in the Islamic revival. I was en route to Iran. I made subsequent trips, but finally moved to the most fascinating and troubled region in the world in 1981.

This book basically covers the wave that struck the Middle East in the aftermath of the Iranian revolution, among both Shia and Sunni, from the first Iranian-backed coup attempt in Bahrain and the assassination of Egyptian President Anwar Sadat in 1981 through the 1985 Israeli withdrawal from Lebanon under pressure from Shi'ite militants—the period I spent traveling the breadth of the region from Morocco in North Africa to, by this time, a very different Iran on the Gulf.

I am neither an Islamic expert nor an Arabist; many learned specialists offer precise histories, on which I have relied heavily. I am merely a Western reporter who lived in the region during the fundamentalist explosion. I witnessed many of the events, and their impact. Among my friends and acquaintances in the Middle East were several victims of the crusade, again a coincidence, but a painful one. Because I am a reporter, I tried to understand why they were maimed or killed, and who was behind it. In the process I also came to meet several of the militant cadre and sheikhs. The result is this book.

The crusade is still in its early days. It may last a long time, or it may not. Much will depend on how it is handled, and how it is understood. This book is an attempt to trace what has been happening, why, and how the crusade operates, not to implicate any specific person or group. Nor is it an attempt to defend the crusade in the court of world public opinion.

This book raises a lot of questions; it has few answers. It is only a preliminary investigation, probing some of the events and people involved in order to put the trend, and Iran's fluctuating role, in perspective. It also attempts to point out some of the mistakes, particularly by the West, that have only provoked the Muslim fundamentalists rather than coped realistically with what they represent. The stakes have never been so high, the potential for misunderstanding and further violence never so great.

2 The Turning Point: Iran

THE MORE PEOPLE WHO DIE FOR OUR CAUSE,
THE STRONGER WE SHALL BECOME.
—*AYATOLLAH KHOMEINI*

THEIR RAGE SUPPLIES THEM WITH WEAPONS.
—*VIRGIL*, AENEID

The pastel walls and rich tapestries at the Tehran Hilton were once an apt backdrop for the Miss Iran competition, the flow of exotic and fleshy beauties parading through the halls every year during the Shah's reign, the highlight of the conference season. But by the spring of 1982 the Hilton had become the Independence Hotel, the entrance walk painted with large American and Soviet flags for guests to tread on. And it was the setting for a very different event.

On a crisp day in March 1982, just as the snow was beginning to soften on the stunning mountain skyline north of Tehran, some 380 men with various religious and revolutionary credentials met at the former Hilton conference hall. Most were wearing large wrapped turbans and austere robes, the severe blacks and browns appropriate for the serious atmosphere, the stern expressions. The occasion was a "seminar" on the seemingly innocuous subject of "the ideal Islamic government."

A few years earlier, the participants had been obscure figures, barely known beyond their own neighborhood mosques in Iran, Kuwait, Saudi Arabia, Lebanon, Bahrain and elsewhere. But with the revolution and the rise of Ayatollah Ruhollah Khomeini in Iran, the title of sheikh, hojatoleslam or sayyid suddenly carried international weight. Before, each had had influence, a local following. Now they had power, and a national base. Together, these men represented one of the newest forces on earth, and one of the oldest. Washington and Paris, Jerusalem and Moscow had only begun to feel its impact. The first scores, of eventual thousands, had died because of its doctrine. The entire Middle East was rumbling under a force that fit no convenient label, no familiar pattern. In the process, the world was learning who the Shi'ites were.

The seminar symbolized a turning point.

"We shall export our revolution to the whole world. Until the cry 'There is no God but God' resounds over the whole world, there will be struggle," Ayatollah Khomeini had said shortly after the 1979 revolution. The founder and spiritual mentor of Iran's transformation from a monarchy to a theocracy also declared, "Islam is the religion of militant individuals who are committed to truth and justice. It is the religion of those who desire freedom and independence. It is the school of those who struggle against imperialism." Within days of the seminar, he added: "Weapons in our hands are used to realize divine and Islamic aspirations."

The Ayatollah often and angrily threatened powers both near and far, warning that Gulf rulers who did not surrender to Islam would be "put to the sword and dispatched to hell, where they shall roast forever." And he pledged total "support for all movements and groups that are fighting to gain liberation from the superpowers of the Left and the Right."

The men at the seminar, hosted by the Association of Militant Clerics and the paramilitary Revolutionary Guards, all preached similar and occasionally even more militant lines. During the conference, they talked of Islam as "a weapon in revolutionary wars against the rich and corrupt. . . . Far from being an opium of the masses," Islam would "wake them up from the sleep of centuries, putting a sword in their hands and sending them into battle against the forces of Satan." Brought together from more than two dozen Arab and Islamic nations, they represented the heart of a movement advocating worldwide Islamic revolution. This comparatively small group of men was to set a course that would affect the world.

The conclusions of the seminar were vaguely worded and riddled with rhetoric. But the crucial bottom line was a declaration: under the guidance of these men, Islamic militants—mainly Shia, but including some Sunnis—would launch a large-scale offensive to cleanse the Islamic world of the "Satanic" Western and Eastern influences that were hindering its progress. To date, they had managed to carry out only a loose, rather haphazard campaign against other Muslim regimes. Now their operations would be intensified and expanded to include the West, specifically those nations that supported and supplied Iran's rivals. In effect, it was the launching of a crusade.

"When they came together," explained Abbass Shekouhi, the Iranian chargé d'affaires in Bahrain, "they agreed, first, that religion should not be separated from politics. Secondly, the only way to achieve true independence was to return to Islamic roots. Third, there should be no reliance on superpowers or other outsiders, and the region should be rid of them. Fourth, they recommended that the Shia should be more active in getting rid of foreign powers."

The timing, three difficult years after the Shah's humiliating demise and the Ayatollah's triumphant return from exile, should have indicated the seminar's importance. If nothing else, the conference, the first of many, should have been probed as an important indicator of a new attitude or mood among a powerful minority in the region.

"The turning point was the ability of Iran to break the back of internal armed opposition and to maintain power during two years of war, and run the economy," said a leading Iraqi financier with the highest Iranian connections. "This coincided with the seminar. People became more certain that the revolution was a successful enterprise. They were willing to commit themselves and more actively to inspire others to follow suit."

It was, in many ways, a heady period for the Iranians. As the mullahs consolidated their hold on government and territory, they demonstrated a new confidence—and an interest in expanding their sights. The combination of Shia Islam and revolution had finally demonstrated its long-standing potential and had been accepted as a dynamic force in the twentieth century.

At the time of the seminar, every party interested in Iran seemed to focus on other developments within that nation's borders. With little access and less success, Western intelligence agencies were scrambling to learn more about the eighteen-month-old war between Iran and Iraq. Hundreds of thousands of Iranian troops had massed along the swampy southwestern border. A new offensive, code-named Operation Fateh, or "conquest," looked as though it might turn the tide of the draining conflict in Iran's favor. Within a month, the offensive had retrieved an enormous chunk of territory, some 8,500 square miles, from the better armed and trained Iraqis, who lost up to twenty thousand men in death and injuries or as prisoners.

Fateh was the bloodiest and most effective campaign since Iraq invaded Iran, technically over the disputed Shatt al Arab waterway, in the fall of 1980. It was a strange conflict, as one wire service reported, fought with the weaponry of the 1980s, the tactics of World War I and the fervor of an Islamic holy war. Iraq, which had originally assumed a quick victory over the strange new fanatic regime, was suddenly losing ground.

Meanwhile, East bloc agencies were equally obsessed with the crackdown on Iran's communists, the powerful Tudeh Party whose members had demonstrated alongside the Shia militants against the Shah and had provided many of the skills for government during the transition. Leftists were now suddenly purged from positions of power, others detained in notorious Evin Prison, and some executed. And the Soviet Union, which shares a long border with Iran, was condemned in the media with the violent disparagement normally reserved for the Americans. At mass celebrations a month after the seminar, held to mark the fourth anniversary of the birth of the Islamic Republic, demonstrators stomped on and spit at the Hammer and Sickle as angrily as at the Stars and Stripes.

In the Arab world, leaders had initially smirked at the arrogant and hated Persians' boasts about exporting their revolution. A series of poorly planned schemes linked to Iran, including a foiled coup in Bahrain four months before the seminar, had all been clumsily conspicuous. Middle East intelligence agencies considered the Ayatollah's Iranian and Arab protégés a mere lunatic fringe of Islam. The "liberation mullahs," as they were derisively nicknamed, were thought to preach a return to the dark ages of the seventh century to Shia Muslims deemed too ignorant or inconsequential politically to count. Their headquarters were in mosques and "husseiniyehs," the uniquely Shia mourning houses and social centers. No Gulf leader in the twentieth century took funeral-parlor politics very seriously. They ignored the fact that these were the only places to which Islam's largest minority, oppressed as heretics by mainstream Sunnis for more than a millennium, turned for comfort and recourse—and to be mobilized.

With attention elsewhere, the seminar passed with little notice. Some foreign quarters wrote it off as merely another gab session among the militants. But the participants were in no hurry. "The leaders of the liberation movements and the mullahs of all the Islamic world, not just Arabs, . . . realized it would not happen in one minute," Shekouhi explained. "It was for every leader at the seminar to take back to his Islamic country and preach to his followers."

Two years later, however, nervous cabinet ministers in oil-rich Gulf States, State Department analysts in Washington, and Soviet envoys in Beirut looked back on the conference with both frustration and concern, all by then trying to find out more about it. For the names of the clergymen who attended that seminar had come back to haunt the vulnerable sheikhdoms as well as the power centers on four continents.

Some Gulf officials later attempted to play down the new strategy that emerged from the Tehran seminar as a reflection of Iran's failure rather than its new strength. The seminar "was a change of tactics, not policy," said Bahrain's unusually candid Minister of Information, Dr. Tariq al Moayyed. "It had to take into account the failure of the revolution to pick up support [outside Iran] on its own steam. The rising masses did not rise. There were no calls to prayer from the roofs of government buildings. It did not happen as they expected. That left one option, to become much more militant than before."

Whether because of success or of failure, Iran did indeed enter a new phase of militancy after the seminar. Within the next three years, Iranian and other fanatic operatives introduced a new modus operandi into the murky annals of terrorism, a trademark that was often the only indicator of who was ultimately responsible for some of the most troubling misadventures of the twentieth century.

What started in Tehran shot through the veins of Islam from Beirut to Baghdad, from oil fields to battlefields.

■   ■   ■

EXACTLY TWO YEARS after the Tehran conference, another seminar was held, this one at the State Department in Washington. It was organized to discuss the terrorist threat emanating from Iran. The United States was finally beginning to recognize the depth of the trend, if for no other reason than the mounting toll of American victims: 52 held hostage in Tehran between 1979 and 1981; 68 killed in embassy bombings in Beirut and Kuwait in 1983; 241 U.S. Marines slaughtered less than five months before the Washington meeting.

Dr. Marvin Zonis, director of the Middle East Institute at the University of Chicago, had a stunning comment about the "Psychological Roots of Shi'ite Muslim Terrorism" at the Washington seminar:

> The message from Iran—no matter how bizarre or trivial it sounds on first, second, fourth or thirty-ninth hearing—is in my opinion the single most impressive political ideology which has been proposed in the 20th century since the Bolshevik Revolution . . . If we accept that Bolshevism is a remnant of the 19th century, then I want to argue that we've had only one good one in the 20th—and it's this one . . . This powerful message will be with us for a very long time—no matter what happens to Ayatollah Khomeini.

The analysis was not outrageous. Others, including both Shi'ites and victims of the fundamentalists' fanaticism, had begun to say the same thing.

At the very least, the West had recovered enough from the shock of the Shah's demise to begin to analyze the scope of what Ayatollah Khomeini had accomplished in Iran. Between 1925 and 1979, a father and son—the first and only ruling members of the Pahlavi dynasty—governed "in the best tradition of Persian kingship." Together, they changed the image and name of the nation, trying to convert underdeveloped Persia into a modernized Iran. Clustered around the Pahlavis, a small Iranian elite often referred to as the

"Thousand Families" monopolized power and resources at the expense of the masses, whose dissent was usually and often brutally suppressed. While the West saw Shah Mohammed Reza Pahlavi as an enlightened moderate, he was viewed as a tyrant by many at home.

For thirty-three years of that era, the United States was Iran's most important ally. The close relationship was perhaps most evident when, threatened with losing his power in 1953, the Shah received CIA assistance in the overthrow of Iranian Prime Minister Mohammed Mosaddegh, who had been successfully undermining the royal family's position. The magnitude of the U.S. role is still disputed, but as one former American diplomat in Iran wrote: "Whatever U.S. involvement actually was, it became an article of faith throughout Iran that the American participation had been critically important, and that therefore the Shah was a U.S. 'puppet.' "

After his return to power, the Shah embarked on a major project to develop Iran. While Iranians may have been ready for modernization, the majority of the fiercely proud population was not prepared to accept the Westernization and the appearance of excessive U.S. domination that came with it. In the end, they rejected the political and cultural price of the Shah's programs—and the United States. Throughout 1978 and 1979, millions took to the streets to protest. The Shah was forced into permanent exile.

Yet to most Westerners, "revolution" was still only a word applied to the end of rule from the Peacock Throne. They did not yet see that the Ayatollah had done something even more remarkable: He had not only used religion as a political base, but also employed its dictates as the means, the tool of action.

■   ■   ■

DECISIONS TAKEN at the Tehran seminar were not difficult to implement. The groundwork for the second phase of the Islamic crusade—the use of Arab cadre, recruited or imported from surrounding countries, to spread the revolution—had already been well prepared at a drab four-story concrete headquarters in downtown Tehran. It had been operational since shortly after the 1979 revolution.

Nicknamed Taleghani Center by foreign intelligence agencies, the building was virtually unapproachable due to the tough bearded

Revolutionary Guards, conspicuous by the simple pale-blue badges on the breasts of their dull-green fatigues, posted at all corners of the building. The lights behind the shades usually burned late at Taleghani.

The preachers of the most extreme fundamentalist dogma, Shia and some Sunnis, and including many of those who attended the 1982 seminar, worked out of Taleghani. Some even slept there. The pretentious-sounding Islamic Front for the Liberation of Bahrain was on the same floor as an Iraqi Shia movement as were, for unknown reasons, the Moros of the Philippines. Kuwaiti, Saudi, North African and Lebanese clerics were in other sections. Taleghani was the nerve center of the revolutionary crusade. It served as the communications and organization headquarters, a place where plans for recruiting and deploying the fraternity of the faithful had gained momentum.

Most of the foreign groups housed at Taleghani, each with its own leadership and militia arm, came under the umbrella of the "Council for the Islamic Revolution" supervised by Ayatollah Hussein Ali Montazeri, the heir apparent of Ayatollah Khomeini—another indication of the movement's prominence. Although most of the council's members were clerics, it also included secular members as well as regular "advisors" from Syrian and Libyan intelligence agencies. Both countries supported the crusade in different ways and for different reasons. The council reportedly received more than $1 billion annually—contributions from the faithful in other countries as well as Iranian government allocations—to support the various branches.

The crusade was also institutionalized within the Revolutionary Guard Corps and Iran's Foreign Ministry, under men such as Hossein Sheikholeslam. The U.S.-educated youth had been one of the student leaders behind the taking of the U.S. Embassy in Tehran in November 1979, and was later appointed to a high post in government. The ministry was reportedly involved in roles both major and minor, including regular liaison with militant clerics from other countries, such as those who attended the seminar, and providing false passports and visas for recruits.

The same month as the seminar, Iranian President Ali Khamenei boasted, "We have aided the liberation movements in the best possible manner, and no government has had the right or power to tell us that we have intervened in their internal affairs. . . . No one can tell us to stop publicizing our version of Islam or stop us from describing our revolution to the people of the world."

The combined efforts made dramatic headway. Incomplete tallies of Gulf governments indicate that several thousand youths had flocked to this center. "Nineteen eighty and 'eighty-one were bad times," said one Bahraini official. "Students in the Gulf had a tendency to drop their books and go to Tehran to join the call. Many had gone to become mullahs. They wanted to participate in a religious way, but they were siphoned off to the liberation camps for training and fighting."

They were not all students. The vast majority were poor, from large and devout families willing to lose a breadwinner in the name of The Cause. Some were idealistic middle-class rebels against families or the system; most were between sixteen and thirty years old. But they all had a common motive: they wanted radical change in the name of Islam. They came from every country in the region, and often beyond. The largest group was Iraqi, mainly because of the tens of thousands of Shia who either fled to Iran or were forced into exile after the Gulf war broke out in 1980.

The young men sneaked across the Gulf waters, human cargo for the booming, usually illegal dhow trade between the sheikhdoms and Iran. They drove over arduous roads through Turkey or Pakistan. And sometimes they arrived by plane via Damascus or Dubai, two of the few places in the Arab world that had maintained air links with Tehran. The traffic was so heavy that one Taleghani official waited full time at Mehrabad airport—where the airport terminal greeted arrivals with a huge "Death to the U.S.A." sign—to channel the new recruits to camps, or "schools of death," as they were nicknamed in the Gulf.

The volunteers were dispersed to camps throughout Iran, all run by the Revolutionary Guards. Libyans, North Koreans, Pakistanis, South Yemenis and guerrillas of the Palestine Liberation Organization were also among the trainers. There were three bases in Tehran alone. Later, a wing of the former U.S. compound, which was converted into a Revolutionary Guards school, was also used for the foreign commandos. Another facility, specializing in intelligence training, was in the confiscated villa of General Nematollah Nasiri, the chief of the Shah's draconian secret police, SAVAK, who had been summarily executed within weeks of the revolution. Other primary camps were in Ahwaz, Isfahan, Qom, Shiraz, Mashad, and in a facility converted in 1984 near the southern naval base at Bushire, where Iranian warplanes took off to hit Gulf oil tankers when the war on land spread to the sea. Conditions were rough, row after row of bunk beds squeezed into cavernous rooms badly in need of paint and scrubbing.

The training was basic. The Shia commandos drilled on automatic rifles, American M-16s as well as Soviet AK-47s, machine guns and grenade launchers. Few learned about heavy artillery; the high caliber was rarely needed for their operations. More important were the delicate formulations of explosives and the mechanics of trucks, a combination so regularly used in their schemes. The elite "volunteers for martyrdom," elsewhere known as suicide squads, were separated from the majority. They were identifiable from the ordinary recruits by sweatsuits with an Iranian crest embroidered on the left breast, and by red bandanas painted with Koranic scriptures tied around their foreheads.

In early 1984, the respected French magazine *Jeune Afrique* carried a chilling picture of the volunteers undergoing the religious indoctrination so pivotal to the crusade. Each of the bearded young men was plugged into a portable stereo, intently listening to lectures extolling the virtues of death. Pictures of Ayatollah Khomeini were pinned over their hearts. "I can in one week assemble five hundred faithful ready to throw themselves into suicide operations. No frontier will stop them," Mohammed Taki Moudarrissi, leader of the broad-based "Islamic Amal" movement, boasted in a rare interview in 1984.

Once trained and dispatched back into the Arab world, the cadre often trained others, then set up local networks. The cells were so secretive that crack teams of foreign investigators were usually unable to penetrate them or prove with concrete evidence the suspected linkage to either Iran or the seminar participants from other countries. An American professor and a French businessman held captive in Lebanon by Shia extremists for sixty-six days were never able to identify who kidnapped them. Kuwaiti security police might never have unraveled the lower layer of operatives behind six explosions if it had not been for the lone thumb left behind by an inefficient suicide bomber.

"America is now facing the real revolutionaries, not the phony revolutionaries who want to be on the cover of *Time* magazine," explained Lebanon's leading historian, Kamal Salabi. "For a change we are witnessing something genuine. These people are content with being anonymous. They thrive on the inner satisfaction of watching Reagan squirm."

Indeed, there was something different about this seemingly mystical, unstoppable force. Nothing in modern history had presented such a broad threat to both East and West, or to all religious and secular ideologies.

■   ■   ■

"WARS COME to provide martyrs and that God may prove those who believe," the Koran says. "Paradise is only to be attained when God knows who will really strive and endure." Khomeini and the radical mullahs in his court used these and other lines to legitimize and promote self-sacrifice among followers, the Iranian youth for the war with Iraq, and the Arab cadre for the crusade elsewhere.

Most Islamic scholars argue vehemently that the Koran actually forbids suicide. But to these Shia fundamentalists, sacrifice in defense of the faith was not suicide, just as bombings and assassinations were never seen as terrorism. One became a martyr, a "soldier for God." And martyrdom was a ticket to heaven. Terrorism became honorable in the war against Satan.

One of the most frequently told stories in the Gulf involves a 15-year-old Iranian fighter captured by the Iraqis. He was bleeding and weeping. When an Iraqi officer told him not to worry because his wounds were not serious, he cried even harder. "That is not why I cry. I didn't die," he sobbed. "God does not want me."

The last note left by one young Iranian soldier who died in the war with Iraq reflected the depth of commitment. "My wedding is at the front and my bride is martyrdom," wrote Mohsen Naeemi. "The sermon will be uttered by the roar of guns. I shall attire myself in my blood for this ceremony. My bride, martyrdom, shall give birth to my son, freedom. I leave this son in your safekeeping. Keep him well."

During the Fateh offensive, I toured the southwest front on the Iranian side and saw scores of boys, aged anywhere from nine to sixteen, who said with staggering and seemingly genuine enthusiasm that they had volunteered to become martyrs. Regular army troops, the paramilitary Revolutionary Guards and mullahs all lauded these youths, known as baseeji, for having played the most dangerous role in breaking through Iraqi lines. They had led the way, running over fields of mines to clear the ground for the Iranian ground assault. Wearing white headbands to signify the embracing of death, and shouting, *"Shaheed, shaheed"* ("Martyr, martyr"), they literally blew their way into heaven. Their numbers were never disclosed. But a walk through the residential suburbs of Iranian cities provided a clue. Window after window, block after block, displayed black-bordered photographs of teenage or pre-teen youths.

A Western official struggling to keep tabs on Tehran remarked, "As we are learning, these are not the odd men out. Whatever hardship stories come out of Iran, it remains a source of pride to the Shia. In one place in the world, they are on top. They truly live in a different world, their thinking totally alien and incomprehensible to the Western mind. We keep thinking they will come to their senses and realize this foolhardiness will cost them their one and only life. What is hard for us to fathom is that this is what life is all about to them, a gateway to heaven that must be earned."

■   ■   ■

A THIRTEEN-CENTURY-OLD PARABLE explains how Shi'ism promotes the concept of conscious martyrdom, or purification through death, which is at the root of the faith. The parable centers around one of the three figures most revered by the Shia throughout history.

In A.D. 680 Hussein, grandson of the Prophet Mohammed, and a small band of followers set out to defend the right of his family's line to the role of caliph—the Prophet's successor or Islam's chief "representative" on earth—which had been taken by the Sunnis. The Caliph of the Umayyad dynasty had thousands of troops; Hussein had fewer than one hundred fighters and a handful of women and children. His advisors all warned Hussein that the overwhelming odds against him guaranteed his defeat and death. But to Hussein it was more honorable to die for belief than to live with injustice. At the

Iraqi town of Karbala, they were all massacred by the Caliph's army. It was the precedent for a tradition that not only survived, but grew in importance with time.

Hussein became the Supreme Martyr, the symbol of man's struggle against tyranny. Husseiniyehs, the mourning houses and religious study centers, were named after him. And each year since his death, a reenactment of the events at Karbala marks the most important religious celebration for Shia throughout the Middle East. In each Shia community, the ten days of Ashura end with the "passion play" of Hussein's death.

"The Imam Hussein was a revolutionary hero who gave his life in the struggle, not as a purely symbolic gesture, but with a real social objective," explained British writer Edward Mortimer in *Faith and Power.* "The duty of Muslims today was to carry on the struggle, to create a classless society and abolish all forms of capitalism, despotism and imperialism."

Hussein left a legacy of "the ultimate protest," the roots of a movement centered around revolt as a duty to and in the name of God. The inherited and constantly reinforced belief was that the Shia were victims of authority and persecution, that they had an ongoing mission either to resist or to challenge the system. "Hussein sacrificed his life and those of his followers in the seventh century in an effort to realize Shi'ite rule over all Muslims. Khomeini has revived the goal of self-sacrifice as a means of achieving Islamic goals," added Dr. Zonis. Martyrdom was the best and most honorable defense of their faith, attacks on rivals or challengers were noble and heroic, not acts of desperation or bloodthirsty terrorism.

■   ■   ■

BUT THE AYATOLLAH was not the first to revitalize the original strategy of the Shi'ite faith. At least once before the Iranian revolution, a branch of the Shia had taken this doctrine to an extreme. And that was nine hundred years ago.

The word "assassin" actually originated with a Shia sect, the hashashin, murderous suicide attackers who launched daring raids against both Christian Crusaders and Sunni Muslim opponents throughout the Middle East. Legend and *The Oxford Dictionary* claim that the word evolved from the hashish administered to the young killers before their missions. The drugs induced a state of euphoria and provided "a foretaste of the delights of heaven" awaiting their success. Islamic scholars argue that the name more likely was an expression of contempt by other Muslims for the fanatical beliefs and outrageous behavior of the Assassins.

The first Assassins can be traced to the year 1090 and to a man named Hasan al Sabbah. His mountain fortress of Alamut, in what is now Iran, led to his revered title as the "Old Man of the Mountain." As a young man and, as lore would have it, a classmate of Omar Khayyam, Sabbah converted to the Ismaili sect, an offshoot of Shi'ism. Although there is little firsthand history about him, he appears to have been a visionary and a man of immense energy, hungry for personal power.

In his fiery preaching to hundreds, maybe thousands, during travels in the area, Sabbah stressed the principle of blind obedience and total commitment to the faith. Some historians conclude it was his charisma and conviction, rather than his doctrine, that drew a large following of converts.

Retreating after a decade to an impregnable compound near the Caspian Sea, Sabbah built a corps of followers. They were men infused with a sense of expectation and exhilaration—prepared to die for their faith, or sometimes, apparently, for Sabbah's whim. Schooled and trained from youth in the isolation of the mountain, these men provided a network of fighters to carry out secret single missions. Armed only with daggers or swords, the young men were usually assigned to murder Turkish or Abbasid potentates and officers who dared to challenge the Old Man or trespass in his region. The odds against Sabbah's corps were reportedly always overwhelming, death in the line of duty almost certain. But in return for their martyrdom, Sabbah promised them a place in Paradise.

Marco Polo was one of the few outsiders who managed to penetrate the fortress. He wrote about his visit with one of Sabbah's successors in 1273:

> He kept at his court a number of the youths of the country, from twelve to twenty years of age, such as had a taste for soldiering, and to these he used to tell tales about Paradise . . . Then he would introduce them into his garden, some four or six or ten at a time, having first

made them drink a certain potion which cast them into a deep sleep, and then causing them to be lifted and carried in. So when they awoke, they found themselves in the garden ... so charming, they deemed that it was Paradise.

Now, this prince, whom we call the Old One, kept his court in grand and noble style, and made those simple hill folks about him believe firmly that he was a great prophet. And when he wanted one of his "Ashisin" to send on any mission, he would cause the potion whereof I spoke to be given to one of the youths in the garden, and then had him carried into his palace. So when the young man awoke, he found himself in the castle and no longer in Paradise; whereat he was not over well pleased ...

So when the Old Man would have any prince slain, he would say to such a youth: "Go thou and slay so and so; and when thou returnest my angels shall bear thee into Paradise. And should'st thou die, nevertheless even so will I send my angels to carry thee back into Paradise." So he caused them to believe; and thus there was no order of his that they would not affront any peril to execute, for the great desire they had to get into that Paradise of his. And in this manner the Old One got his people to murder anyone whom he desired to get rid of.

By the thirteenth century, "assassin" no longer referred to a devotee, but to a trained professional killer. Thanks to terrified Christian Crusaders, the word became commonplace in Western usage. Young troubadours of Provencal in France crooned, "You have me more fully in your power than the Old Man has his Assassins." And an unidentified Frenchman wrote to his beloved, "I am your Assassin, who hopes to win Paradise through doing your commands."

The antagonism and the fear can be traced in part to the murder in 1192 of Conrad of Montferrat, a leader of the Crusaders and later King of the Latin Kingdom of Jerusalem. He was just one of many victims in the Assassins' campaign to intimidate the foreigners into leaving the Islamic lands. A German priest known as Brocardus wrote an analysis of the potential dangers of a new crusade for King Philip VI of France in 1332: "I name the Assassins, who are to be cursed and fled. They sell themselves, are thirsty for blood, kill the innocent for a price and care nothing for either life or salvation."

The protection and spread of Sabbah's Ismaili faith against the far larger and more powerful Sunni sect—and any other force that challenged him—was the original motive for his militant fanaticism. But this was seldom recognized by the Westerners, themselves obsessed with the preservation and expansion of their religion.

The Assassins' sect remained a potent force in the Middle East for two centuries, establishing a network of Assassin fortresses in Iran, Iraq, Syria and what is today Lebanon, until conquering Mongols eventually pushed the Assassins into obscurity. But the tales of their power were often dragged out of history books in the early 1980s— after a new wave of bombings, hijackings and kidnappings began. The comparisons of their tactics with those of the Islamic Republic of Iran were sometimes falsely and sometimes accurately described.

■   ■   ■

YET IT WOULD BE STRETCHING HISTORY and the truth to say that the Assassins are the models for today's Shia commandos. They did share an anxious and zealous desire to purge their communities of foreign encroachment or influence. And both employed the most extreme tactics to accomplish it. But today's Islamic crusade differs deeply from the earlier brand of militancy or fundamentalism. The radical clergy in Iran and their supporters elsewhere have a more specific program. Its tenets and appeal are not simply reactive and negative, but positive. It propounds a course of action leading to a concrete alternative, answers (of whatever debatable nature) to issues and problems for Muslims today.

Ayatollah Khomeini described the goal: "It is our duty now to implement and put into practice the plan of government established by Islam . . . We will create a strong new current of thought and a powerful popular movement that will result in the establishment of an Islamic government." If he had been referring only to Iran, this brand of militant Islam might not have shaken up the Middle East or frightened the rest of the world.

"The Islamic revolutionaries of Iran, and their supporters elsewhere, did not see their revolution as confined to Iran," explained Mortimer.

> Iran was the vanguard or nucleus around which the Islamic umma [the Muslim community] could be reconstructed as successive Muslim countries threw off their chains and restored authentic Islamic government. . . . Like the French Revolution of 1789 and the Russian revolution of 1917, the Iranian revolution was based on principles of

universal applicability, and implicitly threatened all the regimes in
the neighborhood, if not in the whole world.

Imam Khomeini's "vision" has had such powerful effect, partly
because he gave himself the title "Valayat-e Faqih," which means
Guardian of Religious Lawmaking, the most authoritative title of any
Shi'ite leader on earth, and one with strong political overtones as
well. It allows him to speak as the chief authority until the missing
twelfth Shi'ite Imam returns to earth. Since Iran was the first nation
to accept the Shi'ite faith as a state religion, in 1502, and remains the
only major Shia-dominated power in the world, the Guardian can
claim influence over far more than Iran. His specific power and more
ephemeral appeal were such that a widely respected British analyst
predicted about the Ayatollah in 1979: "He is not merely the man
who brought down the Shah, he is seen to portend a chain of upheavals whose cumulative effect would pose the greatest challenge to the
existing internal order since the second world war."

Ultimately, Iran would like to see the original Islamic world re-
united, the dividing boundaries dissolved between the Muslims in
Asian, Arab and African states. "Boundaries should not be considered
as the means of separation of the school of thoughts," Ayatollah
Khomeini said within months of the revolution. "Not only does Islam
refuse to recognize any difference between Muslim countries, it is
the champion of all oppressed people."

Certainly the Sunni, who have been numerically and politically
dominant throughout the Muslim world for thirteen centuries, resist
this interpretation of Islam. Major disputes have also erupted about
what percentage of Iranians and Shia elsewhere, including members
of the clergy, truly support Ayatollah Khomeini's militant program.
But because of the passion and doctrine of Shi'ism, Khomeini's title
arguably gives him more de facto power over a religious constitu-
ency than any other leader in the world. "Islam wants all the world
to be one family," he said.

Islam, while respecting one's homeland, which is one's place of
birth, does not place it before Islam. . . . The notion that we are Iranian and they are Lebanese or from some other place is not propounded in Islam. . . . There are no separate accounts . . .
Islam has come to unite all the peoples of the world, whether Arab

or non-Arab, Turk or Persian, with each other into a great umma called the umma of Islam and to establish it in the world so that those who want to gain control of these Islamic governments and Islamic centers will be unable to do so.

Taking one country, some one thousand miles away, as an example, he said: "We consider Lebanon to be a part of Iran because we are not separate from each other. We are as they and they are as us."

Yet the Persian extremists claim they are not prepared to promote their revolution by use of conventional military strength. "The western media is trying to frighten the world about the export of the Islamic revolution of Iran," charged Ali Akbar Hashemi Rafsanjani, the cleric who is also speaker of Iran's mullah-dominated parliament. "We have announced that we are for the export of the revolution and have explained what we mean by this. We have launched an Islamic movement and Islam must prevail in the region. . . . We will never conquer a country through the use of our army, unless that country commits an act of aggression against us."

The Iranians have been shrewd enough to realize that, to make a true revolution, the roots must grow from within, not be implanted by external force. Conventional arms did not overthrow the Shah, which is one of the reasons that revolution was so awesome. The Shah had been the police chief of the Gulf, his army the strongest by far in the whole region. Nor will regular troops be used to try to bring down rulers elsewhere—except perhaps in Iraq, which initiated a war. Yet the militant Shia, lacking both the willingness and the ability to launch an outright military onslaught, are still among the most aggressive and ambitious forces in the world.

The crusade operates in two ways, differing dramatically for those within and forces outside the faith—as outlined again in the conclusions of the Tehran seminar. The outside world notices the crusade mainly because of its terror, a bombing here, a hijacking there, assorted kidnappings. These are the crusade's reactions to foreign pressures and intrusions, real or imagined. It amounts to a liberation movement, a purifying process, designed to free the Islamic territory and mind of the physical, intellectual and spiritual influences from non-Islamic cultures. For this effort, the crusade's means are, like the Assassins, often destructive.

But for the average Shia, and many Sunni, in the Middle East, the crusade offers something positive. The fundamentalist doctrine is an attempt to reorient all aspects of everyday life—politics, economics, the law and social mores—around the teachings of Islam. Ridding the Muslim world of its foreign imitations is but a small part of the goal. The top priorities are writing new constitutions, distributing national resources more equitably, and restructuring tax systems so they will be less exploitive or burdensome. These goals have great appeal.

For the individual, weighted by the feeling of injustice, fundamentalism has offered a renewed sense of confidence and direction. The appeal has been reinforced by regular contacts and reinforcements from the clergy, messages of support for the oppressed minorities at Friday prayers and in the media, solutions in the Koran to the questions, big and little, of life. As the Iranian ambassador to Lebanon explained in early 1985, "The most prominent achievement of the Islamic revolution in Iran . . . is the molding of a new Muslim man capable of rising up to the challenge, standing fast and winning victory."

In a secular age—of test tube babies and moon landings, the computer ranking as *Time*'s "Man of the Year," and apocalyptic weaponry spawning fears of a nuclear winter—the challenge is, appropriately, fundamental. Like Jerry Falwell's Champions of Christ, the appeal centers on the questioning of basic values and the orientation of life: What is life, and what do you want of it? What serves as your model?

"We have arrived at the end of the world," said Mohammed Taki al Moudarrissi, one of a pair of Iraqi-born Shi'ite brothers who figure prominently in the crusade's headquarters in Tehran. "The presidents and the ministers are devouring themselves. The armies are traitors. Society is corrupt. The privileged, the notables do not concern themselves with the poor. Only Islam can give us hope."

A Gulf cabinet minister, who is Sunni, acknowledged the attraction in a 1984 interview: "There is a halo of respect for the thirty years of Mohammed and the first caliphs, their lives of devotion and poverty, living in humility and away from materialism, demonstrating a willingness to die [for the faith]. When Khomeini emerged, he symbolized all those things. He was worshiped by the Arabs and all the Islamic world. He was a source of inspiration for all. He captured the admiration of all."

The weapon, like the goal, is Islam. "You know and have seen from history that Muslims at the advent of Islam, with a small but united and devout number of people, in less than half a century achieved victory and conquered almost all of the world of that time," Ayatollah Khomeini has preached. The re-creation of a past, one of glory and independence for Muslims, is thus to be accomplished by the means of a bygone era: total commitment, literally, of one's life to the crusade.

"They were one with each other. The weapon of faith was held in their hands. When will we hold this abandoned weapon of faith in our hands?" the Ayatollah asked. "God willing, the Lord will help us Muslims to awaken, will help us Muslims to familiarize ourselves with our Islamic and divine duties."

"God willing," and with a big assist from the temporal authorities in Iran and their allies. As the Iranian leader predicted in a speech to senior government officials, "We have reached a point where nations have become aware of us. The nations have awakened to the matter. They will further awaken."

3 The Roots: A Profile

DO BATTLE IN THE PATH OF GOD AGAINST THOSE WHO BATTLE YOU.

—*THE KORAN*

THE MOST POWERFUL SINGLE FORCE IN THE WORLD TODAY IS NEITHER COMMUNISM NOR CAPITALISM, NEITHER THE H-BOMB NOR THE GUIDED MISSILES—IT IS MAN'S ETERNAL DESIRE TO BE FREE AND INDEPENDENT.

—*SENATOR JOHN F. KENNEDY, 1957*

Les Bradley is a tough twenty-year veteran of the Royal Air Force, a burly fighter pilot whose face was entirely reconstructed after a crash. Later, as a commercial pilot, he was one of the few daring enough after the outbreak of Lebanon's civil war in 1975 to fly dozens of mercy missions of food, blankets and medicine from Cyprus to Beirut International Airport. Bullets once hit the fin of his aircraft.

But the day Bradley remembers most vividly is February 24, 1982. It had been a bad flight for Kuwait Airways 561. It was a milk run from Kuwait to Lebanon, on to Libya and Tunisia, and back by the same route. On the trip out, officials under Libya's eccentric Moammar Qaddafi had bumped passengers from the flight in order to make space for some deportees. Then on the way back from Tunis, the same Libyan officials refused to accept a group of disembarking Indian laborers who had been promised jobs and given visas. Bradley was forced to keep them on board.

There were usually hitches on this run, Bradley later recalled stoically. As he set down in Beirut at teatime that day, he was thinking, Only one more leg and we're home. He began shutting down the engines, allowing passengers to disembark.

Then all hell broke loose. Bradley's co-pilot was the first to see the black Mercedes racing across the tarmac toward the plane. But it happened too quickly for any warning. Bradley was reaching for paperwork when the panel suddenly lit up. "Pieces of glass sprayed in the cockpit. Some hit me. Someone was firing into the plane. At first, I couldn't believe they were firing at me, but they were. The instrument panel blocked some of the bullets.

"I tried to look outside to see what was happening," he said. "There were guys running around the nose of the plane chasing disembarking passengers back on board." It all happened too quickly to do anything. Five young men armed with submachine pistols and Soviet-made AK-47 automatic rifles rushed to the stairs and burst into the cockpit. Seven more were fanning out around the plane on the tarmac.

Bradley realized at once that the scruffy kids meant business. At the orders of the full-bearded commander, large packets of dynamite were speedily attached to the front and rear doors of the Boeing 707. Terrified passengers were ordered to remain in their seats. "The first hour was real dicey," Bradley said. "You could tell their adrenaline was really going. I had the impression that if I made one move they'd blow me away. I was getting ready for the big nothing." When Lebanese airport officials refused demands to move military vehicles encircling the aircraft, the attackers fired off rocket-propelled grenades at the control tower to prove their determination.

To the astonishment of the press, by then frantically scrambling outside the terminal for information, the leader finally identified himself to Bradley and the control tower as Hamza, the Shi'ite Muslim youth who just seventy-nine days earlier had commandeered a

Libyan Arab Airlines 727 in midair between Zurich and Tripoli for what turned out to be one of the longest hijackings in aviation history. It was a six-thousand-mile odyssey, with stops in Beirut, then Athens, Rome, Beirut again, and Tehran before ending peacefully on its third stop in Lebanon three days later.

The Kuwait plane was Hamza's sixth airline heist.

Like all the previous Hamza hijackings, this one was motivated by the disappearance of a religious leader, Imam Musa al Sadr, the Iranian-born friend and colleague of Ayatollah Khomeini. Imam Sadr was a captivating figure whose green eyes, unusual in the region, added to his mystique. He had become the spiritual leader of the more than one-million-strong Shi'ite Muslim community in Lebanon in the late 1960s. In September 1978, the Imam had traveled throughout the Arab world to appeal for aid and political support for the Shia, oppressed in southern Lebanon under either Israeli occupation or Palestinian domination. Libya was his last stop. After talks with Qaddafi, the Imam and two aides reportedly went to the airport to fly to Rome. Their baggage arrived in Italy. But the Imam and his companions were never seen again.

Since his mysterious disappearance, the missing Imam had become a *cause célèbre* among the Shia, the motive for a long series of violent attacks, hijackings and kidnappings against Libyan targets and those who did business with Tripoli. Qaddafi had repeatedly and vehemently denied any knowledge of Imam Sadr's whereabouts, despite his long record of antagonism toward the Lebanese figure. Three weeks before the sixth hijacking, a Rome magistrate had shelved an inquiry into Imam Sadr's fate, announcing that investigations had found that "no crime was committed against Sadr on Italian territory." This decision, plus his fruitless previous hijackings, had prompted Hamza to try again.

His basic demand, once again, was the release of the Imam. "He is our *Imam*," Hamza stressed in solemn tones to Bradley, as a Catholic might talk of a cardinal, a Tibetan Buddhist about the Dalai Lama. It was as if that fact alone should provide justification to steal Bradley's plane. Hamza also told the pilot that the hijacking was all he could do at the moment, since he had no other recourse in a region prone to violence as a basic means of expression. "He wanted so desperately for the rest of the world to know he had a point," Bradley said.

In between frantic pleas from the control tower and brief shoot-outs, Hamza demanded that a delegation go to Libya to discuss the Sadr case. Then he called on the Lebanese government to sever relations with Qaddafi, and on the United Nations to tackle the case as an urgent issue of business. Hamza warned the control tower that he had a large amount of explosives on board, and that there would be a "disaster" if his demands were not met. He announced that his group was known as the "Sons of Musa al Sadr."

The drama unfolded like a grim version of a Keystone Kops episode, haphazardly bizarre and, looking back from the vantage point of two years, occasionally hilarious, Bradley recalled. The young hijackers turned the cabin into a classroom, putting up posters and pictures of the Imam in the aisles, using the public-address system to give lectures on Islam to the 105 passengers, more than half of whom did not speak Arabic. Among the passengers was George Hawi, chief of the Lebanese Communist Party.

Hamza spoke often with Bradley in English, as if he cared what the pilot thought. "He knew it was a waste of time preaching to me as he and the others did with passengers, but I felt he also sincerely wanted me to understand why this was happening. My impression was that he was actually a gentle man, while all the others seemed like thugs. There was a kind of angry thoughtfulness about him," Bradley said. "I sensed that he did not really intend to hurt anyone, despite threats to kill passengers every so often if his demands were not met. It was maximum publicity he was after."

There was one close call, however, when airport officials refused to remove troops and vehicles around the blue-and-white plane. One of Hamza's henchmen hauled a Jordanian teenager out of his seat and put a knife to his throat, threatening to kill him first, with others to follow, if the Lebanese authorities did not meet the hijackers' demands. Bradley turned to Hamza. "I said, 'In the name of God, what kind of obscenity is this?' Hamza became very quiet. I think it was the use of 'God' that struck him. He turned to me and said, 'OK, Captain, for you.' " He ordered the Jordanian returned to his seat, and there were no further threats to the passengers.

The hours dragged on into night, with various negotiators from the Lebanese Army and government, as well as Shia religious figures, trying to talk the hijackers into a compromise. At one stage, Sheikh

Abdul Amir Qabalan, a Shia cleric, took over the control tower microphone. "By everything that is holy to us, listen to my words," he exhorted. "This is not a Libyan plane. It is a Kuwaiti plane. Oh, brother Hamza, this will not help the cause of the Imam Musa Sadr. Let us try to solve this peacefully, with wisdom and spirituality." From the cockpit, Hamza replied, "It is not possible for us to come out of this plane even two months from now, until the Imam Musa Sadr returns safe and sound."

Eyewitnesses were convinced that Sheikh Qabalan and Hamza knew each other, probably very well. The cleric's tone alternated between firmness and friendly familiarity, and Hamza once replied with a joke. Indeed, the Shia militiamen acting as bodyguards to the Sheikh were also "standing by to make sure no one tried in earnest to storm the plane," one eyewitness reported. "The terrorists aboard were, after all, Shi'ites."

Despite his experience as an air pirate, Hamza occasionally acted hopelessly naïve. He wondered aloud why his men had been fired upon when they emerged from the plane to accept a delivery of food and water for the hostages, an Italian passenger said later. And Hamza criticized the negotiators for being unfair, actually telling passengers that the gunmen did not like being shot at any more than the captives.

Yet he was not inhibited about using firepower to make his point. Responding once to several rounds of incoming rifle fire, Hamza and his men opened up briefly on the glass-enclosed control tower, forcing Sheikh Qabalan to dive headlong into a human pile of Lebanese cabinet ministers, bodyguards and reporters all scrambling for cover. Bullets streaked through the windows and into the acoustical-tile ceiling.

In all five previous hijackings, Hamza and his various partners had negotiated their way off the planes, never facing either trial or incarceration. As midnight passed, it was finally the missing Imam's sister, Rebab, who persuaded Hamza to abandon the aircraft. Sheikh Qabalan promised that appeals would be launched at the United Nations, the Arab League and the World Court to find Imam Sadr.

Before leaving the plane for the terminal with nine Libyan passengers as temporary hostages, Hamza first apologized to the passengers. "The leader was a real gentleman," said hostage Gretta Bernotte

Rustico, wife of an Italian diplomat, after it was over. Then he made
a special effort to say goodbye to Bradley. He took the pilot aside to
advise him to get the plane out as fast as possible. "You are the only
one [airline] that flies the Libya–Beirut route. All Kuwait planes are
in danger. Do not come back," Hamza advised Bradley in a confi-
dential, almost brotherly way.

"It intrigued me at the time, definitely. I realized when they mentioned Sadr's name that they were fundamentalists, and they seemed
already as if they had clout. The whole thing seemed staged. Lots of
people seemed to know it was happening and was going to happen.
This was not an isolated gang. They gave me the impression that this
was a movement with a lot of power, because they sure as hell were
not apprehensive."

Bradley had indeed recognized the broad potential of the Shia
commandos, and the new fanaticism igniting passions and politics
throughout the Middle East. But, despite the Iranian revolution and
the traumatic 444-day ordeal of the American Embassy hostages in
Tehran, the outbreak of the Gulf war and a foiled coup in Bahrain,
many Western governments, or their diplomats stationed in the region, did not sense that something larger was afoot. They ignored the
small but important indications of a mass movement in the Middle
East. They did not recognize the beginnings of the Islamic crusade.

"I knew I would hear about them again, and probably often,"
Bradley said afterward. "This was no fly-by-night organization. They
spoke with confidence. They knew what they were doing." Two
years later, Bradley was not surprised to see television news footage
of Hamza operating as commander of a militia in Beirut.

■   ■   ■

HAMZA HAS RAPIDLY become one of the legends in the Shia community of the Middle East.* The largest Shia movement in Lebanon is
Amal, founded by Imam Sadr in the early 1970s. Amal is the Arabic
word for "hope," as well as an acronym for Afwaj al Muqawimal al
Lubnaniya, which means "Lebanese Resistance Battalions." At the
time of the hijackings, Amal leader Nabih Berri, who took over after
Imam Sadr's disappearance, denied all knowledge of Hamza. He

---

* Hamza became known by his first name because, until 1984, he refused to reveal his sur-
name to protect his family.

condemned the various heists, even though performed in the name of his predecessor, and disclaimed responsibility. But in 1984 Hamza was officially appointed Amal's military commander.

His full name is Hamza akl Hamieh. About six feet three and solidly built, he is a handsome and, in context of his environment, an oddly winsome figure who has won the devotion of both moderates and militants. In a region of awesome male pride, fighters vie openly for his attention. Many copy the way he dresses, the way he moves. And they take pride in showing pictures of Hamza in displays of martial arts, fondling recoilless rifles or small artillery, handling explosives or using his own preferred Czech-made antipersonnel grenade launcher.

Hamza explains much about the Shia movement, and its motives, which seem so alien to the Western mind. His family history, his attitudes toward his brethren as well as the West, and the course of his life all make him in some ways typical of the trend throughout the region.

He was not strictly "against" either Americans or Westerners. In 1984, Hamza led the attack on a building to free Frank Regier, professor of engineering at the American University of Beirut, held captive for sixty-six days. Most Lebanese believe that other Shia, hard-core extremists, were responsible for the abduction of Professor Regier as well as the kidnappings of seven other American civilians.

Several months later, Hamza played down the incident. "We do not believe in kidnappings and such things. They are wrong," said the man who had hijacked six planes. At a press conference after the release, Hamza stood in a corner while Berri, U.S. Ambassador Reginald Bartholomew and Professor Regier absorbed the limelight of cameras and televisions. As strange as it might seem, Hamza had in this instance turned out to be a moderate by the standards of Shia militancy.

Yet Hamza also led an attack in January 1984 on the U.S. Marine contingent of the Multi-National Force (MNF) of peacekeepers. The American troops had been stationed around the Beirut airport since the fall of 1982 as part of a mission to help support the Lebanese government and the resurrected Lebanese Army after the Israeli invasion. Relations between the Shia and the twelve hundred Marines were already tense because of the 1983 bombing at battalion headquarters. The 1984 clash was triggered when gunfire hit a bus moving through the Shi'ite southern suburb of Hay al Salloum, nicknamed "Hooterville" by Marines who could not pronounce the original.

"Today at nine o'clock, suddenly the Marines, the American soldiers, began sending their bombs to our area," Hamza told NBC. "The students were going to their schools. The workers were going to their work. There was nothing [fighting] today. Suddenly they opened up and made a battle. Till now we didn't shoot. We are asking all the leaders of the Marines what they want from us. If they want a battle, we are ready." For Hamza there was a clear distinction between the plight of a lone American professor and the challenge from a military arm of the U.S. government. (Sadly, it was probably the Lebanese Army stationed next to the U.S. contingent that was the original source of fire. Marine policy was to fire only in self-defense. As with hundreds of clashes in Beirut, the reason for the outbreak of fighting that day—whether retaliation or provocation—was never recorded. Each side blamed the other.)

Armed with a rifle and a walkie-talkie to coordinate small bands of fighters, Hamza launched a counterattack on airport positions from the maze of concrete shanties that make up the southern slums of squatters and refugees. Emerging from behind a home destroyed during the earlier Israeli invasion, Hamza walked to the front-line between the U.S. position and the Shi'ite suburbs to sight Marine locations, using binoculars hung around his neck, ignoring the gunfire around him. He then ordered a jeep, with a recoilless rifle mounted on the rear, to move in and fire.

Outgunned and outmanned by the U.S. contingent—fourteen hundred men on the ground and more than a dozen warships just off-shore—Hamza and his motley lot of militiamen nevertheless showed little reservation about taking on the Marines. One Marine was killed and four wounded during that three-hour exchange. Hamza's role was that of commander, ducking and dashing from sector to sector to plot the assault, providing direction and timing, and occasionally stopping to fire his own grenades.

Hamza's intense enthusiasm, righteous anger, and commitment typified the strain of militancy of the Shia cadre. It was, however, not totally alien from other practices in other parts of the world. As an

Israeli analyst mused, how different is the committed Shia from a Marine who runs up the hill in the face of gunfire to single-handedly take out a machine-gun nest, or an IRA prisoner who starves himself to death in protest? "Never mind to be killed," Hamza told NBC that day, "because at least we are going to meet our God."

After the bombing of the Marine headquarters the previous October, when rumors were rife that the Marines were being prepared to counterattack the southern suburbs, Hamza told CNN, "None of us are afraid. God is with us and gives us strength. We are making a race like horses to see who goes to God first. I want to die before my friends. They want to die before me. We want to see our God. We welcome the bombs of Reagan," he said to the camera with a big smile. Earlier that month he had explained, "They are depending on their good weapons. But they must know our people depend on good faith."

For Hamza this was not rhetoric. For him and thousands of others scattered through at least six countries of the Middle East, their campaigns are jihads, holy battles against forces out to suppress them.

In the thirteen-century-old lexicon of Islam, jihad is a struggle against an aggressive foreign force or an offensive in the name of the faith. The Koran incites Muslims to battle, for those who believe in God should fight for Him. It is "an obligation on the true believer, because only in a free country can there be righteous self-respect." In the seventh century, jihad was considered by early Muslims to be the most effective means of conquering lands for the new Islamic empire. Holy wars were not, however, designed to coerce conversion of believers in other monotheistic faiths.

"Fighters went into battle not under the color of some new territorial entity but under the green banner of the Prophet," Godfrey Jansen explained. "The only symbol carried before them was the Koran; the battle cry was not the equivalent of 'God for England' but the simple chant of Turkish soldiers used when they went in with the bayonet against the Koreans: *Din, din, din.* The faith, the faith, the faith." Jihad is such a basic tenet of the faith that the Kharijis, one of the earliest fanatical sects, unsuccessfully tried to make jihad the sixth pillar of Islam.

From his exile in Medina, a city now part of Saudi Arabia, Mohammed, the Prophet, preached holy war in his seventh-century campaigns to spread the faith and increase the territory under Muslim control. During his lifetime, he led the first Muslims to victories throughout the Arabian peninsula. Within one hundred years, Islamic crusaders had penetrated and held a land mass spreading from Central Asia through the Middle East and North Africa to Spain. This was the largest and fastest military victory purely in the name of religion in the history of the world.

In Arabic, *jihad* originally meant "effort." It was a rallying cry for the masses to advance the world's newest monotheistic religion, under threat of the sword, against unbelievers. But as time and causes passed, it came to mean, more loosely, a "righteous war," which could be fought even against other Muslims who disobeyed the Sharia, the religious code of conduct and obligations.

In strict interpretation, jihad is no longer possible, except perhaps against Israel, for the original Islamic empire has broken down into diverse and disparate political entities. Mohammed's intention was for all Muslims to be one in "Dar al Islam," the Haven of Islam, with no borders dividing true believers. No figure except a religious man would lead the flock. And no law but that of God, as revealed by the angel Gabriel to Mohammed and recorded in the Koran, would govern any aspect of life.

In practice, many Shia have broadly interpreted jihad, especially in the late twentieth century. To Ayatollah Khomeini, the war with neighboring Iraq has been a jihad. Capturing the U.S. Embassy in November 1979 and holding its staff hostage was a kind of jihad. The campaign of underground terror against the Sunni-dominated Gulf states was a third form of holy war. The word has lost much of its original meaning, and in the process has done unprecedented damage to Islam. It has stressed the differences between various Muslim sects, and has led many Muslims to see their primary loyalty to a political leader rather than to the faith.

Militant Shia of the 1980s do not seem to feel bound by the original definition of jihad. After almost thirteen centuries of following their own path, oppressed more often than not by the Sunni majority, this group of Shi'ites' anger, frustration and bitterness have changed their perspective. Their militant faith has evolved into a general militancy, unparalleled among the major sects of the now much divided religion. The alteration has been fundamental to the past decade of developments in the Arab world and elsewhere.

Whatever the theological correctness, for Hamza his hijackings and his attack against the Marines were forms of holy warfare. During an interview in July 1984, I expressed some surprise at the fact Hamza had never been charged or jailed for violations of both local and international law, nor injured during his bold aircraft thefts. "God wants this. God helps us," Hamza explained. "For what will we be afraid, because at last we want to face our God." For Hamza, God is not dead.

■   ■   ■

HAMZA COULD just as easily have been a doctor or an engineer as a militant crusader. His life is the product, a case history, of thirteen centuries of brooding and bitterness. It also parallels cathartic changes among the Shia during the 1960s and the 1970s that are being so widely felt in the 1980s, not just in the Middle East.

Born in 1954, Hamza moved at an early age with his family to Beirut from the ancient city of Baalbeck in Lebanon's eastern Bekaa valley, an area rich with Greek and Roman ruins. Baalbeck is one of three Shi'ite strongholds in Lebanon, which include South Lebanon and the southern suburbs of Beirut. They are also the poorest parts of the country, where the standards of education, income and social services are the lowest, where most residents hold jobs as laborers and small-scale farmers or merchants. As Hamza was growing up, discrimination against the Shia, particularly by Christians and Sunni Muslims, was rampant.

Hamza's father, a laborer, moved to the capital because he needed work. Hamza originally had great ambitions. "In 1975 I was a student and I wanted to go to Canada or America in order to gain a certificate to be a doctor or engineer. My people, my environment were poor. So I was obliged to stay here and work for a while. Then the war began in Lebanon," he said. The applications submitted to an Ottawa college, and others prepared for U.S. schools, were abandoned. Now there is probably no turning back.

Various influences, local and regional, took hold of his life. The civil war of 1975–76 split Lebanon wide open as Muslims and Christians fought out their differences over reforms that would even the balance of power among the country's seventeen officially recognized sects. Government had been dominated by minority Maronite Christians at the expense of the majority Muslims under the terms of an unwritten agreement made among the nation's chief politicos at the time of independence. Power had been distributed on the basis of a 1932 census that forty years later was seriously outdated.

Hamza first took up arms alongside leftists—mainly Muslim Sunnis, Palestinians and Druze, the small but active sect that does not accept converts and whose doctrine is secret—against Christian rightists. He was then barely twenty, and the issue in his mind was one of survival. It evolved gradually into politics after he joined Imam Sadr's movement, and then into religion. But it was a phase that set him permanently on a course as a warrior.

His first targets were Christians who saw Lebanon, the heralded "Switzerland of the Middle East" and the "bridge between East and West," as the outpost of the Christian world on its eastern extremity. For Muslims, and for Hamza, the Levant was the western edge of the Orient. The religious rivalry had simmered since the Christian Crusades nine hundred years earlier, and with it the question of national identity—eastern or western. For a good Muslim, there could be no question.

Hamza's focus was later refined. The 1975–76 burst of warfare ended with intervention by Syrian peacekeepers, so Imam Sadr and his followers, including Hamza, moved to the traditional Shia strongholds in southern Lebanon. They wanted to get away from a conflict run largely by Palestinians and Sunni Muslims. "It was time to take care of our own," Hamza explained. "There was much social work to be done."

Imam Sadr, of Lebanese descent but Iranian birth and training, had formed the "Movement of the Disinherited" in 1974 in Beirut to mobilize the Shia and improve the social standing of the sect. The Shia had, by then, grown from Lebanon's third-largest to the largest population group—almost 40 percent of the estimated 3.5 million population.* Hamza was one of Imam Sadr's most promising students, and in the southern town of Tyre they continued their sessions begun earlier in Beirut. Hamza also took up arms again, this time

* There has never been an official update on the 1932 census, owing in part to Christian fears of proving the unofficial estimates.

against the Palestinians who increasingly were trying to dominate the southern Shia villages and lands because of their strategic proximity to the Israeli border. "These years there were many problems with the Palestinians. We told them it is illegal to fight us, that this is our land."

Ironically, the Palestine Liberation Organization (PLO) had first trained and armed the southern Shia, anxious to beef up the anti-Israeli forces with men already living on the front lines. While the Shia were initially prepared to fight their common foe alongside the Palestinians, they were not willing to be dominated on their own turf. Their fight against the aggressive Palestinians unified the Shia and asserted their separate identity. It also underlined just how little "Arab solidarity" the Shia felt.

In early 1974, Imam Sadr gave two now famous speeches in which he converted a basically social movement into an armed faction, reflecting the frustrations of a people who previously had been deceivingly passive. "Today, we shout out loud the wrongs against us, that cloud of injustice that has followed us since the beginning of our history. Starting from today, we will no longer complain or cry. Our name is not *mitwali* [a name for the Shia that has become derogatory]. Our name is 'men of refusal,' 'men of vengeance,' 'men who revolt against all tyranny,' even though this costs us our blood and our lives. Hussein faced the enemy with seventy men. The enemy was very numerous. Today we are more than seventy, and our enemy is not the quarter of the whole world," the Imam declared.

In Baalbeck a month later, the broad-shouldered cleric spoke with the kind of passion that had already roused tens of thousands to his side. "Arms are man's beauty," he said as if it were a religious ruling, to a crowd estimated at 75,000, many of them carrying weapons. "What does the government expect? What does it expect except rage and except revolution?" For hundreds of Shia youths, this was an official call to war. It was no longer a political or social struggle, but one sanctioned by their precious faith.

For Hamza, Israel prompted another challenge in 1978 by briefly invading Lebanon, its powerful army storming up to the Litani River to clean out pockets of Palestinians firing artillery across the Lebanese–Israeli border. The flashier and better known PLO made the headlines, but the still little-publicized Shia were in the midst of most battles, too. They also took most of the casualties. Once again, Hamza fought.

In the aftermath, with the Shia squeezed between Palestinians and Israelis, Imam Sadr took the Shia plight to the "Arab nation," a tour through several states to seek recognition and help. "We don't know what happened when Musa al Sadr went to all the Arabian capitals in order to help the south," Hamza said in 1984. "At last he went to Libya, and he stayed there. Until now we are waiting for him to come back. In the meantime, we are fighting for the sake of his thoughts and our home."

Less than five months after Imam Sadr disappeared, Hamza hijacked the first of six planes. He claimed that he was acting on his own initiative. He knew the airport well. After his family moved to Beirut, his father had worked at the terminal.

The Iranian revolution in 1979 galvanized the Shia in Lebanon and elsewhere, inspiring their beleaguered hopes. It was not merely what happened, but how it happened. Iran should have been the most difficult place for an unarmed uprising. Ayatollah Ruhollah Khomeini had no sophisticated network of intelligence, no communications system, to work with during his fourteen years in exile. Indeed, cassettes of his sermons and messages were banned by the Shah, and colleagues preaching the same line back home were imprisoned. He had no arms to speak of, no treasure chest to tap for his campaign.

But he had followers. Sheer numbers forced the Shah from the Peacock throne. The passion of the Iranian masses, the underdog psychology of a thousand years, overwhelmed one of the most efficient and best-equipped armies in the world. Most troops eventually succumbed. Not even the combined intelligence, political and financial resources of a superpower could counter the Ayatollah's spell.

Despite deep differences between Arabs and Persians, the revolution sparked a kind of exhilaration among most Shia and even many Sunnis. Here was an example, a model of what could be done. In Iran, a group of pious leaders had acted against perceived injustices, and won. Maybe, others thought, the same thing could be done elsewhere. On the cold February day that the Ayatollah and his entourage returned triumphantly to Tehran, people danced in the streets of Kuwait and celebrated in Bahrain and the eastern Hasa province of Saudi Arabia. In Lebanon, young Shia fighters fired in the air, their traditional expression of either joy or sorrow.

With Iran as a sowing ground, the Shia crusade quickly sprouted throughout the region.

Links between Iran and Lebanon were particularly strong from trade and migrations over the centuries. More recently, exiled Iranians had set up temporary shop in Beirut, men such as Mustafa Chamran. Chamran, educated at Berkeley, was an important behind-the-scenes figure in Amal after Imam Sadr's disappearance. He also became one of Hamza's instructors. After the revolution, he returned to Iran, where he served as chairman of the Supreme Defense Council and Minister of Defense. He co-sponsored the creation of a militia to enforce and monitor the revolution, a militia which eventually became the fearsome Revolutionary Guards. Chamran then summoned Hamza.

"In 1981, I went to Iran for about one year," Hamza said. "I went to fight. I was at Dezful, Susangaard, Ahwaz." He was clearly a premier cadet among the hundreds of young militants from every Middle East state who were training at bases throughout Iran. These were the cadre who helped cement a powerful link between the Iranian and Arab Shia, a basic component in the campaign to export the revolution.

In Tehran, his lessons with Chamran resumed. Under the sponsorship of the powerful Iranian, Hamza dined with men such as Hojatoleslam Mohammed Baqr Hakim in the holy city of Qom. The Hojatoleslam, an Iraqi, was the most publicized of Arab Shia "liberation leaders," a man crucial to the Islamic crusade. One of Hamza's prize possessions is a picture from a meeting Chamran set up for him with the Ayatollah. Three years after his Iranian visit Hamza said, "There are two [main] cultures: the West and the East, the U.S. and the U.S.S.R. Islam is a third, a balance. Ayatollah Khomeini is the leader of all Muslims in the world. And also my leader. Of course I feel close to those in Iran. I am one of them." His first child, born in 1984, was named Chamran.

•   •   •

ALTHOUGH AMAL is a Shia movement, its policies through 1984 were comparatively moderate and secular. Nabih Berri, the Amal leader, repeatedly tried to defuse the fears of other Lebanese sects, notably Christian. "We support the Islamic revolution in Iran, but not on sectarian grounds. And we do not want an Islamic revolution in Lebanon. Our special relations with the Iranian revolution are based more on principle than on sectarian compatibility," he said.

Indeed, Berri did not have warm relations with the Iranian leadership, and was frightened by the intentions of the militants. That may have been one of the reasons he later adjusted his line somewhat. The Amal leader began to echo the words of the paper presented by Dr. Zonis at the State Department seminar: "We look to the Iranian revolution, in my opinion, as the third great revolution in history. First there was the French, then the Russian, and now the Islamic revolution, which is changing many things in the world. . . . It has renewed the way for Mohammed."

The former lawyer advocated negotiations over violence whenever possible. And his basic political demand was merely for a fifty-fifty division of secular power between the majority Muslims (of three sects) and minority Christians, despite the new Shi'ite demographic edge. Several times that moderation almost cost Berri and the first generation of activist Shia leaders in Lebanon their hold on the movement. The young were also suspicious of the fact that he held a green card giving him eligibility for eventual American citizenship, and that his ex-wife and children lived in Dearborn, Michigan.

The younger generation was increasingly attracted to militancy and the perceived "purity" of Iran's revolution. In late 1983 Berri admitted, "I am afraid myself that every moderate will be replaced by another who is extremist." At the same time a close friend of Berri's said, "The mullahs are close, very close, to taking over the Shi'ite movement."

Amal underwent a rupture in 1982 when one of Hamza's predecessors, Hussein Musawi, stormed out of the Beirut headquarters. The last straws had been Berri's willingness to go along with U.S. mediation in Lebanon, his membership in the National Salvation Council alongside the Christians, and Amal's lack of resistance against the Israeli invaders. The open split on three key positions during the summer of 1982 led to an official break. Musawi claimed he quit, while Amal officials said he was expelled. Musawi moved to Baalbeck, another Shi'ite stronghold, and established close ties with Iranian Revolutionary Guards in eastern Lebanon. He then created his own extremist "Islamic Amal" movement.

Twice, in 1983 and 1984, Berri's preferred policy of nonviolence led to disillusionment and dissipation of his influence among the fighters. Membership of the Shi'ite movements was unusual, almost amorphous, by Western standards, since there were no cards issued or formal lists kept. Under the leadership, there was a large body of supporters or sympathizers of unknown numbers. During this critical period, many Amal followers developed dual loyalties, cooperating with smaller radical or fundamentalist factions. Only major new battles, which diverted attention from internal politicking, kept Berri on top. But the youth of Amal, its backbone, were increasingly wandering along their own path.

"I see the future of my people must be determined by blood," said Hamza shortly after he was appointed Amal commander. "Our leaders in history said we must refuse the tyrants and the inequality. The Shia in all the universe now fight for equality . . . We must fight together to help all poor men in the world. And we must all fight to go back to Jerusalem." The crusade was beginning to take on broader goals than simple freedom or dignity within their own borders. And taking Jerusalem was not strictly related to the Palestinian cause; the Shia wanted it in Muslim hands because of the holy city's Islamic history.

When pressed, Hamza also admitted that he favored Islamic rule in Lebanon and the rest of the Arab world "because Islam makes equality to all the people, true Islam, not the kind in Saudi Arabia." To Hamza, a practicing Muslim who prays piously five times daily and neither smokes nor drinks, this was the most natural goal. "Islam is not a danger to anyone."

Indeed, to be a true Muslim was to be a militant and a fundamentalist, as Islam was originally propagated. "To be a Muslim is not simply a matter of individual will; it means participating in the effort to implement God's will on earth." And it was to the origins of the faith that Hamza and others were turning, trying to shed the dilutions of the centuries, for answers.

■   ■   ■

"ISLAM IS NOT A RELIGION," some have argued. "It is a complete way
of life." It is also a total identity, combining politics, religion and
culture. The Koran, the Hadith (traditions) and Sharia (laws) offer
practical instruction on every aspect of life. They cover conduct, hy-
giene and health, a formula to divide all inheritances, marriage rights
and duties, family obligations, a method of governance, dress and
etiquette, the way to do business.

For the Shia, Islam in practice is even more binding. The Sunni
believe man's relationship with God is personal, face to face, not
conducted through a priesthood. But the minority Shia follow mullahs who mediate and guide between man and Allah. "For us Sunni,
it's direct dialing," a Pakistani official once explained. "The Shia go
through the operator." Sunnis have more latitude in personal practice of the faith, whereas the Shia are technically obliged to obey
their clerics.

This difference, the greatest schism in Islam's thirteen-hundred-
year history, happened within thirty years of the Prophet's death. It
was originally a political dispute over succession. Shia, or, as originally written, "Shi'at Ali," means "follower of Ali." Ali was the
fourth Caliph, or Islamic "representative" on earth. He was also the
cousin of Mohammed, and his son-in-law through marriage to Mohammed's daughter Fatima. Because of blood and family links, many
early Muslims felt he should have immediately succeeded Mohammed. The Prophet, unfortunately, had left no instructions.

The single strain of Islam split after Ali was murdered in 661,
when the dominant Sunnis again chose a leader outside "the family."
The first Shia saw authority descending through Ali, and he became
the first of the Shi'ites' Twelve Imams. All twelve were descendants
of the Prophet through the Ali-Fatima line. To succeed Ali, they recognized his son, Hussein. And then Hussein was killed.*

For the Shia, "every day in his life is a day of battle in which he
must seek either triumph or martyrdom," explained Professor Hamid
Algar, an Islamic expert at Berkeley. "Shi'ism is all about protest
against authority, passion, constant rebellion," said Professor Hasan
Askari, a Shi'ite teaching at the Center for the Study of Islam in
England.

* Ali's first son, Hassan, was actually the second Imam, but he resigned and was then murdered.

The romantic concepts of Shi'ism grew during the reign of the Twelfth Imam. He disappeared mysteriously in 874. The Shia believe he is in "occultation," or hidden from view, but will eventually return to earth in a resurrection. Ideologically, the Shia since then had not accepted temporal rule—until the Iranian revolution. While waiting for the Twelfth Imam to return, a leading Shia cleric on earth serves as his regent.

While Sunnis deplore religious excess, particularly in public, the Shia thrive on it. The Shi'ites' wailing and weeping and bloody self-flagellation during the month of Muharram, at celebrations marking the martyrdom of Hussein, are a sharp contrast to the sedate pilgrimage of Hajj to Mecca and Medina, which both sects perform.

The mind-set of martyrdom, the sense of injustice to their sect, and the fierce loyalty to religious leaders have shaped the Shia into a fiercely militant branch of the faith. Over the years, the Sunni majority was comparatively content with the order of their world, while the Shia were not. Indeed, the Shia are the main inheritors of the revolutionary fervor of the age of Mohammed. For thirteen centuries, until a religious ruling by an Egyptian cleric in 1949 accepted the Shia as equal members of the faith, they nursed their grievances while the Sunnis scorned them as heretics. And the intervening years of domination by Mongols, Turks and eventually European colonialists, who paid them little heed, only ground in their bitterness. Shia history and the Iranian revolution combined to encourage Hamza, and others, to once again act out the role of Hussein.

■   ■   ■

THE HISTORY of the Shia and the campaign of Ayatollah Khomeini are not the only causes of the Shia crusade, or of the resurgence of fundamentalism among all Muslim sects. Frustration was also at the center of the movement. Three specific factors helped ignite their zeal, each playing off the others.

The first was conflict with foreign ideologies. Britain and France had installed their systems of government and introduced their culture in the Arab world during the era of European colonialism. "By the end of World War I," wrote Edward Mortimer in *Faith and Power: The Politics of Islam,* there was scarcely such a thing left as a Muslim state not dominated by the Christian West. How could this happen? Only two answers were possible. Either the claims of Islam were false and the Christian or post-Christian West had finally come up with another system that was superior, or Islam had failed through not being true to itself.

Foreign ideologies and value systems were inherited, adapted sometimes radically, by the newly independent Middle East governments between 1943 and 1962, and usually also with an eye to Western goals: personal prosperity, industrial development, technological advancement, sophisticated armies. Two ideologies dominated: the pan-Arab nationalism of Egypt's eloquent and charismatic President Gamal Abdel Nasser and the socialist Baathism of Syria and Iraq. But the Western formulas combining secularism and modernization each failed. The underdeveloped countries remained poor and weak— while growing increasingly resentful about imported ways of life and government.

For Muslims, the failure was emphasized during the 1967 war with Israel, when the little Jewish state so swiftly humiliated Egypt, Jordan and Syria. In six days, Israel more than doubled the land under its control, capturing strategic pieces from each of the three. But most precious was historic Jerusalem, the loss of which grieved the faithful in all seventy nations of Dar al Islam. In light of their combined manpower and resources, many Muslims felt that something basic must have been wrong. After all, their history had been conquest and success, never such total defeat. That war led to the demise of what had become known as "Nasserism." The Arab world groped for an alternative.

The loss of morale and confidence in public institutions slowly, almost unnoticed at first, led many Muslims, Shia and Sunni, to turn inward. And inward they found Islam. It offered no strange new slogans or complicated alien ideology, nor reliance on an outside force that compromised their independence. And, best of all, there were ready answers to every major question, every issue. "This phenomenon in Lebanon is not separated from what is going on generally in the Arab and Islamic worlds," explained Sheikh Mohammed Mehdi Shamseddine, one of the most influential Lebanese Shi'ite clerics. The Islamic revival was "a response to the challenge of the defeat and failures of past formulas and ideologies."

Mortimer added:

The religious reaction to the 1967 defeat was deeper and broader.
Nasser himself, in his first public speech after the defeat, drew "an ex-
ceptionally enthusiastic roar of applause" when he said that religion
should play a more important role in society. A religious explanation
for the defeat was widely offered: the Jews had deserved victory by
being truer to their religion than the Arabs had been to theirs.

The second spark for Islam was the 1973 Yom Kippur War between Israel and its Arab neighbors, which also fell during the Islamic holy month of Ramadan. The Arab offensive had been
code-named "Badr," after Mohammed's first victory in 623. This
fourth modern Arab–Israeli war was fought in the name of Islam
rather than the pan-Arab cause. The battle cry of the 1967 conflict
had been "Land, Sea and Air," "implying faith in equipment and the
tactics of the military engagement. In 1973 the cry was more expli-
citly Muslim, the call of 'God is Great.' " And it was more successful.
The attacking Syrians and Egyptians fought well, managing to shatter the Israeli image of invincibility. They lost militarily, but they
achieved many of the key Arab political objectives. "Heightened religious fervor had yielded manifest results," argued a noted Arabist.
And one author concluded that the two wars together had created "a
renascent sense of an international Islamic identity."

Mortimer explained:

Above all, the morale and self-respect of the Arabs and Egyptians
had been restored, and many were convinced that they owed their
success to divine providence, vouch-safed to them in recognition of
their repentance and at least the beginnings of reform. Soldiers
claimed, perhaps inevitably, to have seen angels fighting alongside
them.

The third form of inspiration came from oil, which also drew attention to Islam. The Gulf oil-producing states' dramatic decision to
quadruple the price of oil, to cut back on production and to embargo
sales to the U.S. made the entire world sit up and take notice. And it
all happened just as winter was setting in. Oil, Arabs and Islam became synonymous—and powerful.

"The Islamic spirit, increasingly intense after 1970," said Daniel
Pipes in *In the Path of God,*

entered a new phase; Muslims felt they had finally stopped, and perhaps reversed, their long decline. Starved for two centuries for some worldly sign of their special standing before God, for Muslims the achievements of late 1973 appeared to be a vindication of their faith and a reward for their long-suffering steadfastness. . . . These events marked a turning point in Muslim consciousness, convincing many that the umma (Islamic community) had begun its long-awaited resurgence, and improving Muslim attitudes toward themselves, their cultural traditions and Islam.

Britain's former Foreign Secretary Lord Carrington once noted how surprised he was during a 1980 conversation with his Princeton- and Oxford-educated counterpart in Saudi Arabia, Prince Saud al Faisal. The Saudi cabinet minister had spoken thoughtfully to Carrington for four hours about various Middle East problems when he casually referred to his belief that oil was indeed a gift from God to the Islamic faithful.

But there were two steps to this phase. First came the expectation that oil wealth could make Islam proud and powerful again. The boom succeeded in some ways, particularly in building the attention given to Sunni Islam, but it also produced some ugly byproducts during the 1970s. "The expectations of the early 1970s that oil wealth would enable the Arab world to transform itself have been dashed," explained a respected Middle East correspondent. "This has produced cynicism and a sense of impotence, and has created a wide opening for frustration. In many cases, this void has been filled by extreme religious fundamentalism offering a messianic solution that secular politics has failed to deliver."

The clout and profits of oil in the post-1973 period only further angered the Shia, for most of the massive wealth that flowed through the oil pipelines was siphoned off by their Sunni masters. It went for new airports or new armaments or new palaces, but rarely for the social services, schools or health centers badly needed in the poorest parts of each country where the Shia lived. Even in Iran, the Shi'ite Shah's modernization programs diverted funds from the masses at the bottom. The practice applied also in the non-oil Arab states, which received big boosts in aid with the surplus of petrodollars. In Lebanon, Gulf aid both before and after the civil war was divided between the Christian and Sunni centers, only token sums ending up in the Shia bases in the south and the east.

Left out yet again, the average Shia became more militant at the abuse of the Islamic stricture of equality among Muslims. Not spreading the wealth was a major miscalculation by the governments in the oil-rich nations, for it served to "prove" to the angry Shia that these leaders were not working in the true interests of Islam. Once the Shia crusade was launched, it was aimed as much at those Sunni regimes who had "betrayed" them as at the "imperialist" challenges from the East and the West.

Thus, in the context of recent history, Hamza was not exceptional. "The seeming extremist is usually just an extension of our ordinary society," said Fuad Ajami, the foremost expert on the Shia in the United States. "The only difference is that the so-called extremist takes the frustrations of the people around him and plays out their wrath to the limits and beyond."

In mid-1984, Hamza put it in personal terms. "We are like the blacks of South Africa. For myself, I don't have any future except to stay a fighter," he said from a sickbed at his uncle's home. He was on an intravenous drip of glucose, suffering from exhaustion. Several of his commandos stood at the side of the bed, listening to every word of the conversation even though most did not understand English. His baby son, Chamran, lay in a rag hammock above the bed, which Hamza occasionally rocked with his free hand to quiet his crying. "But for the future of my child, I hate to see him live as a slave. My child has the right to live well, to go to university and to be an officer in engineering. He has a right to be equal."

One week after that interview, pilot Les Bradley was in Kuwait packing up. He had just lost his flying license, and his job with Kuwait Airways. Bradley said doctors told him an irregular heartbeat had become too much of a problem, and they would have to disqualify him. The doctors traced it to the trauma of the hijacking more than two years earlier.

Party of God's twelve-foot poster in West Beirut. "The fire of Islam will burn those who are responsible for these practices [against Islam]. We have been dominated by the U.S. government and others for too long." Page 23. [Courtesy of the *Daily Star*, Beirut]

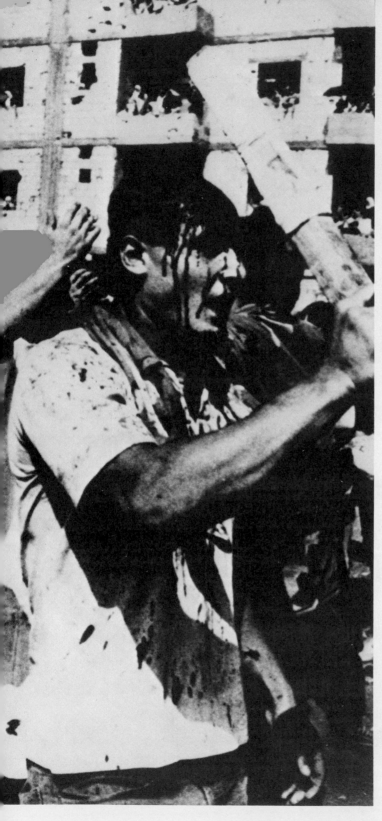

Militant cadre training in Iran. "I can in one week assemble 500 faithful ready to throw themselves into suicide operations. No frontier will stop them." Page 35. [Jeune Afrique/Gamma-Liaison]

Ashura, Shi'ite commemoration of Hussein's martyrdom. "Hussein sacrificed his life and those of his followers in the seventeenth century in an effort to realize Shi'ite rule over all Muslims. Khomeini has revived the goal of self-sacrifice as a means of achieving Islamic goals." Page 38. [AP/Wide World Photos]

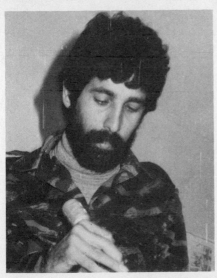

Hamza akl Hamieh, hijacker and militia commander. "We are making a race like horses to see who goes to God first. I want to die before my friends. They want to die before me. We welcome the bombs of Reagan." Page 54. [Courtesy of Hamza akl Hamieh]

Les Bradley, hijacked pilot. "I knew I would hear about them again and probably often. This was no. fly-by-night operation. They knew what they were doing." Page 51. [Courtesy of Les Bradley]

Nabih Berri, leader of Amal Party. "We look to the Iranian revolution, in my opinion, as the third great revolution in history. First there was the French, then the Russian, and now the Islamic revolution, which is changing many things in the world. It has renewed the way for Mohammed." Page 61. [Courtesy of the *Daily Star*, Beirut]

Poster of Musa al Sadr, Lebanese Imam. "Today we shout out loud the wrongs against us, the cloud of injustice that has followed us since the beginning of our history. Starting from today, we will no longer complain or cry. What does government expect except rage and revolution?" Page 58.

1983 U.S. Embassy bombing in Beirut. "We will make America face a severe defeat. . . . God willing, this century will be the period of victory for the oppressed over the oppressors." Page 69. [AP/Wide World Photos]

1983 U.S. Marine bombing in Beirut. "[The suicide driver] looked right at me . . . smiled, that's it. . . . Soon as I saw [the truck] over here, I knew what was going to happen." Page 71. [AP/Wide World Photos]

Marine compound after bombing. "It's sad to see a bunker mentality. But how can you complain when we're so naked everywhere?" Page 244. [Courtesy of the *Daily Star*, Beirut]

Hussein Musawi (seated), leader of Islamic Amal. "If America kills my people, then my people must kill Americans. We have already said that if self-defense and if the stand against American, Israeli and French oppression constitute terrorism, then we are terrorists." Page 83. [AP/Wide World Photos]

Hossein Shiekholeslam (center), Iranian Deputy Foreign Minister. An Iranian colleague said: "It is a post that puts him in charge of exporting the revolution." An American official said: "We know he is one of the top two or three in the regime on terrorism." Page 87. [AP/Wide World Photos]

◀ **Sheikh Mohammed Fadlallah, Lebanese cleric.** "I believe that in all cases violence is like a surgical operation that the doctor should only resort to after he has exhausted all other methods." Page 96. [Courtesy of the *Daily Star*, Beirut]

Aftermath of 1985 bombing near Sheikh Fadlallah's home. After *The Washington Post* reported that the bombing was carried out by people connected with Lebanese units being trained by the CIA, a U.S. official said: "We maintained contact, intelligence contact, with Lebanese intelligence and of course we talked about counter-terrorism and planned things together. But this was not our operation and it was nothing we planned or knew about." Page 97. [AP/Wide World Photos]

▼

U.S. warship firing at Muslim militias in Lebanon. "The recent American casualties in Beirut were as good as inflicted by the [U.S.S.] *New Jersey*'s guns. Terrorism does not spring from a vacuum, nor does it exist without a logic, one that can seem very compelling from the wrong end of the gun barrel." Page 103. [Courtesy of the *Daiy Star*, Beirut]

Four Americans and two French hostages held in Lebanon by Islamic Jihad as of May 1985. *Top, left to right:* ***Terry Anderson, William Buckley, Marcel Fontaine.*** *Bottom, left to right:* ***Rev. Benjamin Weir, Rev. Lawrence Jenco, Marcel Carton.*** "The Islamic Jihad organization claims it is responsible for the abduction in order to renew our acceptance of Reagan's challenge and to confirm our commitment of the statement made public after the bombing of the Marine headquarters that we will not leave any American on Lebanese soil." Page 104. [AP/Wide World Photos]

1983 U.S. Embassy bombing in Kuwait. "I don't believe such missions can be prevented. It's hard to imagine any kind of complete guarantees no matter what we do. We can handle the Tehran [hostage] model. Now we have to work on the Beirut and Kuwait [bombing] models." Page 123. [AP/Wide World Photos]

U.S. hostage William Stanford (in white shirt), minutes before death in 1984 Kuwaiti hijacking. "It is the aggressive policies of the U.S. that caused the death of the Americans. The Americans still think that feudalism rules the world and therefore demand that Iran explain its handling of the hijacking affair. If Reagan thought about what happened to Carter, then he would understand that Iran explains nothing to anyone but God." Page 142. [AP/Wide World Photos]

Grand Mosque of Mecca in Saudi Arabia, Islam's holiest shrine. "Our belief is that the continued rule [by the House of Saud] is a destruction of God's religion even if they pretend to uphold Islam. We ask God to relieve us of them all. They have brought upon the Muslims all evil and corruption." Page 153. [AP/Wide World Photos]

Former President Jafaar Nimeiri of Sudan. "Islam has come. We shall follow the rules of the Prophet Mohammed or we shall die for it. There is no alternative to God's Sharia." Page 211. [AP/Wide World Photos]

Egyptian President Anwar Sadat minutes before his assassination. "This is not religion. This is obscenity. These are lies, the criminal use of religious power to misguide people." Page 175. [AP/Wide World Photos]

Egyptian militant shooting at President Anwar Sadat. "Today's leaders have become apostates of Islam. The peak of worship is jihad. We are asked to do God's bidding and not worry about the results." Page 183. [AP/Wide World Photos]

Defendants at Egypt's "Jihad 302" trial. "If we cannot form an Islamic nation except by fighting, we have to fight. The first battlefield in our jihad is to uproot the infidel leadership." Page 183. [AP/Wide World Photos]

Army tank on Tunis streets after 1984 "revolution of the loaf." [AP/Wide World Photos]

Morocco's King Hassan showing Khomeini leaflets on television. "The fundamentalists in Tunisia and Morocco may admire Ayatollah Khomeini, and the Iranian revolution has obviously been a great stimulus to their movements, but there is no evidence of an organizational link. The link is one of similar motivation, a drive for a return to traditional Islam and a rejection of imported Western values that can now be found throughout the Muslim world." Page 196. [AP/Wide World Photos]

▲ *Khalil Jaradi, "martyred" Lebanese militant.* "Just like the Shah, Israel will be overturned in south Lebanon. The views of Khalil Jaradi will be in every attack on Israel until liberation. We used to fight to liberate our lands, but now we will fight to avenge their deaths." Page 231. [Courtesy of *Daily Star*, Beirut]

Funeral of Israeli soldier Allon Tsur. "This Lebanon is eating our children. How long will we sit there? Allon was the 600th killed and thousands have been hurt. We are a settlement that suffered from [Palestinian] infiltrators and we say today: Take us out of Lebanon." Page 216. [AP/Wide World Photos] ▶

Twelve Israelis killed in 1985 suicide attack on IDF convoy. "If as a result of the war in Lebanon, we replace PLO terror in south Lebanon with Shi'ite terror, we have done the worst [thing] in our struggle with terrorism. In 20 years of PLO terror, not one PLO terrorist made himself [into] a live bomb. The Shi'ites have the potential for a kind of terrorism that we have not yet experienced." Page 233. [AP/Wide World Photos]

▶ *Protest in Maarakeh after Israeli "iron fist" raid.* "Tell them we are going to get them. Someday we will watch Israeli mothers cry like our mothers." Page 235. [AP/Wide World Photos]

Aftermath of bombing at Maarakeh Muslim center two days later. "From now on, whenever a southern village is attacked, a Galilean village will be hit." Page 236. [AP/Wide World Photos]

▼

Israeli Army column withdrawing from Lebanon in 1985. "The Lebanon war gives proof for the first time that Israel can be forced to retreat from Arab territory through guerrilla warfare. This has far-reaching implications for the West Bank, Gaza and the Arab-Israeli conflict in general." Page 238. [AP/Wide World Photos]

Israel's three-phase withdrawal from Lebanon between February and June 1985. (The three phases are numbered and indicated with broken lines.) [Joan Forbes in The Christian Science Monitor © 1985 TCSPS]

Boy pulls Lebanese flag from south Lebanon rubble. "The most powerful single force in the world today is neither communism nor capitalism, neither the H-bomb nor the guided missile—it is man's eternal desire to be free and independent." Page 46. [Courtesy the *Daily Star*, Beirut]

4 The Toll: Lebanon

I AM THE WOUND AND THE KNIFE!
I AM THE BLOW AND THE CHEEK!
I AM THE LIMBS AND THE WHEEL—
THE VICTIM AND THE EXECUTIONER!
—*BAUDELAIRE*, LES FLEURS DU MAL

WE WILL MAKE AMERICA FACE A SEVERE DEFEAT . . . GOD WILL-
ING, THIS CENTURY WILL BE THE PERIOD OF VICTORY FOR THE
OPPRESSED OVER THE OPPRESSORS.
—*SIGN ON THE MAIN GATE OF THE FORMER U.S. EMBASSY*
IN TEHRAN, 1984

No one slept through it.

The sound early that Sunday in the sultry October of 1983 ripped through Beirut, just as the morning sun's first rays bounced off the Mediterranean coastline.

Seven-year-old Rania Yamout ran screaming into her parents' bedroom, terrified by the almost visible waves of impact that blew window glass all over her bed. A long time passed before she left her father's arms.

Sitting outside sipping coffee, banker Hassan Sabeh leapt to his feet when he saw the massive mushroom cloud grow into the sky, then cover it. All he could think of was the picture of Hiroshima in his childhood textbook.

Ghassan Harmouche, an apartment manager, thought it was the end of the world. As with the assassination of John Kennedy in the United States, everyone in the Lebanese capital had a story about where he was or what he did when that horrendous dull roar went off.

Colonel Tom Fintel, chief of the U.S. Army training mission in Lebanon, heard it clear across town as he lay in bed sipping coffee. His first reaction was that the Syrians had fired one of their new SS-21 Soviet-made ground-to-ground missiles. He dashed to a balcony window, where he could see, and smell, the rancid black smoke. He was horrified, but still not aware of the target.

It stunned me out of bed, the beat of adrenaline and the chill of fear a discomforting mixture, despite two years in Beirut.

It was the single largest nonnuclear explosion on earth since World War II, FBI forensic investigators eventually reported. The equivalent of six tons of dynamite, twelve thousand pounds of explosives, went into that bomb—at least twelve thousand, they later qualified. It may also have been the single most effective terrorist attack in Middle East history. The death toll was only a small element in terms of eventual impact.

Lance Corporal Robert Calhoun from San Antonio, Texas, was a slight, freckled-faced twenty-one-year-old on October 23, 1983. His voice cracking with emotion, he explained in an interview the next day what happened: "I heard a crash. It was like a roaring truck. And then I heard something hit like sandbags. Then I heard an explosion. I was behind sandbags on the roof, and stuff was falling. I was praying to God. It was like I got to be hurt, and this is the time it's going to happen.

"As soon as everything stopped, I waited about twenty more seconds. I got up and my friend Joe Martucci was beside me, and he was trapped. I unburied him. As soon as we got up, you heard about a thousand people screaming, 'Help me. God help me.' "

More than three hundred Marines and Navy personnel had been asleep at 6:20 A.M., ten minutes before reveille, which was usually delayed by a half hour on Sundays. Only the cooks, preparing breakfast, were up. Most of the troops were crushed in their beds when the building collapsed into a single grotesque pile of concrete and twisted steel. A few luckier men were blown out of the building like floppy bags of hay.

Corporal Martucci, who had been asleep on the roof, was abruptly awakened. "There was an explosion. We saw the center of the roof actually lift, blow out. It was a type of skyline in the center of the roof. There was a delay between the actual explosion, and the building, the floor, was going down in approximately three or four seconds. . . . We rode the roof down."

But only one survivor saw how it all happened. Lance Corporal Eddie DiFranco saw the big Mercedes truck as it circled in the parking lot outside the Marine compound, rather strangely gaining speed. It was not unusual to see heavy vehicles passing, for the compound was next to the airport's cargo area. But suddenly the yellow truck broke and headed at full speed toward the battalion headquarters. DiFranco, who was on guard duty, will always remember the expression on the driver's face. "He looked right at me . . . smiled, that's it. . . . Soon as I saw [the truck] over here, I knew what was going to happen."

The site was a massive four-story building on the edge of Beirut International Airport, a reinforced-concrete structure that once served as the Aviation Safety Center. It had already been badly damaged in the summer of 1982 by invading Israeli artillery and tanks. But it takes a lot of shells to destroy such a solid structure. It was sufficiently intact that the U.S. Marines decided to make it their battalion headquarters when they returned to Lebanon in the aftermath of the assassination of the nation's new President-elect and the Palestinian massacres. Both tragedies had happened within days of the original departure of the Multi-National Force.*

This time, someone had figured out how to destroy the building

* The first MNF from the U.S., France and Italy had arrived in late August to oversee the evacuation of PLO guerrillas from Beirut. The original mandate was thirty days, but after the evacuation ended, the U.S. decided to pull out after only seventeen days, and France and Italy followed suit. A few days later, Lebanon's President-elect Bashir Gemayel was blown up by a bomb planted in his headquarters. The Israelis invaded West Beirut the next day. Two days later, Christian militiamen began an orgy of bloodletting against an estimated eight hundred Palestinians in the Sabra and Shatila refugee camps. The massacre led the three MNF nations to return, for what they thought would be a brief mission.

completely. It was the worst disaster for the U.S. military since the end of the Vietnam war. After a week of sifting through the tons of rubble, often by hand and small tools in case anyone might be alive below, rescuers had to give up on the last few. Like the suicide truck driver, they had been turned into dust. The final death toll was 241 U.S. troops.

Twenty seconds after the Marine bombing and four miles down the road, a second bomb went off in an eight-story building occupied by a rifle company of the French MNF contingent. Again, sentries did not have sufficient time to stop the truck. The entire structure blew over on its side, looking like a tilted concrete deck of cards. It was the worst single military loss for the French since the end of the Algerian war twenty-two years earlier. Fifty-eight paratroopers were dead.

Washington reacted with fury. "Those who directed this atrocity must be dealt justice, and they will be," President Reagan pledged in a nationally televised speech. "We cannot allow international criminals and thugs to undermine the peace," he told a group of reporters. General John W. Vessey, Jr., chairman of the Joint Chiefs of Staff, said in a similar warning that "justice" would be administered to "those who directed" the attack against the peacekeeping force.

But time passed, without reprisals, and the issue seemed to have been permanently dropped. Part of the problem was finding the phantom force responsible, for, despite all the public speculation and private leaks from U.S. officials, there was little hard evidence. As in the blast at the U.S. Embassy in Beirut six months earlier—which had the same modus operandi—special FBI investigation teams found no major clues in the thirty-foot-wide, ten-foot-deep crater the bomb created. Or, as one official admitted, "There are no smoking pistols."

Defense Secretary Caspar Weinberger's early conclusion that "there is a lot of circumstantial evidence that points toward Iran" was left hanging in midair. In a CBS *Face the Nation* interview just hours after the suicide mission, he also mentioned Syria and its chief arms supplier, the Soviet Union. "I am not convinced the Soviets are not involved. The Soviets love to fish in troubled waters." The

United States was groping, implicating any rival or foe, due more to anger than to information.

As the U.S. and France were to find, the attacks were, in effect, perfect crimes, for all the hard evidence had been blown up with the peacekeepers. The sophistication of the operation was immediately obvious. "To prepare an action like this required a lot of information," explained Lieutenant Colonel Hisham Jaber, the Lebanese Army liaison officer with the Marines. "You needed to know how the building was built, where it was structurally weak, and what the behavior of the guards was." It also required knowledge of how to get through Lebanese Army roadblocks ringing the U.S. position, and that the Marines slept late on Sundays. It was no lucky fluke that the smiling bomber made it all the way to the Marines' front door.

Within hours of the double blasts, an anonymous spokesman telephoned Agence France Presse in Beirut. "We are the soldiers of God," said a male voice in classical Arabic on behalf of "Islamic Jihad," a mysterious group about which virtually nothing was known. "We are neither Iranians, Syrians nor Palestinians, but Muslims who follow the precepts of the Koran." Islamic Jihad had also claimed responsibility for the U.S. Embassy bombing in which sixty-three had died. The movement's demand was that all Americans leave Lebanon or face the bloody consequences. "We said after that [embassy bombing] that we would strike more violently still. Now they understand with what they are dealing. Violence will remain our only way," the voice concluded, then hung up.

Ten days later another bomb-laden truck plowed its way into a yellow two-story building in the southern Lebanese city of Tyre, one of the headquarters of the occupying Israeli Defense Forces (IDF). Twenty-nine Israeli troops and more than thirty Palestinian and Lebanese prisoners held in the tightly guarded building were killed.

An angry Moshe Arens, the Israeli Defense Minister, pledged, "Lebanon is one big nest, a network of murderers against whom we will strike." And they did: waves of warplanes dropped bombs on Palestinian strongholds in eastern Lebanon—despite the lack of hard evidence at that stage about who was behind the bombing. Someone purporting to speak for Islamic Jihad called a few days later to boast of its role in this attack as well. So the Israeli Air Force staged additional raids on pro-Iranian Shi'ite bases, again at a time when Israeli officials said in private they had no solid information beyond the claim itself. Two days later French warplanes followed suit.

Phil Taubman of *The New York Times* revealed eighteen months later, in early 1985, that the French air strike was originally conceived and planned as a joint American–French raid. "It was the first time an American President had approved a counterterrorist strike," he wrote. But U.S. participation "was aborted because the final go-ahead was not issued in time by the Defense Department." U.S. Navy planes stationed on Sixth Fleet ships off the Lebanese coast never took off for the Bekaa valley—for reasons that remain classified. The fourteen French Super Etendards flew alone.

The United States instead looked inward, as both the House of Representatives and the Pentagon launched official inquiries into the military command structure and the security measures at the Marine compound. The Congressional report said the Marine commander, Colonel Timothy J. Geraghty, "bears the principal responsibility for the inadequacy of security." It added that there were "very serious errors of judgment" by officials on the ground and through the chain of command. The dissenting view on the House report was more understanding:

> The 20-20 hindsight condemnation of the Marines' security is not so clear when viewed in conjunction with the successful terrorist attack on the Israeli position on Tyre on Nov. 4. . . . The Israelis are not, nor have they been, limited in their preparedness or actions by a mission described as a "presence." . . . Yet—given the experience of the Israelis in dealing with terrorist threats over the years, their extensive intelligence capabilities and many of the same defenses which the Marines, in retrospect, were criticized for not having—on Nov. 4, ten days after the American and French attacks, a carbon copy attack was successfully carried out against the Israelis.

The more accurate view is that no practical security measures could stop a lone man willing to lose his life in a suicide mission. Neither the U.S. inquiries nor the Israeli and French reprisals realistically dealt with the disasters. Both dealt with *what* happened rather than *why*. Under pressure, the Marines moved their entire "peacekeeping" operation underground, hiding troops in shipping containers converted into bunkers, and the Israelis launched three more air raids. Just as Washington and Tel Aviv had ignored the host of indications of what was to come, they failed to understand, from history both ancient and recent, how to come to grips with the situation around them after the bombings.

■ ■ ■

TWO EPISODES were mainly responsible for lighting the fuse at the Marine compound on October 23, 1983. And, in broader terms, they typified the resentment of the West throughout the Arab world which had been building up throughout the second half of the twentieth century. These two events were finally to polarize the characters in the Lebanese drama: the Shia commandos against the Western forces propping up the Christian-dominated Lebanese government.

Initially, the Marines had been as welcomed by the Shia as they were by other factions in Lebanon, as a presence that would help restore stability and end eight years of war, domestic and regional. Of all the groups in Lebanon, the Shia had suffered the most at the hands of Christians, Palestinians and Israelis in each stage of strife. But beneath the surface simmered anger and suspicion, common to almost all Muslims in the Middle East. Until the summer of 1983, the U.S. forces were still perceived as having been essentially neutral. Then came the first of two fateful events.

In the biggest internal battle fought in Beirut since the 1975–76 civil war, Amal and the extremist Shia blew West Beirut wide open. It began over a small incident. On Sunday, August 28, 1983, Shia youths were putting up posters of Imam Musa al Sadr, the Shia spiritual leader, for the fifth anniversary of his disappearance in Libya. Gunmen in a passing car opened fire, killing one and injuring another. Shi'ite and MNF sources claimed the gunmen were right-wing Christian Phalangists, a group founded and led by the father of Lebanese President Amin Gemayel. The Phalangists had recently been trying to establish offices in the Shia neighborhoods. Amal gunmen took to the streets in pursuit of the Christians. Militias dug up weapons they had buried in basements and backyards instead of turning in during the previous year of comparative calm, as the government had ordered. The little battles then drew in the Lebanese Army.

The clashes intensified because the Shia, and other Muslim groups, had long charged that the Army was actively against them. The Army was U.S.-trained and was dominated by minority Christians, many with loyalties to the Phalange, who were thought to have initiated the trouble.* State troops quickly became the primary target of retaliation. Within twenty-four hours, thirteen thousand soldiers—40 percent of the Lebanese Army—had been called in to fight what U.S. military advisors described as the biggest engagement in the army's history.

The fighting was raw, almost primitive, unlike the Israeli–Palestinian conflict one year earlier when targets were obvious. The Shia, later joined by Druze and Sunni Muslim militias, took on army tanks and artillery with only rifles, machine guns and rocket-propelled grenades. They fought with daring and abandon from rooftops and street corners, their faces often concealed by pillowcase hoods and macabre Halloween-style masks. As one Amal fighter explained, "We will fight with whatever we have. Life is not worth living without our rights."

The battle raged throughout the densely populated commercial and residential areas for four days. Despite its vast superiority in weaponry, training and numbers, the Army lost thirty-six killed and 160 wounded. The crossfire also killed two Marines, four French soldiers, and more than ninety civilians, even though the whole Muslim half of town had fled underground.

By massive force, the Army finally regained partial control. It moved back into positions in the heart of West Beirut, but not into the seventeen-square-mile district in the southern suburbs dominated by the Shia, the area surrounding the airport and the Marine compound. For the first time, and despite tremendous odds, the Shi'ite militia was in the forefront of the opposition's challenge to the government.

Either ignored or scorned by Christians and other Muslims during

---

* U.S. military trainers began helping to rebuild the Lebanese Army in 1982, arriving shortly after the Multi-National Force. They remained after the MNF left, and were still in Lebanon as of the time of this book's final revisions.

Lebanon's forty years of independence, the Shia were now running the show. They held territory. Diplomats and foreign correspondents wanted to hear what their officials had to say. Despite its powerful U.S. support, the government could no longer challenge them without significant loss of life, equipment and standing. In Lebanon, the Shia counted. And among their ranks, still behind the scenes, were the extremists.

By September 1983, the status of the United States and its Marines was eroding uncomfortably as the Shia "emerged." On September 4, the Israelis pulled out from the Chouf Mountains surrounding the capital to a more defensible line twenty-two miles south along the Awali River. The withdrawal was the spark for the second event, unleashing hatred between Christian and Druze militias, which had been engaged in sporadic and brutally bloody conflicts for more than a century. Since the end of the Israeli invasion, the United States had tried to encourage peace, at this stage guided by special trouble-shooter Robert McFarlane. As usual with mediation in Lebanon, attention was once again diverted from the major issues to the domestic squabbling that triggered renewed violence. The "Mountain War" was to become far bigger than the August battle in the capital.

The dramatic and idyllic Chouf, Lebanon's heartland, overlooks Beirut International Airport. Two more Marines were killed in both spillover and retaliatory fire during the Mountain War, which in turn initiated intervention by the American contingent as well as U.S. Sixth Fleet gunships offshore. Originally a ceremonial or psychological presence, the Marines were slowly sucked into the domestic strife—but so far only in self-defense.

As tension around the Marine complex heightened, the United States dramatically increased its force. The troops onshore remained between 1,200 and 1,400, but the naval contingent off the Mediterranean coast soared to 12,400 men and more than a dozen ships, not including the U.S.S. *New Jersey*. That craft, the only operational battleship in the world, and its escorts were dispatched to Lebanon by the Pentagon as the Druze–Christian war broke out, but had not yet arrived. The U.S. "peacekeeping" force now could call in strikes from the sea whenever there was "an imminent danger to U.S. lives."

Despite early predictions that they could not last long, the Druze made rapid headway, pushing the Christian "Lebanese Forces" militia out of at least 85 percent of the scenic mountains. Then, almost overnight, the Druze were besieging Souk al Gharb. The former resort suddenly became the most strategic territory in the Chouf, for it was the last stronghold of the Lebanese Army and the gateway to the Christian East Beirut suburb of Baabda, and the Presidential Palace. Panic-stricken, the Army appealed to the United States to help hold Souk al Gharb. Frightened commanders claimed that the Army could not hold out another thirty minutes. McFarlane agreed.

Colonel Geraghty, who was considered by diplomats and other MNF commanders to be the coolest and most thoughtful of the three Marine commanders to serve in Beirut, was flabbergasted when he received the order on September 19: American naval and air fire was called in *not* to defend the Marines, but to support the besieged Lebanese Army in Souk al Gharb. In effect, the Marines would be going on the offensive for the first time, taking sides in the Lebanese conflict.

Two officers present as Geraghty answered his radio phone said he argued vehemently against it: "Sir, I can't do that. This will cost us our neutrality. Do you realize if you do that, we'll get slaughtered down here? We could be severely attacked. We're totally vulnerable. We're sitting ducks." But Colonel Geraghty was overruled. The U.S.S. *Virginia*, a nuclear-powered cruiser, fired more than seventy deafening rounds against the Druze militia. American warplanes, already in the air, were turned back only at the last minute.

Tragically, the shelling was probably not necessary. McFarlane and Saudi Arabian mediators did finally negotiate a truce a week later, but Druze and Syrian sources said it was despite the U.S. involvement, not because of it. Colonel Fintel, the chief U.S. trainer of the Lebanese Army, admitted eighteen days after the *Virginia*'s shelling that the Army could probably have held Souk al Gharb without U.S. intervention. The Christian command of the Army had simply but fatally overreacted. Indeed, as the Americans learned after the fact, only eight Lebanese soldiers had died at Souk al Gharb. But eighteen days later it was too late.

The move came back to haunt Washington as a major miscalculation. Some American diplomats conceded that it was the last straw in the growing antagonism between the United States and Muslim groups.

Through those two events—the first Shia military victory and the intervention by the United States in Lebanon's domestic war—the U.S. had lost its credibility and neutrality in Lebanon. American advisors were seen as pro-Christian. The Marines were viewed as just another faction, what one Beirut newspaper called "the international militia" of Lebanon. The Marines, as the most visible symbol of U.S. policy, suddenly came under fierce attack, verbal and literal, by an alliance of Muslim groups. Enmeshed in the civil war as combatants, the Marines were no longer peacekeepers. Indeed, there was no peace to keep.

The Shia, being the closest to the U.S. complex, were the most active. One Shi'ite fighter, nicknamed "Castro" by the Marines because of his full scraggly beard, led a Shia band that regularly sniped at the American troops. Dozens of others, less visible, targeted the exposed U.S. position from the shanties of "Hooterville."

Amal leader Nabih Berri repeatedly disclaimed his forces' responsibility. He occasionally sent his militiamen down to "clean out" the snipers' nests. While some of the Shi'ite marksmen were indeed self-professed members of Amal, others were not. In the West Beirut shanties surrounding the Marine compound, fanatics from a variety of groups had moved in in recent weeks, waiting for the right moment, ready to take advantage of the mood to advance their cause.

The physical strength of the U.S. forces—including the "flying Volkswagens," the 2,700-pound shells from the *New Jersey*'s guns— was powerless against the little snipers, the car-bombers and the assassins. It was not an issue of quantity or quality as much as of commitment, the suicide fanaticism of Shia commandos that has often given them an edge over most conventional arms and tactics.

Thirty-four days after Souk al Gharb, the smiling bomber and his Mercedes truck blew the sleeping Marines sky high.

■   ■   ■

AN INNOCUOUS LITTLE ROAD, really not much more than a single track, runs through the mountain range along the Lebanese–Syrian border. In recent years, it has been the primary route for smugglers of hashish and stolen cars. It begins in the former mountain resort of

Zebdani in western Syria, where local legend has it that Noah's Ark and Adam's tomb are located, and ends in the Bekaa valley of eastern Lebanon.

American suspicions about the link between Iran, Syria and the bombings centered on this road. An Iranian presence so far from home dated to the June 1982 Israeli invasion, when Ayatollah Khomeini and his theocrats had reacted with fury and speed to the bold Israeli move. Indeed, the Persians initially appeared to be doing more militarily to aid the Palestinians and the Lebanese than any of the Arabs, except Syria. In hindsight, however, the Iranian move may have been a pretext for other long-term intentions.

A few days after Israel launched "Operation Peace for Galilee"— and sixteen months before the MNF bombings—Iran dispatched more than one thousand Revolutionary Guards, or Pasdaran, to the region. The guards were volunteers in the powerful but poorly trained paramilitary unit created after the Iranian revolution to provide force to back up the mullahs' words. In Zebdani they established the largest single base of operations outside Iran, taking over a "youth camp" on the outskirts of town with the permission, and maybe encouragement, of Syria. Zebdani was the operational, logistics and supply headquarters for a fluctuating three to six hundred Pasdaran, who were stationed in scattered buildings just across the border on the Bekaa plains. The remainder of the Pasdaran either worked at the Zebdani camp or waited there for rotation into Lebanon.

The dirt road was the physical link, one that was to become increasingly important over the next twenty months. It was first the land line connecting the Iranians' headquarters in Syria and their troops stationed around the ancient city of Baalbeck in Lebanon. It quickly became the route for operations by the Lebanese militants.

On July 19, 1982, David Dodge, acting president of the American University of Beirut, was abducted on campus by unidentified gunmen. In the chaos of the invasion, with West Beirut under siege by the Israelis, it was virtually impossible for American diplomats to trace him. Not until after his release 366 days later, negotiated through the Syrians, did the world learn he had been whisked out of Beirut and taken to Iran. U.S. diplomatic sources later said Dodge was spirited out on the old road to Zebdani.

Intelligence sources with three of the four nations participating in the MNF—the United States, France, Italy and Britain—eventually admitted that in late 1982 U.S. satellites began keeping regular surveillance over both Zebdani and the old road because of mounting anxiety about exactly what the Iranians and their local followers were doing. Despite propaganda out of Tehran, the Pasdaran had actually done little to confront the Israelis based some thirty-five miles south. Most of their activities appeared to serve other priorities. They were missionaries more than fighters.

"Our only goal is to Islamicize the place and, as the Imam Khomeini says, we have to export the Islamic revolution to the world. So, like any other Muslims, we have come here with the aim of saving the deprived," one Iranian told a British reporter in a rare interview.

The Pasdaran had quickly tightened their grip around Baalbeck, a predominantly Shi'ite Muslim area. They entrenched themselves in three major offices, taking over the Lebanese Army's regional headquarters in the Sheikh Abdullah barracks, as well as a modern clinic renamed "Hospital Khomeini" and the Hotel Khayyam. But they were active in many places, including schools, where they propagated Islamic doctrine.

Although Syria theoretically controlled the eastern Lebanese areas, Baalbeck particularly resembled a little Tehran. Within months after the Pasdaran arrived in 1982, increasing numbers of women took to wearing the black shrouds known as chadors, which cover all but the face. Vivid posters and wall paintings depicted Khomeini leading bloodstained Islamic warriors fighting for Jerusalem. Liquor disappeared from shop shelves. And well-armed Revolutionary Guards roaming the streets usually had the last word on any issue.

Very quickly the Iranians also found an effective Lebanese ally in Hussein Musawi, the former chemistry teacher turned militia commander who had just defected from Lebanon's largest Shi'ite movement, Nabih Berri's Amal. The link-up was natural, for Musawi had been trained in Iran. He was another of the elite protégées of Mustafa Chamran, the Iranian Defense Minister who had worked in Lebanon with Amal before the Shah's overthrow.

Musawi had angrily condemned Berri for his moderation and for committing the cardinal sin of succumbing to U.S. diplomatic efforts to end the Israeli siege of West Beirut, which was also Amal's stronghold. Like many militants, Musawi held the Americans responsible for supporting Israel to such a degree that it could invade Lebanon. He was also disillusioned by Berri's lack of support for the Iranian revolution, launched by their brethren Shia. After several heated sessions, Musawi split with Berri, taking his followers to a new base in Baalbeck. Under Iranian sponsorship, he formed the extremist Islamic Amal ("Islamic Hope") party.

Within months, a second and looser group, called Hizbollah, or "Party of God," gathered around the local Shia clergy, modeled on a militia group with the same name in Iran. "Hizbollah" derives from a verse in the Koran that promises triumph for those who join "the party of God." For the Prophet Mohammed, it was the means of spreading the faith. Now it was the vehicle for spreading the revolution.

Hizbollah's following mushroomed as both the Iranians and their local allies indoctrinated the young and the poor Shia peasants through films and "ideological seminars." The decorous Ran el Ain Mosque soon blazoned a sign: "Martyrdom's Headquarters." And banners and signs in the streets declaimed: "Death to America," "Martyrdom is the aim and hope of God's worshipers" and "Our revolution is Islamic before being Iranian, and it is the revolution of the oppressed throughout the world." For eight hours a day, a local radio transmitted "The Voice of the Iranian Revolution," sermons, songs, and interviews with supporters.

Lacking any official structure or membership list, Hizbollah was not a political party in the Western sense, although it served many of the same purposes. It was similar in "structure" to the religious organizations in Iran, its membership fluid and dependent upon the message and personal appeal of religious leaders. Musawi said of it, "Hizbollah is the people's march. It is a popular state. In other words, every believer who fights Israel in the south and who defends the honor of the Muslims in Beirut or the Bekaa Valley and has links with the Islamic revolution belongs to Hizbollah. . . . We [in Islamic Amal] work for Islam and are bound to the Islamic revolution. Therefore, we are part of Hizbollah."

Through Islamic Amal and Hizbollah, the Iranians had firmly established their forward outpost on a Western flank, in Lebanon, to propagate their revolution. It was quickly to grow.

Shortly before the U.S. and French bombings, Musawi described Iran's relationship with these groups as that of "a mother to a son. We are her children. We are seeking to formulate an Islamic society which in the final analysis will produce an Islamic state." Indeed, the aims he listed were far broader than merely bringing Lebanon into the fold. "The Islamic revolution will march to liberate Palestine and Jerusalem, and the Islamic state will then spread its authority over the region of which Lebanon is only a part."

Sheikh Ibrahim al Amin, one of Hizbollah's leading lights, was more specific: "We aspire for and seek an ideological and political society that will give Lebanon its proper position in the world struggle. We cannot consider the Lebanese society to be sound and clean when it is tied to an agreement with Israel and subject to American designs in the region."

■　　　　■　　　　■

LESS THAN A WEEK after the MNF bombings, Washington pointed a finger at Musawi, who was allegedly working with Iranian support and Syrian acquiescence. By this time, Musawi had become so feared by Westerners and Arab moderates that he was referred to as the Shi'ite "Carlos," a reference to the notorious international terrorist. But Musawi frequently and vehemently denied responsibility, while commending those who carried it out. "I salute this good act, and I consider it a good deed and a legitimate right, and I bow to the spirits of the martyrs who carried out this operation," he said in Baalbeck.

He also claimed that Iran had played no part. "Iran had nothing to do with what happened in Beirut. The wind of the Islamic revolution created new revolutionary currents that threw the U.S. and France out of Lebanon. The same currents will in the future throw Israel out of Lebanon."

"If America kills my people, then my people must kill Americans," Musawi said later. "We have already said that if self-defense and if the stand against American, Israeli and French oppression constitute terrorism, then we are terrorists in that context. This path is the path of blood, the path of martyrdom. For us death is easier than smoking a cigarette if it comes while fighting for the cause of God and while defending the oppressed."

Whatever the truth of Musawi's denials, it is clear that, from the fall of 1982 into 1983, the Baalbeck movements had quickly grown and quietly spread, no longer simply on the fringe of the Lebanese furor. The growth of militant fundamentalism in Lebanon was the biggest success to date for Iran's campaign to export the revolution, and offered the first and most detailed insight into the inner workings of the crusade.

By August of 1983, two months before the bombings, cadre of Musawi's Islamic Amal and Hizbollah—which were effectively becoming one under the Hizbollah label—had infiltrated the chaotic maze of West Beirut's poor Shi'ite suburbs. An Amal official admitted, "There used to be 100 different organizations in these neighborhoods in the pay of all different kinds of people. No one can say they are all gone or expect us to be able to control them all 100 percent." Not even the group theoretically ruling the Shia territory knew what fanatic undercurrents were emerging.

At the same time, the August and Mountain wars coincided with particularly heavy traffic by Lebanese, Syrians and Iranians on the old mountain road from Zebdani into Lebanon, according to worried Western intelligence sources and U.S. satellites monitoring the hive of activity. Heavy trucks and military vehicles were hauling in men, materiel and blueprints for use on four fronts in the battered and battling nation, items too sensitive or secret for the normal Damascus-to-Beirut highway. This traffic was to prove the Syrian link.

In the north, the equipment and the forces aided PLO rebels challenging PLO chairman Yasir Arafat, who was then trying grimly to hold on to the port city of Tripoli. In the south, they were supporting Shia activists against Israeli occupying forces, until the Israelis sealed off the area. And in the central Chouf mountains and Beirut, they backed Muslim militias against the MNF, particularly the Americans.

Colonel Ghazi Kenaan, of Syria's G-2 military intelligence, was one of the connections, U.S. intelligence sources said. Colonel Kenaan supervised the various operations and the distribution of materiel. From his base in the eastern Lebanese town of Shtoura, he worked out the logistics for Syrian President Hafez Assad, a ruthless tactician who shrewdly manipulated surrogates and various allies to fulfill his own goals. High on Assad's list of friends were the Iranian and radical Lebanese Shia commandos.

Since the outbreak of the Iran–Iraq War in 1980, Syria had been Iran's main ally among the very few Arab states willing to side with the non-Arab Persians. But their common goals, changing the regimes in Baghdad and Beirut, were for entirely different reasons.

In Lebanon, President Assad wanted to rid the country of the Americans, who were threatening to entrench de-facto Christian supremacy over the majority Muslims and to shape the tiny nation into a Western mold. He felt Lebanon belonged to the Orient, specifically the Arab bloc. But the Syrian leader's ambitions, like his rule, were totally secular.* The Iranians and their local allies had an entirely different dream. They wanted to spread militant Islam throughout the Arab world, ridding all these states of "infidels" from both East and West.

Baalbeck and the various military training camps within a fifteen-mile radius became the staging ground for this deadly political game. Islamic Jihad had claimed credit for the Beirut bombings, but increasingly the anonymous callers—sometimes the same voice, but not always—appeared to be the only "members," making Islamic Holy War more of an information network for a variety of cells or movements rather than a cohesive or structured independent group of extremists. It was unlike any of the other lethal movements—the Baader-Meinhof Gang, the Red Brigades, the Irish Republican Army or the Japanese Red Army—that the world had endured.

Although the modus operandi was identical in many of the attacks, there were few other indications, at least in the early stages, of an established chain of command that linked them all, or of firm connections between the individuals or groups behind the various terrorist operations. Islamic Jihad was clearly pro-Iranian in ideology, but some doubts existed among both Muslim moderates and Western diplomats about whether it was actually directed by Iran rather than home-grown.

---

* The 1973 constitution of Syria, a land Mohammed's crusaders captured in the seventh century, would have appalled the Prophet: it refers to Islam only once, and only as the result of public pressure. A single clause specifies that the president must be a Muslim.

The Iranian training camps—which instructed militants from other nations with the clear hope that they would use their new skills at home—were proof that the terrorism was "state-sponsored," but not necessarily in the way many Westerners assumed. The Iranians had provided instruction on ways to back up the campaign to terrorize Western governments into either withdrawing from or cutting back on their involvement in the region.

But even some U.S. officials acknowledged that they were not fully convinced a specific order had been handed down from one government leader in Tehran to blow up the American Marines and French paratroopers. However, even if there was no specific order, the message in general from Iranian theocrats and Islamic militants in other nations was that Western governments, which they felt were challenging or trying to repress Islam, should be banished from Islamic lands. The controversial presence of the Multi-National Force, particularly after the August and Mountain wars, was clearly considered an offensive thorn to militants, and therefore made the Western troops an obvious target.

And a few signs did indicate that Iranian individuals, sometimes with assistance from Syrian and Libyan individuals, became involved once attacks were planned, by providing resources and/or funds, or putting the planners in touch with others who had a needed expertise to help—not necessarily fully aware of exactly what was to happen.

As the MNF bombings and later incidents were to indicate, the callers claiming to represent Islamic Jihad did appear to have some if not complete advance knowledge, and perhaps loose links to members of the cells responsible for the attacks. But in other cases, the callers seemed to be exploiting the activities of groups that had no apparent ties to Islamic Jihad.

The movement, if it could even be called that, was amorphous, more of a concatenation, probably linking cells that were aware that Islamic Jihad would claim responsibility on their behalf, as well as others who were later openly angered by usurpation of credit. The effect, creating an aura of a single omnipotent force in the region, may have been all that the anonymous callers sought. They did, indeed, succeed in that goal.

Piecemeal clues provided some insight into the diversity of forces—Lebanese, Iranian and Syrian—allegedly linked to the militants who carried out the bombings. The first came from those who used the dusty track between Zebdani and Baalbeck, a cast of characters both long and multinational. Several have been implicated in the MNF attacks. The evidence remains circumstantial, and the connections are murky, but some of the names on the list provide useful insight into the style and rhythm of the crusade.

One often mentioned was Hossein Sheikholeslam, who had also been a leading figure among the students who took over the U.S. Embassy in Tehran and held fifty-two diplomats and security personnel hostage for 444 days. The hostages had nicknamed him "gaptooth"—for an obvious reason. Afterward he moved on to the Iranian Foreign Ministry in the prestigious post of assistant for political affairs. "It is a post that puts him in charge of exporting the revolution," explained Abbass Shekouhi, the Iranian chargé d'affaires in Bahrain, one of his colleagues. In early 1985, a key U.S. official added: "We know he is one of the top two or three in the regime involved in terrorism."

The assignment called for Sheikholeslam, still in his twenties and a graduate of the University of California at Berkeley, to travel often to Syria and Lebanon, where he usually visited Zebdani and Baalbeck. In the week before the bombing in Beirut, the young Iranian official checked in to the Sheraton Hotel in Damascus, where he stayed down the hall from Reuters correspondent Mike Sheridan. His trip appeared to be related to business involving the Syrian-Iranian oil deal. But Sheridan saw him riding in a black Mercedes with Lebanese plates. And other Western officials said he was seen heading into Lebanon. Sheikholeslam had been expected to stay in Syria until October 24 or 25. But he checked out of the Sheraton, apparently on very short notice, on Saturday, October 22, the day before the explosions at the Marine and French compounds.

Another Syrian link was established through radical Palestinians, a few members of hard-line factions or the new rebel group that opposed Arafat. Most were under Syrian tutelage. They may have been tapped for their knowledge about the assembly of sophisticated bombs, the location of PLO materiel left over in Beirut, or possibly the Palestinian safehouses and subterranean complexes that could conceal operatives and equipment. As the Pentagon inquiry into the bombing reported: "Stockpiles of explosives, built up over a decade prior to the Israeli invasion of June 1982, are reportedly still in place and available for future terrorist operations in and around Beirut." But more than one intelligence source indicated it was unlikely that this level of operatives was aware of the target.

An important Lebanese middleman appears to have been Abu Haidar Musawi. Intelligence sources suggested that Abu Haidar Musawi was a relative of Islamic Amal leader Hussein Musawi, although Musawi is a common Arabic name. At any rate, Abu Haidar Musawi was well known in Beirut as a prominent member of a radical Shia group known as the "Hussein Suicide Squad."

U.S. military sources in Beirut and Washington saw him as a link between the Beirut bombings and the Shia fundamentalists in Baalbeck, and through them to Syria and Iran. Intelligence agencies probing the bombings claim he arranged to get trucks similar to those used to carry goods to the airport cargo area near the Marines. (The red van that carried the 1,100-pound bomb into the French paratroopers' building was also identical to one driven by a vegetable vendor in the neighborhood who catered to the French, an MNF official said.) Obtaining the trucks was one indication of the complicated planning that went into what looked like a simple operation.

The small cell of hardened fighters to which Abu Haidar belonged was one of the many that either spun off from or were nurtured by the Baalbeck group. It also had ties to the oldest and largest Shia opposition group in the Middle East, Dawa—in full, Al Dawa al Islamiya, "the Islamic Call"—which was now based in Tehran. Musawi reportedly went to the Bekaa to consult on the operation with Hussein Musawi. He bragged to others that he was going to "explode the situation" in Beirut.

U.S. intelligence agencies tried diligently to establish more specific ties between the Islamic Republic of Iran and the bombings. Iranian Chargé d'Affaires Majid Kamal angrily denied culpability in an interview three days after the bombing: "Unfortunately, every time America has a loss in the region, it blames Iran. They are all lying. Some of this is a joke. We strongly reject these charges of involvement." Yet within a week after the blasts, U.S. sources were citing surveillance reports that could implicate the Iranian Embassy in Beirut.

Roughly ten minutes after the explosions, cars full of men were seen driving from the embassy at high speed. The timing, 6:32 A.M., was more suspicious than the speed, since drivers in Lebanon tend to race rather than ramble on even the narrowest, shell-cratered roads. Moreover, the embassy was directly across the street from the French MNF headquarters. But it seemed an impractical, indeed unsafe, place to have a command central. It had, like the American mission, been under guard by Lebanese gendarmes at two separate gates. At the side had been a company headquarters for the Lebanese Army. And the embassy was comparatively small. Since Israeli shells had badly wrecked the original five-story embassy the year before, Iranian diplomats had moved into the ambassador's villa, which had no special antenna on the roof for independent communications.

In contrast, the Iranian Embassy in Damascus was the most imposing and well-staffed Iranian mission in the Middle East, dubbed "Iran's foreign brain center" even before the attacks. The new four-story building, pink, red and white begonias dripping from window boxes, hid behind a high fence and cordons of Revolutionary Guards.

Intelligence agents from both Arab and Western nations had pinpointed three men from this embassy as pivotal link men with the extremists. First, on the operational side, was Hussein Ahromi Zadeh, the Iranian military attaché, who had duties often outside Syria, in Lebanon's Bekaa valley. Zadeh served as liaison between the embassy and the two main Iranian bases in Baalbeck and Zebdani.

His counterparts in European and Arab embassies claimed that Zadeh would spend up to five days each week supervising the Revolutionary Guards and their Lebanese allies. He often told other diplomats that Iran would not leave Lebanon because it was on a "cultural mission."

Second on the intelligence list was Ali Akbar Mushtashimi, the Iranian Ambassador to Syria and believed to be a top coordinator of Iranian-backed missions to spread the revolution in the Arab world. Western intelligence sources said he made "liberal" use of the diplomatic pouch, which is immune from inspection by the host country, to bring in sensitive material. One source noted: "The pouch was a euphemism. He brought in crates of stuff," which often went to Zebdani or into Lebanon.

Three months after the Beirut blasts, Mushtashimi received a gift parcel containing a book on Shia holy places. As he opened the package, it detonated, blowing off a hand and severely wounding him. "It could have been any number of people," said an envoy from a Muslim country who had close contacts among the Iranians about the source of the book bomb. "There were a lot of people who would have liked to see him suffer. He was considered a prime mover behind many questionable activities." Mushtashimi, who was medivaced to Europe for treatment, was out of action for six months, but he did eventually return to Damascus.

The third was Sayyid Ahmed al Fihri, the Ayatollah's personal representative in Syria. He was so revered that when I requested an interview in Damascus the embassy said he never saw "outsiders."

The cleric's influence was evident at the Tomb of Zeinab outside Damascus. The mausoleum holds the remains of the prophet Mohammed's granddaughter, who gained a revered place in Shia history because of her heroic efforts to keep the faith alive after the Karbala massacre led by her brother Hussein. The ornately tiled Shi'ite shrine, which contains an eight-foot-high solid silver tomb, more than a dozen crystal chandeliers, and two doors of solid gold, is the site of regular pilgrimages by Shia from Iran and many Arab countries. The walls outside the surrounding courtyard are covered with posters of Ayatollah Khomeini and Imam Musa al Sadr, as well as of political groups such as Dawa. Banners in Arabic, Farsi and English advertise daily Islamic instructions, many of which are reportedly taught by Fihri.

He did not work out of the embassy. But he clearly was kept busy with "insiders," for Syrian and Lebanese sources claim he oversaw the campaign to propagate the faith among Muslims, an assignment with greater long-term importance for the crusade than the specific plots against Western targets. He was another who reportedly often traveled to eastern Lebanon to preach the message of militant Islam to the young crusaders.

■   ■   ■

SINCE 1981, a sandbagged guard emplacement has fronted the ten-story apartment building in the Bir Abid suburb of Beirut where Sheikh Mohammed Hussein Fadlallah lives. Scruffy young men in mismatched fatigues cradle Soviet-made AK-47 rifles. A walkie-talkie connects the guard post with the Sheikh's fifth-floor flat, and any-one who visits is searched—except women, who are asked to wear Is-lamic dress and head cover. Fadlallah is a Shi'ite leader with strong Iranian connections who has repeatedly been fingered for a promi-nent part in the bombings.

In the apartment, in 1983, were several armed men. One young man introduced himself as Mohammed Ali Amelli, and he wanted to talk. On his breast pocket was a small green button identifying "the Islamic Republic of Iran" in Farsi and English. He proudly showed off books that were helping him learn the Iranian tongue. An enor-mous scar ran the length of his left arm, from injuries suffered during the civil war, he said. He then pulled up the trouser leg of his unusual fatigues, green with brown leopard spots, to show off his leg, hid-eously mauled. "They are all right now," he said. "I was operated on three times here, and once in the Soviet Union." Trying to find out who Amelli was working for, or who paid him, was not easy. He de-nied membership in any of the large movements or small cells. "I work only for God," he said with such seriousness that one believed he believed it. In fact, the man for whom he was working directly was one of the most powerful figures in the Middle East.

Sheikh Fadlallah is a grandfatherly type. Without his black turban and flowing brown robes, the short, stout Muslim might pass for a professor. He looks out from behind big brown glasses and, unlike the usually severe Shia mullahs, often and easily smiles. Before the bombings, he was obscure except within the Shia community. The cleric was respected for his learning and had a big following at the mosque in Beirut's Bir Abid suburb, and in Iraq, where he spent sev-eral years.

But after the bombings, Fadlallah overnight became one of the best-known and most feared men in the region. In calculated leaks, the Christian "Lebanese Forces" militia alleged that he had possibly provided but definitely blessed the two "smiling" kamikaze drivers in a special ceremony on the eve of their attacks on the Marines and French forces. Israeli and U.S. sources gave strong credence to the report, while admitting they had nothing firsthand. But whether or not Sheikh Fadlallah actually supported the Beirut bombings is al-most secondary to the broad impact he has had on the Shia funda-mentalists throughout the region. Gulf security officials said that his name came up in both the interrogations and the closed-door trial of the twenty-five men accused of detonating the six bombs in Kuwait, including one each at the U.S. and French embassies, seven weeks after the Beirut bombs. The Kuwaiti bombers—like growing numbers of both activists and ordinary Shia—had been "admirers" of the sheikh.

During a visit to the most militant mosque in Kuwait in May 1984, I tried to talk to several worshipers, who were at first reluctant to speak with a Western woman. But my residence in Beirut opened the door, for almost to a man each wanted to know about Sheikh Fadlallah. It was the same in Bahrain. A prominent Iraqi who is associated with several of the Shia extremist groups compared Sheikh Fadlallah to Ayatollah Khomeini in 1978: "He has an enormous following, but no official organization."

The chief representative in Damascus of Dawa, the most influential Shia fanatic group, also said Sheikh Fadlallah was not a member, much less a leader. "He is a high believer and a scientific one. He does not need to belong. He works at a higher level influencing the lives of all Shia, providing direction and spiritual guidance," explained Dr. Abu Asseal, who uses a nom de guerre.

Sheikh Fadlallah also denied any formal affiliations or involvement. In an interview a month after the explosions, he brought up the subject first. "What propaganda that I blessed the people who did it. This is silly. Suicide in such a way is forbidden in our religion. . . . We don't believe in what's happening now. We reject it. All over the world the Shia are thought of as devils, snakes. We are *not* dangerous. . . . I do not know the parties or who did it." And he claimed that after the retaliatory Israeli and French air strikes he was besieged by angry people who appealed for revenge. "I advised against it, and so far there has been none." He even went as far as to welcome a continued MNF presence—as long as the French and the Americans ended their "aggressiveness" and returned to the original terms of their mission. And he denied having any contact or connection with Hussein Musawi.

In a second interview a year later, the sheikh added, "I don't work for any political movement, not Dawa, not Hizbollah. But my thoughts, which I write in books or preach, have spread in the world. Some assume I am Dawa or Hizbollah due to the thoughts and the books. I have been working and writing for Islam for thirty years, so I have affected the people. These people may or may not be in Hizbollah or Dawa. . . . People come to me about Amal and Hizbollah and, because of my influence, I am somewhat helpful to people who have problems. I believe a person should hold highly his responsibility. I am not a believer of Hizbollah. Why should I not come forward if I were?"

Sheikh Fadlallah described himself as only a "spiritual reference" in Lebanon. And he said of the Shia cadre, "The majority in the resistance are believers. A small portion follow Marxist or nationalist thought. Some operations are organized and others are personal initiatives." And he said of Islamic Jihad, "It's a cover not for one group but different groups. It should be evident that it does not exist, because international intelligence services have not yet produced or pointed to any single person. It is not natural to have this wide organization, which claims acts in Indonesia, the Red Sea and Lebanon, and not have been found out by any intelligence service. This is why I do not believe there is an Islamic Jihad." To a local paper, he added that the invisible movement "has entered the political dictionary and each faction, seeking to promote a certain political objective, tries to use it as a cover."

Sheikh Fadlallah's position explains much about the Shia "structure." In a system where religion and politics are so totally one, the clergy sets the philosophy and the tone. Others, in formal groups or informal cells, carry out the specifics of certain principles as they see fit. It would have been highly unusual—according to both Shia tradition and his own history—if he had been knowingly involved in the Beirut bombings. As the Dawa official had said, the sheikh was actually more important than that. He was a thinker, not a doer.

In October 1983, for instance, Sheikh Mohammed Mehdi Shamseddine, another influential Shia cleric in Beirut, issued a *fatwa,* or religious edict, declaring that Shia attacks on Israeli forces in southern Lebanon were "a religious duty." Anti-Israeli attacks increased in quantity and intensity. But not even the Israelis ever charged that Sheikh Shamseddine was responsible for organizing the campaign.

The Italian peacekeepers' experience illustrates Sheikh Fadlallah's specific influence. The largest of all contingents and the most dangerously exposed in Shia and Palestinian neighborhoods, the Italians had initiated direct contact with him. A military emissary made it clear they wanted good relations with the Shia. Dozens of Italian troops donated blood to clinics run by the Shia religious council, which led one of the sheikh's colleagues to preach in a mosque that the Italians should be seen as friends and "blood brothers." During the seventeen-month MNF presence, the Italians had only one soldier killed in an early attack.

Sheikh Fadlallah did indeed have close ties with Iran, and with Iranian diplomats in Beirut until the Lebanese expelled them after the bombings. (Relations were reestablished seven months later.) Three months after the bombings, he traveled to Iran, as he had often done in the past, for "consultations." He was much heralded on the front pages of Tehran papers and on television. He met with the Ayatollah, with whom he had been in contact for more than twenty years, as well as President Ali Khamenei and Speaker of Parliament Hojatoleslam Ali Akbar Hashemi Rafsanjani. The sheikh also said during the interview that he had talked with Sheikholeslam. "It was not an official visit," he said, "merely a special trip. The Western publicity said I went to Iran to give a report and take information from there. This is not true. My position does not allow me to do such things."

The sheikh's primary contributions to militant Islam are two volumes, of twenty he has written, that have become basic philosophical texts for Shia revolutionaries in the Arab world. They are available in mosques and Islamic study centers throughout the Gulf and in Syria and Lebanon. The most famous is entitled *Islam and the Logic of Force.* "My books encourage Muslims to live Islamic lives and make Islamic governments, but not by violent means," he explained. "I encourage peaceful and scientific ways."

"Islam is a tenet," he said, "a law and a method of life. Our youth have been influenced by its atmosphere. I am one of those who have helped formulate the Islamic concepts of this generation over the past eighteen years. The generation has now begun to carry Islam far from the traditions which held that Islam was just a way of knowledge."

But Sheikh Fadlallah denied that the Shia were by nature religious revolutionaries. "The present state of violence that has engulfed the Shi'ites is not a Shi'ite feature, but is rather an Oriental state. In other words, it is a state of emotional reaction that grips the Orientals. . . . Many who are analyzing the Shi'ite situation are looking at the Shi'ites out of the context of the conditions that prevail in the area, and in isolation from similar states of other Lebanese communities." And he charged that the Western media and unspecified political quarters were waging psychological warfare against fundamentalists "aimed at promoting rejection of Islam on the grounds that Islam represents terrorism and a terrorist backward political tide."

Yet he readily defended Hizbollah, the most militant Shia faction in Lebanon, which by late 1984 had absorbed all the known major extremist groups: Islamic Amal, Dawa, the Hussein Suicide Squad, Jundallah (Soldiers of God) and the Islamic Students Union. Indeed, some intelligence sources speculated that Islamic Jihad was actually the activist arm of Hizbollah, as Black September had been of Arafat's Fatah faction within the PLO.

"Hizbollah was born in the atmosphere of the Islamic Revolution in Iran . . . It is an organization born from Islamic concepts that are trying to face political reality. . . . The birth of Hizbollah in Lebanon is part of the overall Islamic challenge of the existing regimes and imperialism in its old and new forms," the sheikh said. "Hizbollah is a party, just like other parties in Lebanon which resort to the use of arms. It might be responsible for infractions and violations of the law, and they might have made mistakes, even though their mistakes are far less than those of others."

And the sheikh also was able to rationalize the bombing. "Although there are some people who have reservations about these methods, and I am perhaps one of them, they do not view them as negative. Instead they see these methods as correct and representing the free will of people who cannot be stopped by any hurdles or obstacles. . . . In the view of Muslims, for instance, this method is considered as a means of confronting America, France and Israel, which, through pressures, are trying to destroy the country and engender a mood of despair."

Of the Americans he said in early 1985, "We do not support or encourage attacks against purely American cultural institutions, or against American individuals doing normal business in the world. But in the meantime, we feel that when America pressures the Islamic world and Muslims, especially through Israel, it is very natural that the war being waged by those opposed to the policy of the American administration take the form of attacks on strictly political U.S. interests. This is very natural . . . It is a battle between America and all groups which feel that America is usurping their freedom and independence, and exerting pressure on them."

His line on violence could have been taken either way: "I believe that in all cases violence is like a surgical operation that the doctor should only resort to after he has exhausted all other methods." But when pressed, he added, "When it is necessary, I approve of violence. Also, every person needs to defend himself. If a man needs to use violent ways, he must use it."

Sheikh Fadlallah had firsthand experience with violence. Explaining the gunmen in his apartment, he said: "Between 1981 and 1982, there were four assassination attempts on me. So I need protection. There are only eight regulars, and then some volunteers and friends." In a nation where every leader has had a corps of militiamen providing personal security since the early 1970s, it was a comparatively tiny force.

On March 8, 1985, just as crowds of worshipers were leaving Friday prayers at the nearby Bir Abid mosque, a young man parked a pickup truck near Sheikh Fadlallah's apartment block. The cleric's bodyguards demanded he move the vehicle, but the driver asked to be allowed enough time to cross the street and fix a spare tire. Moments later, the truck exploded. Flames engulfed the entire block of high-rise buildings after gas cylinders in shops and homes also ignited. More than eighty people were killed, more than two hundred injured—making it the worst car bombing since the Marine blast. But the cleric, who had returned just a week earlier from another visit to Iran where he and other Middle East religious leaders had an audience with Ayatollah Khomeini, had not been at home.

Many parties had an interest in eliminating him or relaying a message in general to the hub of Shia militancy in West Beirut, including the Christian Phalange, the Israelis, even the United States. But the militant Shia had little question about who they felt was responsible. Afterward, Sheikh Fadlallah commented: "They sent me a letter, and I got the message." The next day he led a mass funeral procession of thousands through the bombed-out street. From the charred frame of one devastated building an enormous sign, in English, boldly declared: "Made in the U.S.A."

Two months after the incident, *The Washington Post* reported that the bombing had been carried out by a team "composed of Lebanese intelligence personnel and other foreigners" hired by a Lebanese unit that had been undergoing CIA training. The training, which had been approved by President Reagan, had been designed to have groups available to strike at suspected terrorists before they could attack U.S. facilities in the region.

Without the U.S. agency's knowledge, the unit had organized others to plant the bomb next to Sheikh Fadlallah's home. A Reagan administration official later told *The New York Times:* "This was a Lebanese operation. We maintained contact, intelligence contact, with Lebanese intelligence and of course we talked about counter-terrorism and planned things together. But this was not our operation and it was nothing we planned or knew about." Alarmed U.S. officials subsequently canceled the covert training operation.

But the denials and the cancellation did not remove the deepening suspicions about U.S. intentions in the minds of the Shia militants. The incident instead fueled fears and bitterness about American intervention on their turf—further justifying and strengthening the crusade.

■   ■   ■

ON FEBRUARY 6, 1984, President Reagan wrote to Seaman John Wandell, twenty, who was stationed on the U.S.S. *Guam* off the Lebanese coast: "Nancy and I enjoyed your poem very much. It really brightened our Christmas. We know that the price of defending freedom is immense. But we know that the alternative in places like Lebanon is acceptance of the rule of terror. We must not abandon those who have relied on our help to build a just and lasting peace." The note was consistent with Reagan's pledge after the bombing to remain in Lebanon and continue peace efforts which were "central to our credibility on a global scale."

But the next night, on nationwide television, the President announced that he had ordered the withdrawal of the U.S. Marines from Beirut. The sudden change of mind, and of U.S. policy, was clearly in part the result of the Shia crusade. Although Syria could

claim some political credit, it took the determination and commitment of the Shia commandos, motivated by their own reasons, to
carry it out on the ground, literally at whatever cost in their own
lives.

On the same day that the President wrote Seaman Wandell, Amal,
with assistance from the extremists, took full control of West Beirut.
A ferocious battle with the Lebanese Army and the Christian militia
left more than two hundred dead, but the Shia managed to wrest the
area not won during the August war. At least 40 percent of the active
Muslim troops in the U.S.–trained Lebanese Army had defected or
had laid down their arms rather than fight against their own people
in the name of a Christian-dominated government. The Lebanese
government, led by President Amin Gemayel, was more beleaguered
than at any other point in the nation's independent history, controlling only one-half of the capital in a country smaller than Connecticut. And the isolated Marine compound was suddenly surrounded by
Shia militiamen, both Amal and the extremists.

Just seven days earlier the new Marine commanding officer, General James R. Joy, had said that he feared Lebanon would "come
apart at the seams" if the Multi-National Force withdrew. He
pledged that the Marines would stay "until the job is done." He
spoke during a lull in the fighting with Shia gunmen in nearby
neighborhoods. One Marine had been killed and four wounded
within a few hours. He was only following the line dictated by Washington. The President had said after the bombing, "Without the
peacekeepers from the U.S., France, Italy, and Britain, the efforts to
find a peaceful solution in Lebanon would collapse." Yet the U.S.
mediation did indeed totally collapse while the Multi-National Force
was there. As Washington discovered, once again, military might
could not necessarily ram a policy down the throats of those who did
not want it and were willing to die to block it.

The period between the October blast and the February "rede-
ployment" to ships offshore saw an increase in the number of attacks.
The Pentagon noted that, from October onward, U.S. intelligence
was flooded with reports that Muslim factions were planning further
hostilities against the Marines, including more car bombs. Some of
them were wild: the U.S. contingent and Sixth Fleet ships were put
on alert for kamikaze hang gliders and balloonists, suicide swimmers

and fishermen. "One day they said we should look out for dogs with TNT strapped to their bellies," recalled Lance Corporal Manson Coleman. "For a few days we were shooting every dog around."

The first public warning came at a rally in Baalbeck exactly a week after the bombings. Sheikh Mohammed Yazbeck, the main speaker, raised the slogan "Death to America" and told the audience, "We are determined to carry it out." The Muslim leader praised the attacks as a "noble action because it shook America's throne and France's might. Let America, Israel and the world know that we have a lust for martyrdom and our motto is being translated into reality. . . . America's fleet will not frighten us. We shall teach it a lesson it will never forget by our faith and our strength."

Shortly thereafter, the Iranian paper *Kayhan* reported that more suicide squads would be recruited from what it called "the Islamic masses" to force the Americans and the French to leave Lebanon. And on November 22, in an interview with the Algerian news agency, the hitherto rather moderate Amal leader Nabih Berri, who had supported U.S. mediation efforts, accused the same two nations of seeking to commit "massacres" against the Lebanese and creating a "climate of racism" against the Shia. Berri, whose green card would eventually qualify him for U.S. citizenship, asked the United States and France to leave Lebanon.

In December 1983, Islamic Jihad phoned in a new threat. The anonymous voice pledged that "the earth would tremble" unless the MNF withdrew by New Year's. President Reagan told a closed meeting of Citizens of America, "We have information right now that they have marshaled a force, particularly of Iranians in Lebanon, that numbers up to one thousand who are all willing to sacrifice their lives in a kamikaze attack."

General Joy said some of them were close to the compound. "Radical elements have moved into these neighborhoods for the specific purpose of firing on the Marines. . . . We do have evidence that the Iranian-backed terrorist elements are planning attacks on MNF contingents, not only on U.S. forces. . . . We have definite evidence that there are some outside agitators. If they are not necessarily non-Lebanese, they are definitely manipulated by elements from outside Lebanon."

About the same time, a Lebanese intelligence report claimed that crates of aircraft parts had been spotted in the camps of radical Shia commandos in the Bekaa valley. The markings allegedly revealed that the country of origin was Iran. The targets would be either the U.S. ships or the Marines. Washington became almost hysterical, although U.S. diplomats in Beirut gave little credence to the sensational publicity. Nothing further ever came of the reports, nor were there ever aerial attacks.

But at Christmas the troops began moving underground. Not even Lebanese Army liaison officers or the American press could get by the entrance without an escort and a search. A five-mile exclusion zone was declared around American ships in the Mediterranean and the Gulf. The various diplomatic New Year's Eve parties in Beirut were canceled as everyone took maximum precautions. U.S. effectiveness, both politically and militarily, was rapidly crumbling.

Despite congressional pressure and skeptical public opinion back home, the Marines might have stayed longer, maybe through the summer of 1984. But the situation on the ground, following the Shia conquest of West Beirut on February 6, made this unrealistic. Already intimidated from the bombing by these seemingly mystically powerful Shia, Washington was not prepared to challenge them any further.

Three weeks after President Reagan wrote to Seaman Wandell, the Marines were gone. It was a commentary on the time that the "most elaborate fortifications built by a foreign army in Lebanon since the crusaders abandoned their magnificent castles seven hundred years ago" were turned over to the Shia.

■   ■   ■

THE MARINE WITHDRAWAL did not, however, end the crusade against the American presence in Lebanon. The Shia commandos instead began a second phase of attacks, as American individuals rather than institutions became the targets. It began three months after the bombing with the swift and spectacular assassination of Dr. Malcolm Kerr, a widely respected Arabist. Born in Beirut, he was seconded from the University of California to become president of the American University of Beirut (AUB). He stepped in after the 1982 kidnapping of David Dodge, the acting president. Although he had spurned personal bodyguards when he first arrived, Dr. Kerr was sufficiently worried by January 1984 to order a security review for the entire staff and campus. It was too late to save his life.

Early on January 18, two young men carrying books asked to see the president. When told he was not in, they waited by the elevator outside his office. A few minutes later, as Dr. Kerr left the elevator, two bullets ripped through his head. A silencer had totally muffled the sound, allowing the gunmen to escape. Only the noise of Dr. Kerr dropping his umbrella and briefcase aroused attention.

Ironically, the friendly and easygoing AUB chief had been a champion of the Arab cause, and had worked throughout his professional life to help the West understand the Arab world. No one was caught or arrested following his murder and initial accusations suggested both Christian and Muslim factions. But Ann Kerr, his wife and an English instructor on campus, summarized the widely held conclusions.

"I suppose it's a group of people who feel bewildered about what's happening in the world today," she said. "They feel imbued with a cause of their own. They don't understand western culture; they feel they have no say in what's going on in the world. It seems to me it's this kind of motivation that drives people to extreme fundamentalism, and to perpetrating the kinds of acts that happened to my husband."

American diplomats and AUB officials concurred that Dr. Kerr himself was not the target. It was his position as the most important local American outside the embassy. "AUB and Kerr are the most visible American institutions here. If anyone wants to shatter this, Kerr is someone who represents the Americans," said Professor Fred Bent, a visiting professor from Cornell University. And Secretary of State George Shultz said of the assassination, "These tactics are aimed at Americans generally."

Yet according to students and faculty, Dr. Kerr's biggest battle in the previous months had been with Shia fundamentalist students who had demanded many changes at the university. They called for an end to Western music as "against God's will." They pressed for rules forbidding "familiar behavior" among male and female students in the tropical gardens of the campus. Once they had commandeered an auditorium for prayers. Several times groups had assembled on campus, usually to mark some holiday or victory, and shouted, "*Allahu Akbar*" (God is great). This occasionally led to skirmishes with other students in the one place in Lebanon where all sects were equals. At the time of his death, Dr. Kerr was trying to persuade the students to delay campus elections due to the restless climate.

Then the voice of Islamic Jihad was soon heard again. "We are responsible for the assassination of the president of AUB, who was a victim of the American military presence in Lebanon. We also vow that not a single American or French will remain on this soil. We shall take no different course. And we shall not waver."

Three weeks later, Frank Regier, an electrical-engineering professor, was kidnapped when he walked off the campus grounds. Another month went by and gunmen opened fire on Colonel Dale Dorman, a Marine officer attached to the embassy, who was walking in civilian clothes along the seafront fifty yards from the U.S. mission. He was hit in the arm and the chest, but survived. Two days later, Jeremy Levin, bureau chief of Cable News Network, disappeared as he walked from his home to his office eight blocks away.* Ten days after that, U.S. Embassy political officer William Buckley was forcibly bundled into a white Renault by unidentified gunmen in front of passersby outside his apartment building on the same block as the International Red Cross headquarters.

Another seven weeks passed. Presbyterian minister Benjamin Weir and his wife, Carol, who had lived in Lebanon since 1958, were out strolling. Suddenly, a block from the local police office, three armed men rushed out of a waiting car and snatched Reverend Weir. "One of them grabbed him by the tie so that his face got red, and then another hit him on the back of the head," his wife said. As the car raced off, "I ran after them, screaming, trying to draw attention to them." The car had no license plates.

Reverend Weir was a particularly odd choice. Although he was a Christian, he had remained in Muslim-dominated West Beirut. He spoke fluent Arabic. He worked closely with various Muslim-oriented charity and relief groups. During the Israeli invasion and

---

* Levin was released on February 14, 1985, under disputed circumstances. He claimed to have escaped, but Shia radicals telephoned a news agency to allege that he had been allowed to escape. The latter version had some credibility, since the U.S. publicly thanked Syria for intervening on Levin's behalf.

siege of the Muslim sector, he and his family had remained. His daughter Chris had nursed up to eighteen hours a day in the underground hospital set up in the Near East Center of Theology where her father worked. All the victims she treated were Muslims, many of them fighters.

Five months after the kidnapping, her husband still missing, Mrs. Weir reflected the thinking of many Americans who had stuck it out in Lebanon: "I don't think my husband's kidnapping was a personal act against him. He's been kept because of our policy. It's a protest against our foreign policy." The kidnappings and bombings "provide more evidence that the U.S. has been unable to maintain an even-handedness in Arab–Israeli matters. The U.S. is losing its credibility as a mediator in the Arab world. The violence which occurs is produced by the U.S.'s inability to look behind the causes of violence and to deal with those causes," she added. "I also see an increased anti-American climate, which makes this kind of violence possible."

Mary Regier, wife of the kidnapped AUB professor, had similar thoughts: "I am sure it wasn't personal. I think what happened: the Americans were being evacuated that day, which reflects on the local people. Perhaps it means [to them] 'We don't trust you.' This happened two or three days after the big *New Jersey* shelling. Here is a tall, fair-haired, obvious American on the street. Perhaps that made someone mad."

The continued use of the world's only operational battleship was considered a major provocation in Lebanon, even by Americans there. Two former AUB instructors wrote an angry letter to *The New York Times*:

> Mr. Reagan, Mr. Shultz, let us put it to you bluntly. The recent American casualties in Beirut were as good as inflicted by the *New Jersey*'s guns. Terrorism does not spring from a vacuum, nor does it exist without a logic, one that can seem very compelling from the wrong end of the gun barrel. . . . So please send the *New Jersey* home. Or, at the very least, do not justify further shelling as protection for American civilians. It is dishonest—and for us a bitter blow—that our undoing should be presented as our salvation.

It was not until two days after the Weir abduction that anyone claimed responsibility. A man phoned Agence France Presse in

Beirut. "In the name of God, the merciful and compassionate," he introduced himself in classical Arabic, making it difficult to trace his origin. "The Islamic Jihad organization claims it is responsible for the abduction" of the Americans, "in order to renew our acceptance of Reagan's challenge and to confirm our commitment of the statement made public after the bombing of the Marine headquarters that we will not leave any American on Lebanese soil."

"Reagan's challenge," presumably, was his pledge to introduce new measures to counter what he dubbed "state-sponsored" terrorism. The voice also warned the mainstream Shia Amal movement "not to interfere in this affair if their members don't want to be harmed." Amal had freed Professor Regier after an accidental tip-off about where he had been hidden.

Then in May 1984, U.S. intelligence sources in Beirut received a hair-raising report. Embassy personnel and American instructors at AUB were quietly warned of a plan to kidnap one hundred U.S. citizens. In light of the hostage ordeal in Iran and the recent kidnappings in Lebanon, most of the victims of which were still missing, the threat of yet more to come by any of the many Shia groups terrified the U.S. Embassy. The new plot reportedly was timed to coincide with the beginning of the Muslim holy month of Ramadan, June 1 by the Western calendar, when the faithful fast and sacrifice from dawn to dusk. But the word quickly leaked, and the story became a sensation.

"Hizbollah will execute kidnapping operation at AUB and the U.S. Embassy," claimed the embassy report, quoted in a Beirut newspaper as having come from unnamed sources.

> The targets will have American identities. Have prepared 100 people for the operation, from which 20 are from inside the university. . . . Some of the elements will have explosives wrapped around them. In case these elements are hit by fire, they and the people they have kidnapped both will be killed by explosion. Purpose of the operation is to put pressure on the U.S. and reduce pressure on Iran, which is surrounded by enemies and unable to export its oil. The operation will be executed from three axes.

The same week, the U.S. Embassy announced that the bulk of its operation would be moving from the Muslim-dominated western sector of Beirut to the Christian-controlled east. The embassy had remained in West Beirut throughout the civil war and during the eleven years that the PLO maintained its main base just a few miles down the road. Although a spokesman claimed it was a move long planned, most other Western embassies conceded that the Americans simply felt that the threat from the Shia radicals was too great.

The Shia takeover of all West Beirut and the growing visibility of Hizbollah in Beirut did not help ease diplomatic qualms. With the Shia in command, the radicals had finally surfaced. Hundreds of Hizbollah fighters moved into strategic positions along the "green line" that divided the two halves of Beirut, sometimes as effectively as the Berlin Wall. Posters went up advertising their presence. Ambulances carried their name in big red letters. They opened three offices. They even started giving interviews to select papers.

The whole personality of West Beirut started to change. Ayatollah Khomeini became a prominent image on Hamra Street, the Champs-Élysées of the Middle East. His visage was plastered on the walls of boutiques and bookshops and banks. *"Kulluna Khomeini"* (All of us are Khomeini) was painted everywhere. Sidewalk salesmen hawked his picture in cardboard miniatures encased in plastic and attached to leather strings, a common sight around the necks of Shia militiamen. Hizbollah was now out in the open.

The familiar frills and dazzling colors of Lebanese women shoppers were increasingly replaced by drab conservative dress, arms covered and hair tucked under big gray or black scarves. The Candybox, Golden and Key Club bars were among dozens that came under attack, sticks of dynamite thrown at their front doors, sudden raids made by gunmen to check identity papers and, occasionally, smash bottles of liquor. By the beginning of Ramadan, even the legendary Commodore Hotel, home of the hard-drinking foreign press corps, had packed away its gin and whiskey.

There were never casualties in those raids, for the bombings always came on the nights the clubs were closed. They were messages. Amal officials, who tried to reassure businesses to remain open, claimed their men were not involved. It was the independent work of extremists, they said.

Yet Hizbollah quickly denied the threat to kidnap Americans. "This is untrue," a distributed statement read. "We are against the imperialist American policy in the world, but we are not against the American people. We are keen on preserving the public and private teaching institutes and on protecting the Muslims, the Christians and the foreigners." It charged that the accusation was "part of a campaign designed to force the most prestigious education institute in the Middle East to move to the eastern Christian sector of Beirut."

On behalf of the Americans, a Lebanese cabinet minister sought out Sheikh Fadlallah for reassurances. The sheikh then went on nationwide radio and television to condemn any violence against foreign targets, as well as Christian Lebanese. He even expressed reservations over the bombing of bars. The mass kidnappings did not take place. Nevertheless, the embassy moved most of its personnel out of the Muslim sector to a hastily prepared annex in the east.

■   ■   ■

SEPTEMBER 20, 1984, was a steamy Mediterranean day, calm by Beirut standards. Kenny Rogers, a big strapping Scot doing temporary duty in Beirut, was standing guard in the parking lot of the American Embassy annex in Christian East Beirut, waiting for British Ambassador David Miers to conclude a courtesy call on his U.S. counterpart, Reginald Bartholomew. A royal military policeman, Rogers was part of the beefed-up security team for British diplomats.

Guard duty seemed so much easier in the Christian sector, which had witnessed comparatively few of the vicious attacks so frequent in the Muslim-dominated west over the previous three years. The site added to the psychology. Aukar is a quiet residential suburb of hillside villas and luxury apartments built along winding little roads, facing the sea. Unlike most other parts of the capital, Aukar was unscarred by a decade of war. But the British ambassador's three bodyguards still had to be on alert at the beige tile-and-concrete annex, where the majority of U.S. diplomats had been rebased just two months.

As he waited near Miers's armored Minster sedan, Rogers's attention was drawn to the end of the cordoned road in front of the annex. "I looked along the road and saw a light-colored Chevrolet van with diplomatic plates," he recalled the next day. "There seemed to be an argument going on between the gate guard and the vehicle. There was a shot fired by the man in the van. The van accelerated down the road in the direction of the embassy [annex]. One of the other guards fired, possibly three rounds, at the van. By this time the van was almost parallel to me."

Then he realized exactly what was about to happen, the greatest fear of foreigners in Lebanon: a bomb-laden vehicle was heading straight for the entrance of a diplomatic facility. "I fired five rounds through the door," Rogers said. "I saw the driver fall over. As he fell over, he pulled the steering wheel to the right. The vehicle slid sideways and hit the American van [parked] at the side." Then it blew up.

Marine Corporal Larry Gill was on duty at Post One, the security desk in the lobby, just before noon on that sunny Thursday. "I heard the shots, and the skidding. Then the lights went out." He was thrown unconscious against the stairs behind him. Staff Sergeant Terry Turrel was on his way to the elevator when the blast went off. The impact broke his jaw, but he managed to get the first flash out on his walkie-talkie to the U.S. trainers of the Lebanese Army based at the Ministry of Defense. Major Alex Franco, who had survived the first embassy bombing seventeen months earlier and been decorated as a hero of the rescue effort, said he would never forget the chilling but familiar words that came over the airwaves from Turrel: "The embassy's gone up."

It was déjà vu of the April 18, 1983, embassy bombing in other respects. Like his predecessor, Ambassador Bartholomew was buried under rubble in his seafront office. Once more, American political officers had to dig by hand to rescue the leading U.S. official in Lebanon. And just as Ambassadors Bartholomew and Miers were being hospitalized for minor injuries, Islamic Jihad once again called in to claim credit.

"In the name of God, the compassionate and merciful. The Islamic Jihad Organization announces that it is responsible for blowing up a car rigged with explosives which was driven by one of our suicide commandos into a housing compound for the employees of the American Embassy in Beirut," an anonymous voice said. "The operation comes to prove that we will carry out our previous promise not to allow a single American to remain on Lebanese soil. When we say Lebanese soil we mean every inch of Lebanese territory. We also want to caution our Lebanese brothers and all citizens to stay away from American institutions and gathering points, especially the embassy. We are the strongest, and we will remain the strongest."

But the Shia commandos may have been disappointed in the results. The heroics of Rogers and a Lebanese guard, who the Americans claimed actually fired the crucial shots, prevented the van, with its three thousand pounds of explosives, from getting within ten yards of the front door—and what an American colonel supervising the aftermath estimated would have been a death toll five times greater. Fourteen were killed, only two of them Americans, and dozens injured.

More damning than the bombing was the fact that it could have happened at all at the annex nicknamed "Fortress America." Yet in the haste to get out of West Beirut, certain security provisions had not been completed at the new building. A massive steel gate which could have blocked the van lay pathetically at the side of the road the day of the bombing, not yet installed. Video cameras perched on the roof had not yet been activated. President Reagan rather glibly remarked, "Anyone that's ever had their kitchen done over knows that it never gets done as soon as you wish it would."

But again, security was not the only issue. The motive for this attack was clear. The attack had not come out of the blue; as with each of the Shia operations, there was cause behind the effect. Two weeks earlier, on September 6, the United States had unilaterally vetoed a United Nations Security Council resolution that called on Jerusalem to end unspecified objectionable "practices" against civilians in Israeli-occupied southern Lebanon. The wording had been greatly weakened—mainly to win U.S. support—from an original condemnation of the two-year occupation in the Shia-dominated territory.

Two days after the veto, Islamic Jihad issued a statement: "This flagrant and continuous defiance of our [Arab] nation will get the appropriate answer. Very soon, we shall strike at one of the vital American installations in the Middle East. . . . Our heroes are prepared to sacrifice their lives to destroy an American or Zionist institution, even though it may be small."

In another warning, a caller addressed President Reagan directly: "You, governor of the White House, await a painful blow before your reelection, more painful than our blows against your embassy and your military headquarters in Beirut." And three days before the bomb, a strange advertisement appeared in a Beirut paper declaring simply: "U.S. Ambassador: wanted dead or alive." After the warnings, it was only a matter of time before another "volunteer for martyrdom" was dispatched against the United States.

The comment of Neff Walker, an American psychology professor at AUB, was typical of the reaction to the veto among the majority of Americans still living in Lebanon. "We were in Greece on vacation. My wife was reading the paper and she said, 'Oh, look, they've vetoed the resolution. I wonder what will happen next to the Americans in Beirut.' It wasn't hard to guess," he added. The focus was on where, rather than what, would happen in retaliation. Ironically, the annex was considered immune, since it had moved to the eastern sector. Like the Marine attack, the danger was recognized, but the obvious target or tactics were overlooked.

After the bombing, Washington publicly tried to put on a brave face. During the presidential campaign, Vice-President George Bush pledged, "Let me assure you of one thing: the United States under this administration will never, never, never let terrorism or fear of terrorism shape or determine the foreign policy of the United States of America. We are not going to move out because terrorists move in. We are too great. We are too strong. We are too proud. And we are too principled to let terrorism shape our foreign policy."

Certain intelligence quarters also tried to sound as if they had a grip on the situation. Washington officials leaked information that Hizbollah was responsible, which elicited only snickers even from Americans stationed in Lebanon. As one well-seasoned envoy commented, "Every Shia in Lebanon is now Hizbollah." Another report said explosives used in recent anti-American attacks had been provided by Iran. In one case, the CIA reportedly monitored the transfer via Syria into Lebanon, but was unable to determine where or when the materiel was to be used, or by whom. Yet other U.S. sources on the ground and in Washington indicated the explosives originated in Libya, leading to an impression of confusion or uncertainty within the administration.

Assistant Secretary of State Richard Murphy was dispatched to Beirut to investigate and offer reassurances of no changes in foreign policy. At a tightly guarded press conference at the ambassador's residence—to which only American reporters, no Lebanese, were invited—Murphy attempted to stand firm. "The attack," he said, "did not succeed in what I assume to have been its goal: to demolish the embassy [annex] and through that destruction and killing to so sap the will of the American government that we would decide it was no longer in our interest to maintain official relations with Lebanon." His rebuke was greeted by yet another Islamic Jihad threat, issued the next day, that "a big operation [would] be carried out against the American interests soon."

With the U.S. elections just six weeks away, the Reagan administration appeared to panic. The West Beirut embassy was closed, vacant of even Marine guards. Anti-aircraft guns were positioned on the residence grounds, which had been converted into a temporary embassy in East Beirut, and air lanes above the ambassador's home were closed to all traffic. U.S. personnel restricted to the east were banned from going out after dark. In small numbers, diplomatic staff were withdrawn by hastily summoned U.S. helicopters to Cyprus, since even Beirut International Airport was off limits. State Department spokesman Brian Carlson said these were only "temporary measures" that could be reversed later "pending the outcome of the embassy reorganization and security enhancement."

A few hours after being awakened with news of the annex bombing, President Reagan told reporters, "We can't . . . crawl in a hole someplace and stop performing." But that is exactly what the United States did. Just a year earlier, the Americans had had the largest and most active presence in Lebanon, with an estimated 190 Americans masterminding local peace efforts. By election day, November 6, 1984, only six diplomats, isolated from the mainstream of political events, were left in Beirut. A ban was issued against U.S. employees mentioning the activities of Ambassador Bartholomew—for good reason, since he had flown secretly to Paris for safety during the final election week.

The Islamic crusade had taken on the United States, and won the first round.

5 The Challenge: Kuwait and Bahrain

The twenty-one young men were all dressed in dark-blue jersey sweaters and baggy canvas trousers, standard prison gear in Kuwait. Under tight security, they filed into the former girls' school now converted into a courtroom. One with a cast on his foot focused on British diplomat Mark Higson in the gallery. Higson was obviously trying to identify him from a chart of names and pictures in the local press. But the pictured men had beards, and these were clean shaven. Peering at Higson, the prisoner said, "Yes, that's me, smiling death." They were the only words spoken aloud in the hushed court as the men who were charged with the biggest terrorist attack in Kuwait's history were put on display.

The atmosphere in the former classroom on February 11, 1984, was electric. Heavily armed troops sealed off the building. Inside there were twice as many guards, even though the defendants were locked in a specially constructed cage. The select few officials and diplomats invited to attend were searched. After opening day, the trial was to be held in secret. But the defendants appeared to think it was a big joke. "They talked to each other, smiled a lot and laughed frequently," one diplomat noted. They acted "like a group of sophomores about to be reprimanded for a prank."

The twenty-one were charged with a ninety-minute wave of explosions the previous December that had shattered the little Gulf city-state, killing six and injuring more than eighty. The coordinated bombings at six key foreign and Kuwaiti installations might have been the worst terrorist episode of the twentieth century in the Middle East, far worse than the Beirut explosions, if the bombs' rigging had not been faulty.

On that tranquil day, December 12, 1983, the first bomb went off at the whitewashed U.S. Embassy compound on the blue-green seafront. A truck laden with forty-five large cylinders of gas connected to plastic explosives careened wildly through the front gates. Before Kuwaiti security guards at the entrance could react, it rammed into the three-story administrative annex. With an enormous roar, half of the L-shaped structure crumbled. Like a rippling earthquake, the shock blew out windows and doors in distant homes and shops. The high-rise Hilton Hotel across the street took an estimated $400,000 worth of damage.

But, either by mistake or by design, the driver had missed the bustling chancellery building—and a heavy toll in casualties. Five of the six deaths that day were at the American compound. Only a quarter of the explosives had ignited. "If everything had gone off, this place would have been a parking lot," said one prominent American diplomat.

The other five bombings were less daring. An hour later, a car parked outside the French Embassy blew up into an enormous ball of flame. Ambassador Jean Bressot missed injury by inches when the impact jarred loose the large crystal chandelier above his desk. The main damage was a massive thirty-foot hole in the security wall around the grounds. Only five people were wounded.

But the biggest catastrophe would have been at the Shuaiba Petro-chemical Plant, the main oil refinery in a nation with reserves that, according to production levels, would last longer than anywhere else in the world. Shuaiba was to get the biggest bomb of all: two hundred gas cylinders rigged in the back of a yellow truck without license plates. The truck exploded 150 yards from the No. 2 refinery, and only a few yards from a highly flammable heap of sulfa-based chemicals. One policeman conceded that the complex "miraculously escaped a catastrophe." And a Western diplomat said five months after the attack, "If all the bombs had gone off, Shuaiba would still be burning today."

Equally important, Shuaiba had the main water-desalination plant in the desert state. "The nation would have gone almost totally dry," the envoy explained. "It would have been totally devastating for Kuwait. The total effect would have crippled one of the most important oil-producing nations in the world." Only ten people were injured. But the close call exposed the indefensibility of the little nation, as well as the extraordinary vulnerability of the entire Gulf region.

Other booby-trapped cars rocked the control tower at Kuwait International Airport, the Electricity Control Center and the living quarters for American employees of the Raytheon Corporation. The U.S. company was installing a missile system in Kuwait, which was feeling jittery because of the neighboring war between Iran and Iraq.

The bombs went off only six weeks after the Beirut Multi-National Force attacks. Intelligence reports had led the U.S. Embassy in Kuwait a month earlier to request tighter security around its full block of diplomatic buildings. The British Embassy was among others receiving threats at the time, mostly by telephone. But the Kuwaitis, confident that security was under control, had turned down the request. The blasts took the Kuwaiti government "completely by surprise," said an official of one of the targeted embassies. "They were dumbfounded, and terrified." That they were terrified was understandable; that they were surprised is more difficult to fathom. The warning had been there for as long as three years.

■   ■   ■

EXACTLY THREE YEARS before the Kuwaiti bombings, in early December 1981, an airport immigration official in the Dubai sheikhdom of the United Arab Emirates had noticed a group of young men sitting in the transit lounge. All were Gulf Arabs. All were waiting for a flight to Bahrain. He might not have thought about them particularly, except that they refused an offer of an earlier flight than the one on which they were booked. Suspicious, he then asked to see their passports. Immediately he found "irregularities." Within a week, Bahrain announced that a coup attempt had been uncovered. The Dubai immigration officer had stumbled onto the plotters, who planned a series of violent attacks allegedly to replace the monarchy with an Islamic republic.

The news stunned the tropical little archipelago, for Bahrain was the smallest and most peaceful of the six Gulf states. Its government and lifestyle were both relaxed and tolerant of dissent. Indeed, it seemed one of the least likely places in the Gulf for either violence or a revolution. Bahrain had one of the earliest civilizations in the region, proven by the ancient burial mounds that dot its thirty-three islands. It had also been one of the first to discover oil—and the first to run out of it. Production was only a trickle in the 1980s. Banking had become the big business, replacing Lebanon when its war scared away clients. Bahrain's primary value was as the back door to Saudi Arabia's oil fields, just five miles away.

Bahrain shows few signs of ostentatious wealth or overdevelopment, especially in comparison with neighboring oil-producing nations. The main island looks like a nation in miniature, a fairyland surprisingly green and balmy. Gulf Arabs and Westerners stationed on the peninsula both use Manama, the capital, as a retreat. Most things forbidden elsewhere are easily available in Bahrain, from liquor to discos and female "escorts." The threat of insurgency was reflected in the size of the Army, smaller than the police force of a large American city. The Air Force consisted of twelve helicopters. The Navy had 200 men, and the Army 2,300.

Bahrain and five of its sister Gulf states—which altogether accounted for just under one-fifth of the free world's oil supplies—were equally shocked by the threat to Bahrain and immediately scrambled to debate the menace to what had seemed their most secure and stable member. Only six months earlier, they had formed the Gulf

Cooperation Council (GCC). The fundamentalists' campaign as well as the reality of the Iran–Iraq war to their north made the six—Bahrain, Saudi Arabia, Kuwait, Oman, Qatar and the United Arab Emirates—feel more vulnerable, both physically and politically.

All the ruling royal families of the six states are Sunni. But in Bahrain the clear majority is Shia. The Shia are about one-quarter of the population in Kuwait, while they account for significant minorities in Saudi Arabia, Qatar and the United Arab Emirates. More importantly, the Shia make up the largest sector living on the oil fields in each state. If neighboring Iran and Iraq are included, the population of the eight key Gulf states is almost 75 percent Shia. Together, the eight nations also represent 370 billion barrels of untapped oil, or 60 percent of the world's known reserves. As James Bill, a U.S. expert on the Gulf, put it, the Gulf is "the world's economic jugular vein."

The six states started the GCC in part to appear more self-reliant, pooling their riches and military resources so that, together, they could confront any threat rather than have to call in outsiders for help. They even talked about building their own arms industry. The coup attempt made it clear that they were not yet equipped to cope with a major challenge.

The plan for coordinated attacks was believed to have been scheduled for the tenth anniversary of Bahrain's independence, December 16. Among the goods secretly sneaked in were police uniforms for disguise. Officials presumed the targets were members of the royal al Khalifa family at the scheduled National Day celebrations, the radio and television station, military installations and other government offices. But the government may never know, for the suspects themselves said they did not. "To this day, we are still not completely sure it was a coup attempt, as the chaps were told to go into Bahrain and lie low and wait to be told where their targets were and when to act," said one GCC security official two years later.

The Dubai discovery had in fact preempted an intelligence operation in Bahrain. "We already had simple evidence, knowledge that trained elements were infiltrating back, lying low. But we wanted to know the target, so we waited," a Bahraini official explained. "We know there were more batches in Kuwait en route here, but after the publicity about the detentions they turned around.

"About one hundred fifty men were to come in to carry out violent acts against senior government people and places. But they were thwarted, with the result that some eighty were apprehended and the balance did not even get here. Most of their arms were not yet in, either." The machine guns, the grenades and the ammunition had been buried, mainly along the coast. Two years later security forces were still uncovering caches.

Most of the seventy-three suspects who were rounded up yielded little information. "You may think they are weak physically," said one officer about all the men subsequently convicted. "They are one hundred percent stubborn and always prepared to die. But they do not cooperate at all with authority. No amount of pressure will get them to talk." Nevertheless, on the basis of some confessions, Bahraini officials unequivocally put the blame on Iran. Bahrain's Prime Minister, Sheikh Khalifa al Khalifa, charged that Tehran "bears full responsibility for training hundreds of nationals from Gulf states in special camps under the supervision of experts on sabotage and demolition."

Officials alleged that the suspects, all Shia Muslims, belonged to the rather pretentious-sounding Islamic Front for the Liberation of Bahrain, headquartered in Tehran. Another link was the Iranian Embassy in Bahrain, where a diplomat had received communication equipment for the plotters in his diplomatic pouch, government sources said. They subsequently asked him to leave Bahrain. Dr. Tariq al Moayyed, the Bahraini Information Minister, commented, "Tehran denies it sponsored the plot, then its radio beams programs over here telling people to rise up and how to make petrol bombs. Who are they trying to fool?"

A few days after the plot was discovered, five armed men delivered a statement to the Bahrain Embassy in Tehran demanding release of the suspects. The gunmen claimed to have planned the subversion. They said they belonged to the Islamic Front for the Liberation of Bahrain. For Iran, despite all the rhetoric about exporting the revolution, no move had ever before been as bold or as obvious as the coup attempt. As one official noted, "Iranian fingerprints were all over the operation. They made the mistake of leaving a trail."

And the trail led directly to Hojatoleslam Hadi al Moudarrissi, one of the most prominent Shia mullahs in the little sheikhdoms. In the

1970s, in exile from Iran during the Shah's rule, he had made a series of lengthy trips to Bahrain, Kuwait and the United Arab Emirates. His earlier stay in Iraq overlapped with that of the exile there of his religious colleague, Ayatollah Khomeini, who wrote a note giving him "responsibility" for Bahrain and the Emirates, said Bahraini officials, who have the original.

Hojatoleslam Moudarrissi has a distinctive face, a full black beard, an aquiline nose and a broad forehead topped with the wrapped black turban of his religious rank. A powerful figure, he undertook this assignment with vigor. Bahraini authorities had been aware of the formation of the Islamic Front, but they had not taken it seriously. "We regarded it as just one of the dozens of Sunni or Shia mushrooms that had grown up in the area over the years," said one official. "You could hardly find a less terrorist-prone nation than this. It is very placid. So we looked at the mushroom groups as pressure groups only."

Moudarrissi rapidly rallied support within the husseiniyehs and the influential Islamic Enlightenment Society, a massive complex of more than one hundred offices that dealt with Shia matters. For all the comparative freedom and tolerance in Bahrain, Shia opportunities there—as in all the Gulf states—were limited. Shia were all but officially banned from the armed forces. Although they represented up to 70 percent of the Bahraini population, they held only token positions in government. Moudarrissi's message fell on receptive ears.

He "preached the message of militant Islam, with the goal of having an Islamic republic here," said one source who had dealings with him. "They were capturing almost in Communist style the religious leaders to bring in youths in groups of three to four hundred. No one here believed the Shia of Iran could throw the Shah off the Peacock Throne. He was supposed to be the policeman of the Gulf. It was a thunderous surprise. When it happened we all had to look at what was happening inside our own countries.

"We all began to wonder which way the wind would blow in the Gulf with the Shia. All the ingredients were present for disaster: spiritual elements, the desire for change, the very religious basis for the whole movement which no Muslim leader could attack. And there was the hope it brought with it that, for the first time since Hussein was massacred at Karbala, the days of suffering for the Shia might be over. That was the beginning of the Shia Islamic crusade, this new chapter we are in now," he added. "Suddenly what had seemed like an insignificant little Islamic Front became a major threat."

Shortly after Ayatollah Khomeini assumed power, Bahrain expelled Hojatoleslam Moudarrissi. He moved on to the Emirates, but was later asked to leave. However, he had had sufficient time to build an infrastructure he could manipulate even at great distance. And he did have a pipeline: his voice was beamed almost daily to Bahrain on Radio Tehran's powerful transmitter.

The contacts between clerics in Iran and the Gulf Shia were difficult to stop. One of the most prominent Western ambassadors on the island told the story of his houseboy's vacation. In passing one day, the envoy asked what the servant, a Shi'ite, had done with his time off. To the ambassador's astonishment, the young man replied that he had gone to Iran. Illegal dhow traffic and the flights via Dubai or Damascus made the trip fairly easy.

The details of the plot were uncovered on the 212-square-mile island chain more than a year after the Hojatoleslam was expelled. The prosecution's statement shortly before the trial specified that the defendants were "communicating and striving with a foreign country, and with an individual working on behalf of that country, to undertake aggressive acts against Bahrain." The highest government sources later named Moudarrissi as the mastermind.

"The coup thing was so badly done. It was something of no great consequence," a Bahraini official claimed. "But it was important as an indication of their intent and potential." As it happened, the Bahraini coup attempt turned out to be a tepid indication of the threat and the potential. The "clumsiness" of it was something that would end after the 1982 Tehran seminar, when the "liberation mullahs" resolved to step up their campaign against Sunni Gulf states as well as Western powers.

The plot did mark a turning point for the Gulf states, what some would later call the opening chapter. During the two years since Iran's religious coup, the easily intimidated Gulf nations had been sensitive to the possibilities about an overspill of fervor from Iran.

But suddenly the threat was a reality. And, just like the Iranian revolution, the threat came not from foreign forces, but from their own people. For the GCC, the frightening, and embarrassing, fact was that the seventy-three saboteurs who were eventually rounded up came from four of the six member nations: Bahrain, Saudi Arabia, Kuwait and Oman. That they were Arab Shia, not Persians who had moved from Iran over the previous two centuries for trade and shipping, had frightening implications for the Gulf sheikhs, emirs and sultans. They could not help but wonder which of them was next. They had their answer in Kuwait.

■   ■   ■

UNDER THE RULING AL SABAH FAMILY, Kuwait had been the most progressive nation of the Gulf oil states. It had the only elected National Assembly, and even considered giving the vote to women. It was the only sheikhdom to maintain relations with and buy arms from the Soviet Union. Women held important jobs in government, education and business, shrouding themselves only by personal choice. Customs officials usually turned a blind eye to foreigners bringing in liquor. Even after the outbreak of the Gulf war in 1980, when it backed Baghdad, Kuwait struggled hard to keep up good relations with Tehran.

In the 1960s and 1970s, the primary voices of dissent had been nationalist in flavor, the underground movements generally leftist or communist. Now the main opposition forces, both visible and invisible, were advocating an Islamic fundamentalist line. In Kuwait's 1981 election for the National Assembly, which had been suspended since 1976, seven fundamentalists—four Sunni and three Shia—won seats in the fifty-member body. In the 1985 elections, three Sunnis lost their seats, while the Shia retained theirs. The count was deceiving, however, for the fundamentalists actually had support from more than a dozen other legislators.

Other signs were far more worrisome. At the University of Kuwait, fundamentalists gradually won control of the student unions. Among their first moves was a push for resegregation of the cafeteria by sex. When the college administration balked, the students took it to the parliament and won. One of the major problems with countering fundamentalism was that no Gulf official dared to reject proposals based on the faith that was the core of the nation's pride and existence.

On campus, both men and women increasingly wore conservative dress. More men grew beards and shed their jeans and Western dress for the traditional dishdash, a long white robe. Shia girls particularly donned scarves, longer or full-length skirts, and long-sleeved shirts. One professor, a Shi'ite woman who had spent years in the United States, reported in 1984 that girls in a political science lecture class had appealed to her to hold a separate session for women only. At the time, the professor said, it did not matter either way, since in most classes men and women had already begun sitting on separate sides of the room, by choice. In late 1984, one student actually appealed for a religious ruling from a prominent Saudi cleric to condemn co-education as contrary to Islam. Kuwaiti scholars and officials were horrified when the cleric agreed, leading Kuwaiti intellectuals to charge that fundamentalists had started engaging in "intellectual terrorism." The university ignored the edict.

After reestablishing a parliament, Sheikh Saad al Abdullah, the Crown Prince and Prime Minister, and his wife began a campaign for female suffrage. It would have been a dramatic step for a Gulf state: under Kuwait's strict and complex electoral laws, less than 10 percent of the native population were then qualified to vote, all men. But the "fundamentalist spirit" led the royal family to drop their reform.

Under pressure from fundamentalists, the government also revoked provisions allowing diplomats to import alcohol, and customs cracked down on all foreigners. Airport officials also began scrutinizing luggage for tape cassettes that might carry messages from Ayatollah Khomeini and other mullahs. Gulf leaders painfully recalled how effective those recordings had been against the Shah.

The parliament introduced legislation to bar non-Muslims from citizenship, which would particularly affect the Christian Palestinians who had lived in Kuwait for decades and were instrumental in running various government agencies. A movement in the parliament also pushed to revise the penal and civil codes to follow the Sharia more closely. But moderates managed to hold off a move to make the Islamic code "the" basis of law, rather than just "a" source of legislation.

Fundamentalists circulated petitions to block a beauty salon from opening up in a new mall, arguing that it violated Islamic strictures.

They warned television programmers against showing too much familiarity on the air. A powerful beam from across the bay now broadcast long hours from Radio Tehran in Farsi and Arabic, sermons from various mullahs, war reports, Islamic music, readings from the Koran, calls to prayer. All had a popular following in the shops and narrow stalls of both the old and new souks.

Earlier, in 1979, the U.S. Embassy had begun to shred all its daily classified cables and intelligence reports. The Iran hostage ordeal had led diplomats to fear a sudden uprising elsewhere. The Americans even shredded the biographical profile of the Russian ambassador in Kuwait. The concern was so deep that one European ambassador speculated, "If Iran really wanted Kuwait under its influence, it would never need to take it militarily. One more big 'gesture,' like taking Basra [in southern Iraq, near the Kuwaiti border], would do it. Then Kuwait would be taken from inside. It would ignite the Shia."

In this atmosphere, the bombs erupted in little Kuwait.

■   ■   ■

IN THE AFTERMATH, the government displayed a sense of helplessness. The only early conclusion had been that "the close coordination of the bombings was indicative of a well-organized and established terror group inside the country," as one minister put it a bit too late to count. In other words, working right under their noses. There had been not a single independent lead from earlier intelligence work or any suspicions, notably about the more than 260 large gas cylinders which had all been purchased locally and accumulated in a single place in the weeks before the attacks. No one had discovered that large quantities of arms had been secretly shipped in from Iran across the bay. Oil barrels were designed to take a dipstick all the way to the bottom; guns and grenades were hidden along the sides under a V-shaped funnel.

The bombings turned the normally relaxed nation into a police state. Guardsmen were ordered to "shoot whoever refuses to stop or be searched." Armored personnel carriers and tanks fanned out around Western and Gulf embassies and public utilities. Soldiers cordoned off the Emir's palace, the Prime Minister's office, and key ministries. Hundreds of foreign workers were rounded up and questioned. All Iranians, Syrians, Lebanese, Jordanians, Palestinians and Iraqis were temporarily barred from leaving the country. Roadblocks and identity checks were everywhere. A government edict forbade women from wearing veils when driving, as a "security precaution," for fear of what, or who, might be hidden beneath. An old law prohibiting any group of more than twenty people from assembling without permission was resurrected.

Governments throughout the rest of the Gulf tightened security at airports and harbors, questioned Shia figures, increased surveillance. All six states handled the bombings as if they had happened in their own backyards. Frantic telephone calls crisscrossed between intelligence officials and chiefs of state for several days. They assumed that a threat to one was a threat to all.

Again the only claim of responsibility taken seriously came from Islamic Jihad, which called the French news agency in Beirut. What was curious was the caller's boast that a seventh bomb would explode later. Kuwaiti police subsequently uncovered and defused a seventh car bomb in front of the Immigration Bureau. The timing of the sequence was important, for it was the first hint that the anonymous callers were at least aware in advance of the plots. Islamic Jihad also had never been active so far from Lebanon, and subsequent events uncovering the links with other Shia groups offered another clue to the "identity" of the phantom group.

The impact was felt as far as Washington. Within days, three-foot-high concrete barriers were erected around the White House, the State Department and the U.S. Mission to the United Nations. Metal detectors were installed at various federal buildings to check parcels. The Pentagon and the CIA tightened their own security. And discussion began immediately within the highest military circles about creating new antiterrorist commando teams.

A bomb left in a corridor near the Senate Chamber of the Capitol the previous month—unrelated to the Middle East—was in part responsible for the nervousness. But more alarming was an unsigned one-page letter the police received in Manassas, Virginia, at around the time of the Kuwaiti blasts. It reported that a plot had been laid to "blow up a place on Pennsylvania Avenue, and at Virginia Avenue and 23rd Street"—the White House and the State Department.

Manassas Police Chief B. R. Reed, who casually remarked that he probably would have thrown the letter away had he been the first to see it, later said he was "under the impression that Iranians were involved" in the threat. The letter also said a truck with explosives would be used. The FBI and the Secret Service immediately intervened.

Predictions became dire. At a conference on terrorism the month of the bombings, Senator Daniel Patrick Moynihan of New York said, "The prospect of 1984 being the year they bring the war to our shores is real. We should assume it and not be surprised by it." Former CIA director Richard Helms noted, "It would be surprising if a wave of terrorism didn't hit the U.S."

Perceived threats from radical factions of the PLO, the Italian Red Brigades, the German Baader-Meinhof Gang and the Japanese Red Army had never triggered such a response. The visible evidence of fear underlined the new and different strain of terrorism. It had become accepted as the most lethal and threatening brand the world had ever known.

Dennis Hays, president of the American Foreign Service Association, said candidly about the suicide bombing of the embassies, "I don't believe such missions can be prevented. It's hard to imagine any kind of complete guarantees no matter what we do." The same was true of government facilities at home. "We can handle the Tehran [hostage] model. Now we have to work on the Beirut and Kuwaiti [bombing] models."

Six months after the blasts, tank traps and extra guards still protected Western and Arab missions in Kuwait. The radio and television station had been cordoned off. Access to six-lane highways in front of government outlets had been cut off, creating enormous traffic jams on smaller side roads.

The high stone fence around the British Embassy, which had not even been a target, had an extra layer of protection. A jeep sat at the front gate with a machine gun locked and loaded. A tent full of troops was stationed at the rear. Weighted yellow-and-black striped barrels blocked the entrance road. Sentries searched the parcels of anyone who entered the grounds. It was the same all over town.

At the sealed-off U.S. compound, schedules often went awry.

"There's been a little bit of a delay," a secretary told me when I arrived for an appointment. "We've had one of our drills this morning"—mock terrorist drills, like fire drills at primary school. They covered every possibility: hostage-taking, bomb threats, and demonstrators storming the grounds. Marine guards would dash through the buildings collecting or mock-destroying documents.

"We have to have these occasionally so we'll know what to do and not be taken by surprise," said the secretary, as if she expected another attack soon. When I asked a diplomat how long the protection and the drills might be necessary, he replied, "Oh, for the foreseeable future, I would think. We can't be seen to be letting our guard down. That may be what they are waiting for."

■   ■   ■

THE TWENTY-ONE MEN responsible for the six bombings in Kuwait might not have been captured at all in the nationwide manhunt if the lone suicide driver at the American complex had blown himself up completely. The single piece of him left behind was a thumb—with a print. That tiny piece of evidence led police to uncover his identity and track some of his accomplices. His name was Raad Muftin Ajeel. But his links were more important than his identity.

Raad Muftin Ajeel was a twenty-five-year-old Iraqi, a Shi'ite Muslim. Four years earlier he and his brother Saad had been active underground members in Iraq of Dawa, that largest and oldest Shia extremist group in the Middle East. Since the 1979 Iranian revolution, Dawa had made its headquarters in Tehran.

In 1982, the Iraqi regime of President Saddam Hussein had launched a dragnet for pro-Iranian sympathizers, particularly the deeply feared Dawa. They were held responsible for a host of assassination attempts on the Iraqi President, Prime Minister and others as well as small attacks on government officials and installations. They were also recruiting young militants from the nation's majority Shia population in a secret campaign against the ruling Sunni majority. Ajeel's brother was one of those picked up and, shortly thereafter, executed. Intelligence sources claimed that Ajeel, also under death sentence if found, escaped to Iran.

All the defendants in Kuwait, including four tried in absentia, were originally accused of membership in Dawa, which Kuwait had outlawed. The strongest charges against them were to be "joining a group whose objectives aim at spreading destructive principles, and the practicing of terrorism."

Abdel Aziz Hussein, cabinet minister and chief government spokesman, called the bombings "the first concentrated Iranian operation to export the revolution and destabilize the Gulf after Iran failed to infiltrate the Iraqi [war] front." It appeared that the link between the wave of terrorism and Iran was finally going to be proven in court. But when the trial opened, the charge had been significantly toned down.

Sheikh Jaber al Ahmed al Sabah, the Kuwaiti ruler, had disclosed that his government had been threatened with further terrorist attacks if the defendants were not released, and Tehran Radio was broadcasting regular warnings from Dawa that Kuwait would face "serious consequences" if the "heroes" standing trial were harmed. Sheikh Jaber boldly declared at the time, "We will not bend to these threats. We will never be shaken. We will never give up our dignity in the face of terror pressures and whoever stood behind them."

But in the end, the twenty-five youths were charged only with "belonging to a group bent on demolishing the basic values of society through criminal means." Terrorism was not mentioned in any of the six charges, nor was Iran, despite abundant references to "another state." When the accusations were read out in court, the men actually protested. Several loudly shouted out their allegiance to Dawa and declared they wanted it reinstated. One diplomat commented, "They were boasting about it, bragging, even though conviction would insure a guilty verdict and the death penalty."

In the final judgment six weeks and forty-six witnesses later, six of the twenty-five, including three still at large, were sentenced to death, seven to life imprisonment, seven to terms between five and fifteen years. Five were found not guilty. But more telling than the sentences was the fact that all twenty-five were acquitted on the single most important charge, and issue, facing them—and Kuwait. They were found *not guilty* of subversion.

■   ■   ■

BENAID AL QARR is a shabby and dusty suburb of Kuwait City with few sidewalks. The sun-bleached two- and three-story buildings, paint usually peeling, do not well suit the nation with the highest per capita income in the world. The cars parked along the narrow streets are old American brands or small Japanese models, not the big Mercedes and BMWs that speed along the palm-fringed boulevards in other parts of Kuwait's capital and only city. Benaid al Qarr is a Shia suburb.

As the crow flies, the main mosque in Benaid al Qarr is two blocks from the U.S. Embassy in one direction and two blocks from the Iranian Embassy in the other. Just down the main road from the mosque is an innocuous and tatty yellowish facade hidden behind a high gate and a concrete courtyard. The only indications that it is a religious building are the loud ululating chants from rusted loudspeakers atop the wall that five times a day call the faithful to prayer. An old-fashioned sink juts incongruously into the street from the exterior wall to provide water for washing before prayer or for the poor who are thirsty.

This is a Shia husseiniyeh, one of the sect's typical social centers and mourning houses where Shi'ites pay respect to the dead. Until 1980, both the mosque and the husseiniyeh were the stronghold of Sheikh Mohammed Shirazi, an enthusiastic and popular Iranian who drew thousands, especially the young, to his lessons and sermons. From this mosque, an angry mob of hundreds marched on the U.S. Embassy in late 1979 to protest alleged American complicity in seizing the Grand Mosque in Saudi Arabia, actually the work of Sunni fundamentalists.

In the Gulf, the Shia "started really to be captured by the spirit of the Islamic revolution at the time the Kuwaitis felt compelled to impose control on the Mohammed Shirazi 'school' in Kuwait," according to a Gulf security source. "For roughly two years before, we had begun to see the teachings coming out of that school and infiltrate down the coast to Bahrain and Qatif and Hasa province" in Saudi Arabia. In 1980, about the time the war broke out between Iran and Iraq, Kuwait expelled Sheikh Shirazi. His husseiniyeh had become too threatening, his militant Shi'ite line too suggestively sectarian.

Unlike most other twentieth-century insurgency movements, the Shia have used totally legitimate channels as centers of operations. As Ayatollah Khomeini had said earlier of Iran, "It was the mosques that created this revolution, the mosques that brought this movement into being." Therefore, those were the first places the Gulf States had begun watching when the Iranian Imam talked of exporting his revolution. The Ayatollah had also said, "The rulers of the Muslim countries are bound to oppose the movement in Iran for the sake of self-preservation. . . . Seeing that an entire population has risen up against the Shah, despite all the power he had at his disposal, the rulers of Dubai, Kuwait and so on naturally ask themselves, 'How can we be sure the same thing will not happen to us?' "

Kuwait also expelled one of its own, withdrawing citizenship from Sheikh Abass al Mahry and eighteen of his followers. "We sent away a person at the beginning of the Khomeini era who was openly supporting Khomeini and attacking our country," explained Sheikh Salim al Jaber al Ahmed, son of the Emir and Deputy Foreign Minister. Sheikh Mahry was considered a firebrand at the Shabaan mosque in another Shi'ite stronghold, a proponent of fundamentalism and the conversion of Kuwait into an Islamic republic.

Both clerics headed for Iran. Yet their influence was still deeply felt in Kuwait four years later. "[Shirazi's] supporters argued and appealed that it was illegal to expel him," said one long-serving diplomat. "When they got no response, they decided not to have readings or sermons until he returned. His mosque particularly remained silent."

More importantly, the two men left behind a small nucleus of followers in cells, young men hand-picked for religious and political indoctrination. "If there is an organization in Kuwait, then it comes through Mahry and Shirazi," one official charged. Sheikh Salim concurred: "Certainly Iran has used Mahry to have information on people they can use in Kuwait. And there are people who will do it, though only a tiny percentage." After pausing briefly, Sheikh Salim added, "But then that's all it takes." Sheikh Shirazi was to become one of the top coordinators of Shia movements throughout the Arab world, based at Taleghani Center.

"The bombers were collected from outside," said a member of Kuwait's ruling al Sabah family about the December 12 explosions. "But the people who supported the bombers came from the hussein-iyehs. This is how the Shia in Kuwait are willing to carry out the orders from Tehran."

Among the little-publicized security steps after the bombing was the closing down of the "Shirazi Mosque," as it had become known among followers. The use of established religious facilities had proved to be one of the greatest strengths of the movement—and the biggest problem for the Gulf intelligence agencies.

"I see the Islamic [fundamentalist] movement as desperately dangerous, as all the tools that exist in the cabinets of the security men around the world cannot cope with this fanaticism," said a leading Gulf security officer. "You simply can't raid a mosque or penetrate a cell centered around a husseiniyeh. It is distasteful, even to the Sunni. And even if you did, you would probably be unable to find anything incriminating beyond a copy of the Koran."

■   ■   ■

BUT THE CRUSADE'S BASIC NETWORK is more elusive, almost ephemeral, and more widespread than just the religious houses. And it is virtually impenetrable, as the story of a Kuwaiti named Abdullah illustrates. He claimed he was once a billionaire. The handsome young Kuwaiti and scores of others made quick fortunes on the Souk al Manakh stock exchange before it crashed in 1982, the loss of an estimated $94 billion ranking as the greatest in financial history. But unlike most other investors, Abdullah had earlier taken much of his money out. It went to Iran, at an average in good times of $1 million a month.

Abdullah supported Ayatollah Khomeini, "as every Shia does," he said in mid-1984. His money was not to fill Iranian government coffers, but to pay for the export of the revolution. He said the funds went for training of commandos, support of the mullahs who ran the indoctrination courses, purchase of weaponry. He claimed he channeled the vast sums through both the Iranian embassy in Kuwait and various Syrian connections.

He was not bragging about it, but telling the story as a fact of everyday life when I commented that I could see few indications of support among the Kuwaiti Shia for what was happening in Iran. "No, you are wrong," he said. "We do things as we can with whatever we have. From me, it is money." He claimed that no one had ever solicited a penny, that the donations were on his own initiative. In checking out Abdullah's story, I found that several Arab and

Western embassies in Kuwait were aware of similar cases. And, historically, it fit the pattern.

The Shia financial system has been one of the main sources of their autonomy from the ruling Sunni religious establishment. In the Gulf States and elsewhere, Sunni priests are, in effect, government civil servants or appointees. The state pays their salaries; the national budget builds their mosques. In many Muslim nations, the Ministry of Religious Works is among the most powerful bureaus. But the Shia pay for their own. Husseiniyehs are often named after the patron who paid for their construction. Contributions of up to a fifth of individual incomes of the faithful support both the mosques and the Shia sheikhs. The Shia supported Khomeini's exile. Moreover, Shia councils provide clinics, schools, relief funds and other social services. Where feasible, the Shia have used the income to form, in effect, a state within a state. This reflects their reluctance to recognize secular power, and their fierce sense of separateness. It has more recently financed the Islamic crusade. The centuries-old system is largely untraceable.

Shia help the crusade in other ways. Six months after the bombings, a Shi'ite employee at Kuwait's Ministry of Health was arrested and charged with stealing large quantities of medicine and drugs from the government pharmacy, allegedly for shipment to Iran. A diplomat cited this incident to explain the quiet purge of Shia from several government posts after the bombings. The network is vast and loose, often without any organization—or so it appears.

Abdel, for instance, worked in one of the many jewelry shops in Kuwait's new air-conditioned souk, a glass-and-concrete American-style shopping mall. In 1982 I probed Abdel's feelings about what was happening in Iran. He began by talking at length about the sale of gold religious jewelry, particularly with lines from the Koran engraved on necklace lavalieres for both men and women, and about how his business had boomed since the revolution. Personally, Abdel said, he quite liked Kuwait's Sheikh Jaber. "He is fair. He is just. I would guess that among the Shia he is popular, maybe very popular. I think he cares about his people." But in the next breath Abdel said he favored strict Islamic rule in Kuwait, a government that would adopt the Sharia as the only law of the land, as the Iranians had done.

"Khomeini has courage. He is doing the right thing for the people. There is equality in Iran."

Abdel had become wealthy from the capitalist and highly subsidized economy in Kuwait, which relied on expensive imports for every aspect of life. But that did not affect his beliefs. "Those things are not important," he said. He was not against the system or the ruling Sunni family. He was, simply, for something vastly different, which he did not find inconsistent. His faith was more important than his income.

"One of the problems in combating this thing is that not even another member of a family can argue against it," a sociologist pointed out. "A father could debate the merits of Arab nationalism or communism with a son, sometimes using Islam and its values. So, who can fight Islam?"

Abdel stressed that he did *not* want the Iranians to take over Kuwait. "This is *our* country," he emphasized. And as he opened up during the conversation, he admitted that Iran had problems. The mass executions particularly disturbed him, and most of the others interviewed. "But we have learned from them, more the good than the bad. We would not make the same mistakes."

When I asked why he wore no religious jewelry and displayed no visible sign of support for the Islamic revolution, Abdel slowly walked over to his wall safe. On the inside of the locked door was a portrait of a stern-faced Khomeini. "Since the [Iran–Iraq] war, we have taken down our pictures and banners," he explained. "People are nervous here. The government is excitable."

In the sweltering open-air alleys of the old souk across the way, Ramadan, a fruit merchant, kept his Khomeini profile inside the cover of an old red plastic accounts book in the corner of his tiny stand. He too wanted an Islamic republic in Kuwait. There were dozens of others. Two years later, Abdullah offered much the same logic. "I am Kuwaiti," he said in a discussion about the royal family. "But I am a Shi'ite." He too wanted Islamic rule in Kuwait.

■   ■   ■

"THE KUWAITIS TOLD US they had broken the back of the movement" after the trial of the bombers in the spring of 1984, said one envoy from an "endangered" embassy. But he and diplomats from several other countries admitted that the evidence was quite the contrary. The day after that interview, I went back to the Benaid al Qarr mosque, which had been allowed to reopen, and encountered several belligerent youths. "We are going to have an explosion in this country, you wait and see," one said angrily. "We are the big question marks in Kuwait."

The potency of the threat was acknowledged throughout the Gulf. "Before the coup plot, we said we were on top of it," said one Bahraini security source. "And in Kuwait no one thought there was a problem before the bombings. On the whole, all of us [in the GCC] were saying that it was really just a law-and-order problem with the Shia. We all were surprised each time. And we are likely to be surprised again." Indeed they were, according to one of the few figures known about the crusaders' strength: by mid-1984, at least five hundred Bahraini youths had gone to Iran for various forms of training, from religious to guerrilla, and often a mixture of both. One of the interesting points of the campaign against the Gulf States was that no Iranians were convicted of major plots; most of those arrested were indigenous or from nearby Arab states.

In terms of future potential, he echoed the European ambassador in Kuwait: "Iran is the only single country that can create problems in these [Gulf] states, almost without doing anything themselves. All it has to do is win a single big battle [in the war with Iraq], then wait to see the streets. It's not something the Rapid Deployment Force can do anything about, as it will all be over in forty-eight hours. Who can do anything? If we shoot at it, it will only aggravate it."

For several months after the bombings, a host of small things indicated that the movement had not been checked. The Interior Minister announced that four Iranian expatriate workers had been arrested for having "simple implements such as tubes and gas cylinders which, used in a special way, could be turned into explosive devices." Kuwait security police had a report that the four men were planning sabotage against local targets, including the Ministry of Information. Two months after the embassy bombers' trial, General Youssef Khorafi, undersecretary of Kuwait's Interior Ministry, said that an average of two hundred people had been deported each month since the bombings "because we feel they are a threat to security and society." He noted that those expelled belonged to unauthorized religious parties.

Diplomats put the figure much higher, and a Gulf cabinet minister claimed that Kuwait had deported more than ten thousand, mainly Shia, in the five years since the Iranian revolution. Yet the problem would still not go away. Indeed, one security official conceded in private that the most disappointing aspect of the trial was the failure to uncover the links inside the country, although the government was still not willing to admit this publicly. Diplomats said the bombers themselves may not have known, since the "cut-out" system characteristically kept operatives from knowing the identity of the planners and the brains or even the lower legmen.

Interestingly, most of the bombers had come into Kuwait legally, obtaining jobs with local firms, their fingerprints on record. Authorities admitted that the sophisticated advance work could not have been done totally without inside help. Of the total twenty-five charged, including four then still at large, only three were Kuwaiti, two of whom were acquitted. The majority, seventeen, were Iraqi. Three were Lebanese, two were of "unknown nationality," probably nomadic Bedouin. All but one were Shia, and he was a Lebanese Christian who had been hired for $30,000 to help with the explosives—a straight mercenary. The others reportedly had little, if any, monetary incentive.

The Lebanese connection was hinted at, not just from the style of the attack, which was identical to those on both the U.S. Embassy and the Marine headquarters in Lebanon. One of those implicated, but still at large, was a Lebanese Shi'ite named Hussein Sayyed Musawi. Intelligence sources claimed he was another relative of Hussein Musawi, head of the extremist Islamic Amal that worked closely with Iran's Revolutionary Guards in eastern Lebanon. Although Musawi is a common name, it could have indicated a Musawi family link between the Beirut and Kuwaiti blasts.

A more dangerous link appeared after the sentencing. Three were sentenced to death, but Kuwait received threats of reprisals on targets in Kuwait and on Kuwaiti establishments abroad if the hangings were carried out. In the meantime, three Americans in Beirut were kidnapped. Immediate speculations by diplomats about linkage between the recent convictions and the kidnappings, and the possibility of demands for an exchange, were an indication of the fear the Shia phenomenon could evoke. Despite repeated U.S. pressure on Kuwait for information about any offers of a swap, the Kuwaitis remained evasive. But the men sentenced to hang within thirty days had not faced the executioner more than a year later. Sheikh Jaber had withheld official approval of the death sentences, required by law.

It seemed unlikely that fanatics alone could topple the Gulf governments; something more dramatic was required to ignite the situation. But through sporadic violence and cultural pressure they had managed to force rulers—theoretically accountable to no one—to become "more Islamic." That in itself was a victory. In the process, the extent of the crusade's impact was being defined in the region most susceptible to its appeal.

The aura gathering around the Shia commandos among so many Arab and Western officials as well as intelligence agencies of diverse political loyalties was such that they automatically acknowledged that the Soldiers of God were capable of anything.

■   ■   ■

SHORTLY BEFORE MIDNIGHT on December 3, 1984, Britain's Princess Anne was waiting at Dubai's posh steel and chrome international airport to board British Caledonia Flight 381 to London, ending a three-day state visit to the United Arab Emirates. Foreign Ministry officials, protocol officers and security guards were preoccupied with ensuring that every courtesy and comfort were provided the English royal, a representative of the nation's former colonial masters. Just a few yards away, no one paid any attention to four Lebanese, who had flown in earlier that evening from Beirut, queueing up with twelve other passengers to join Kuwait Airways Flight 221 bound for Karachi, Pakistan. To the relief of Dubai security, Princess Anne finally got off without any last-minute complications; the Kuwaiti airliner departed unnoticed ten minutes later. The Gulf officials mistakenly thought the potential for crisis was over.

Kuwait Airways Flight 221 was almost a shuttle, a short one-and-a-half-hour, 530-mile hop to Karachi, mainly ferrying Pakistani laborers home from profitable stints in the Gulf. Weather forecasts indicated no serious problems, so it looked as though it would be a pleasant, easy trip. But, fourteen minutes after takeoff, as the Kuwait flight approached cruising altitude and the seat belt signs were turned off, a loud shriek pierced through the aircraft from the first-class section. Then a single gunshot rang out. In the cockpit, British pilot John Clark felt the cold metal of a hand grenade being pressed into the back of his neck by one of the four Lebanese who had boarded during the Dubai stopover. Two of the other Lebanese, brandishing pistols, simultaneously ordered all passengers into the economy section, then confiscated all their passports, tickets and identity papers. Captain Clark was ordered to abort the flight to Karachi and divert to Tehran. It was the third air heist to Iran, the ninth hijacking in the Gulf region, in less than five months.

Iran was initially unreceptive. Air controllers and security at Tehran's Mehrabad Airport refused landing rights, instead dispatching an Iranian fighter to intercept the plane. They eventually agreed, however, "on humanitarian grounds" when Clark told Tehran by radio that the "highly agitated" hijackers had threatened to blow up the plane midair with the 150 passengers and the eleven crew members on board unless it was allowed to land. He was, he added almost as an afterthought, also running out of fuel. The bulky blue-and-white airbus, the interior shades closed, set down at 1:58 GMT Tuesday morning and, under instructions from the air control tower, taxied to a side runway.

Just before dawn, the spectacle began. A crew member of an incoming Iranian flight reported overhearing one of the hijackers tell the control tower over the plane's radio that they would shoot a passenger every fifteen minutes if their demands were not met, a standard ploy of hijackers. But this time the hijackers followed through, as whining shots echoed from inside the plane over the cockpit radio to the control tower. "Minutes after the shooting was heard, the main door was opened and the half-dead body of one of the passengers was thrown out," Iran's news agency reported. Sprawled on the runway, the body was then shot again, and again. Iranian guards retrieved the victim and rushed him to a nearby medical center, but he was pronounced dead on arrival.

It took two days for the United States—acting through Swiss intermediaries, since diplomatic relations with Iran had been broken off during the hostage ordeal—to find out that the dead man was Charles Hegna, an American official of the Agency for International Development (AID) stationed in Pakistan. Hegna's brutal murder was the first in a series of incidents over a literally torturous six days that was to mark this hijacking as the most grisly in history.

The startling murder and the early negotiations for fuel in exchange for hostages diverted attention from the hijackers' demands, which were not publicized until Wednesday, the second full day of the ordeal. They were almost predictable: freedom for the seventeen bombers held in Kuwaiti jails.

Meeting in emergency session and keeping in constant touch with their Gulf and U.S. allies, the Kuwaiti cabinet finally announced it would not accept any of the conditions before all the hostages were freed. Small groups of hostages, first women and children and then mainly Pakistani men, were subsequently released in stages. But the Kuwaitis still balked. The angered hijackers, led by a man who identified himself only as "Abu Saleh," announced that explosives had been planted inside the plane. It would be blown up, passengers and crew still inside, if the prisoners in Kuwait were not immediately released. As the Pakistani ambassador in Iran lamented to reporters, the talks were going "very poorly."

The nightmare grew worse on day three, Thursday. Radio monitors in other Middle East countries picked up the agonized, haunting screams and hysterical crying of one of the hostages, macabre pleading that was subsequently broadcast around the world. Then an American passenger, clearly under orders from one of the masked hijackers standing with a gun at his back, shouted a request that a loudspeaker be delivered to the plane. When it was, the hostage stood at the top of the exit stairway, first introducing himself as the U.S. consul in Karachi, which, curiously enough, he was not. He said the hijackers had begun a countdown, and then he appealed for his life: "Tell the Kuwaiti authorities to provide the hijackers with a pilot and co-pilot, because they are serious about their threats," a reference to the hijackers' demands for a fresh crew to fly them out of Tehran. Then the hijackers pumped six bullets into him at point-blank range.

This second victim was another AID official, William Stanford. His body, again dumped on the tarmac, was so shot up and bloodied that Swiss diplomats had trouble identifying him from the photographs and statistics the United States had by then provided about the four U.S. citizens believed to be on board.

Other shots were heard later inside the aircraft, and when an Iranian cleaning crew and photographer were allowed inside, they saw two bloodied bodies on the floor. By the end of the day, all news agencies were reporting at least four dead, an erroneous report but one which did shrewdly planned psychological damage.

Released hostages later told chilling tales of brutality on board the airbus. In sporadic fits of temper, the hijackers were particularly brutal to the Americans, who, with the Kuwaitis, had been segregated and tied to their seats in the first-class section. John Costa, a fifty-year-old New York businessman, was forced to lie in the aisle while one hijacker stood on his back shouting anti-American slogans. Other times he was "interrogated," lighted cigarettes held against the skin of his face and hands. "What they wanted was for me to say I was from the CIA," Costa said. "That's all they wanted to hear." The hijackers' moods fluctuated wildly. "If they got angry, they would beat you, and then they would offer you orange juice. We could not tell from one minute to the next what they might do and how they would react to anything you might say." The only break they took was for prayers.

British flight engineer Neil Beeston said, "Every five minutes there was a frightening incident. There was no letup at all" by hijackers who screamed at the captives and put gun barrels at their temples. The hijackers told the Kuwaitis they would not kill them, since they were Muslims. But the torture, according to one hostage, "made death look easy." Only one passenger managed to escape: taken to the aircraft door as if to be the next death, a Pakistani jumped and ran to safety as the gunmen opened fire behind him.

Friday, day four, was the most bizarre because of an odd sequence of events in Tehran and elsewhere. A still-unexplained shooting inside the plane crippled the airbus; because thirteen windows were shattered, flying elsewhere was no longer an option. The hijackers also threatened to resume the killings unless a prepared statement was broadcast in Iran and Kuwait. The Iranians eventually agreed.

"We do not have any enmity toward anyone and we do not intend to deny the freedom of anyone or to frighten anyone," the communi-qué read. But then it warned:

A group of personalities [passengers] whom the world considers im-portant, but whom we consider a bunch of criminals, are worthy of execution according to God's and the Koran's decree. There are other individuals, including Americans and Kuwaitis, whom we will not free, and their fate is also liable to be death unless the Kuwaiti govern-ment comes to its senses and frees our enchained brothers. . . . The op-pressive regime in Kuwait and the whole world must know and bear witness to what we have said and we will honestly carry it out. . . . The world will witness a great epic . . . The American masters of Kuwait will see how blood will become victorious over their shaky rule.

The statement ended:

Our hope is that the fate of our enchained brothers in Kuwait and all over the world would meet God's approbation. With hopes of martyrdom, praise be to God, the cherisher and sustainer of the worlds.

Meanwhile, in Beirut, an anonymous caller from Islamic Jihad telephoned a Western news agency. After the usual opening line, "In the name of God, the compassionate and merciful," he made an un-expected statement: "We did *not* commit the Kuwaiti hijacking. But we do support our comrades and announce our readiness to partici-pate in any action likely to achieve their demands." The voice added, "There is no way of turning back after the shock dealt to the West-ern world," apparently referring to the two American deaths. "We hold the oil kings and princes, especially the [Kuwaiti ruling] al Sabah clan responsible for what happened and what is happening." In a separate statement, the Lebanese branch of Dawa threatened to blow up the Kuwaiti Embassy in Beirut if the hijackers' demands were not met. The most prominent voice going against the tide was that of Sheikh Fadlallah, who offered a ruling that all hijackings were "un-Islamic."

In Washington, President Reagan issued his first criticism of the Iranians. They "have not been as helpful as they could be in this situ-ation, or as I think they should have been," he said. But his adminis-

tration then gave curious instructions to the U.S. mission at the
United Nations. In New York, the Political Committee of the General Assembly was voting on a Soviet-sponsored resolution on state-sponsored terrorism, "resolutely condemning policies and practices
of terrorism in relations between states as a method of dealing with
other states and peoples." It urged that "all states take no actions
aimed at military intervention and occupation, forcible change in
or undermining of the sociopolitical system of states, the destabilization and overthrow of their governments, and in particular, initiate
no military action to that end under any pretext whatsoever, and
cease forthwith any such action already in progress." The resolution was adopted overwhelmingly (101–0, with 29 abstentions). But,
charging that the definition of state terrorism was too vague
and left too many loopholes, the United States and most Western
nations abstained. The American position underlined the difficulty
both of defining terrorism, since one nation's "terrorists" are
another's "freedom fighters," and of finding a practical or effective
response.

Sunday crackled with tension as the frustrated hijackers made
their final threats. By this stage, they had released all but the two
Americans, Captain Clark, and four Kuwaiti government officials,
one of them an ambassador, in daily batches, yet they had all of their
major demands rejected by Kuwait. First, they wanted Kuwait to
send a new plane to Tehran to replace the damaged airbus. The hijackers then warned the control tower that they had finished planting explosives at the plane's wing and fuselage and were saying their
"final prayers." This, one said, was the "final warning." They would
blow up the plane, themselves and the seven remaining hostages.
After reading their last will and testament over the cockpit radio to
negotiators, and refusing an offer of food and drinks, they cut off the
radio link. The Iranians were sufficiently worried to declare a state of
emergency at the airport, closing off all incoming air traffic. Fire engines and ambulances encircled the plane—at a safe distance—in
case.

But shortly before midnight of the sixth day, seven hours after they
had said their final prayers, the hijackers resumed radio communications, asking for a doctor and for service workers to clean up the airbus, as well as a power charger. Iranian security forces apparently

saw their chance. Three were dressed as a doctor and two janitors. Cautiously, they approached the plane.

"When they arrived in disguise," the Iranian news agency reported, "they grabbed one of the hijackers and pushed him down the stairs. Three other security men outside lobbed smoke grenades as troops fired their guns to distract the hijackers." Within minutes, the other three hijackers were led down the stairs, hands in the air. The rescuers acted "swiftly enough to prevent any counterattack." Costa, his eyes black and swollen from beating and his face covered with red welts from cigarette burns, said after it was over, "The operation went so fast and unexpectedly that I didn't notice it."

Kuwait politely if coolly thanked the Iranians for ending the ordeal. Greeting the returning hostages in Kuwait, Crown Prince Saad al Abdullah took the opportunity to declare that Kuwait "will never bow to terrorism and blackmail. I want all to understand, especially those who financed the criminals, that Kuwait shoulders its responsibility with dignity and refuses to submit to blackmail." A Kuwaiti paper, however, wanted a firmer indication of Kuwait's commitment to stand up to terrorism. *Al Rai al Aam* said there was a "national demand" that the three saboteurs sentenced to death eight months earlier for the Kuwaiti bombings finally be executed. The government ignored the appeal.

■   ■   ■

BUT THE ORDEAL was not over, for the Americans and the Iranians launched a war of words over responsibility and eventual judgment of the hijackers. Spokesmen for both the White House and the State Department called for Iran to either extradite the air pirates to Kuwait, under terms of the Hague Convention on international hijacking, or try them. And, once the two American survivors had been flown out of Iran, a White House official alleged that Iran had "clearly encouraged extreme behavior by the hijackers."

Others charged that Iran was ultimately responsible for the hijacking. "We have no smoking pistol showing Iran did it," a State Department official told *The New York Times*. "But they created a climate of terrorism in Lebanon and helped organize the terrorist cells. They armed them in Lebanon to kill Westerners. They then try to say that they are not responsible for the hijacking. But we say that

because of what went on in advance, you are responsible even if
there is no evidence to go to court saying that the Iranians planned
the hijacking." He added, "The hijackers took the plane to Iran because they knew they would have a very sympathetic audience there.
The hijackers wanted to force the Kuwaitis to release the pro-Iranian
terrorists. And during the first three days at the airport, the Iranians
tried to pressure the Kuwaitis to comply with the demands. There
was nothing said or done that indicated any unhappiness with the hijackers. . . . It is our judgment, rightly or wrongly, that only when it
was established that the hijacking could not achieve their objectives
was a way found to end the hijacking."

Additional accusations added to the tension. One Kuwaiti and two
Pakistani passengers claimed that the hijackers received additional
weapons and equipment once the plane had landed, including handcuffs and nylon ropes used to tie passengers to their seats. On the first
day, one of the hijackers left the plane and "spent about thirty minutes talking to Iranian officials. The hijacking started with a small
gun and suddenly we saw many more guns, explosives and nylon
rope," said Professor Ahmed al Sharhan of Kuwait University. "Just
how were the hijackers able to obtain these things?" U.S. officials alleged that radio communications monitored by outsiders hinted at
cooperation.

Abolhassan Bani Sadr, the first Iranian President after the 1979
revolution, who had fled to Paris in 1981, quoted unspecified
"sources" as saying that two of the hijackers had also taken part in
the air heist of an Air France 737 to Iran the previous July. (Those
hijackers, who blew up the cockpit, later surrendered and disappeared into Iranian custody.) Another Pakistani said he had seen the
four Lebanese, all with first-class tickets, waved inside by security
men in Dubai without being checked. Western sources in Beirut
claimed that the Lebanese had not gone through checks at Beirut International Airport either. *The New York Times* quoted Washington
officials as saying the four were members of Hizbollah, the pro-Iranian group in Lebanon. And another U.S. official said that the climax
smelled like a set-up surrender. "You do not invite cleaners aboard
an airplane after you have planted explosives, promised to blow up
the plane and read your last will and testament. That is patently ab-
surd."

The Kuwaiti ambassador to the United States, Sheikh Saud Nasir al Sabah, charged, "We tend to lean toward the fact that [the hijacking] was well-planned with extensive intelligence and surveillance because the Airbus jet carried three U.S. AID officials and three Kuwaiti diplomats . . . Suppose they hijacked a plane with no American officials. What would they have bargained with?" And the son of the Kuwaiti ruler called in the foreign diplomatic corps for a two-hour briefing to say privately what the government dared not say in public: Kuwait was convinced Iran was involved, in part to pressure the government to end its financial support for Iraq in the then four-year-old war.

However, most of the hostages indicated otherwise. Costa said there was "no evidence whatsoever" of Iranian complicity. Charles Kapar, the other American survivor, said he had noted no new weapons on the second day or at any other time. Kuwaiti Ambassador-at-large Khalifa Hussein al Muslim had no criticisms: "We sometimes saw certain death in front of our eyes. For me, the Iranian forces were like angels suddenly descended from the sky." Captain Clark commented, "As far as I knew, they did their best. . . . They've been just marvelous. I think the Iranian authorities played it just right, in that they didn't give way to demands. They pacified the hijackers." The pilot added that he felt "nothing but humanity and compassion" from the Iranians, who he never felt were in collusion with the hijackers.

Iran defused the crisis somewhat by announcing that the four would be tried by Islamic law in Tehran. But the government was furious with the American allegations. Even Ayatollah Khomeini became involved. "If any country other than Iran handled an instance of air piracy the way Iran did, the world would have praised it for skillful, responsive and adroit handling of the incident," he said. "The Americans say there is no evidence of Iranian involvement in the operation, and yet declare Iran had organized it. The fact is that they have nothing to announce. The Islamic Republic terrifies them."

And Prime Minister Mir Hussein Musawi countered, "If Iran had not acted in a logical way, but in a gangster-Mafia fashion, probably other passengers would have been killed." And he rejected extradition. "If handing over the hijackers were lawful, they [the West] should hand over the terrorists who have martyred hundreds inside Iran and who are now continuing their activities with the support of the Americans and the French. Then we shall hand over the Kuwait airbus hijackers to them . . . It is the aggressive policies of the United States that caused the death of the Americans." In a final note he cautioned, "The Americans still think that feudalism rules the world and therefore demand that Iran explain its handling of the hijacking affair. . . . If Reagan thought about what happened to Carter, he would understand that Iran explains nothing to anyone but God."

■   ■   ■

WORDS WERE ABOUT ALL the United States could shoot back. Throughout the trauma, Washington was basically helpless. Once again, there was no follow-through on the stream of warnings about U.S. action that had been issued by Reagan administration officials for months before the hijacking. Secretary of State George Shultz had become so vocal in favor of either preemptive raids or retaliatory strikes against extremists that the policy option was dubbed "the Shultz Doctrine."

In fact, U.S. military officials at the Pentagon, at Army Special Operations headquarters in North Carolina, at European Command Headquarters in Stuttgart, West Germany, and in Beirut, Oman, Bahrain and elsewhere were scrambling during the entire six days, preparing contingency plans. Because of the English pilot and engineer, Britain's crack SAS troops were also on full alert. Washington had signaled tentative approval for a commando unit to rescue the hostages if the plane flew to any other destination, as seemed possible on several occasions.

Beirut was considered the most likely stop, due to the anarchy in Lebanon and the Shi'ite domination of West Beirut, especially around the airport. The Lebanese hijackers would almost automatically pick up support from sympathizers. The Americans looked at every option, including some slightly bizarre possibilities. "If it came to Beirut, our biggest fear was that the hijackers might divert and crash into Yarze [the East Beirut suburb where the U.S. ambassador and several other Western envoys live] as it came in for landing," one U.S. official explained. "That would be only ten seconds off the normal course. It would be a 'beautiful' diversion. With thirty-seven thousand miles of fuel, there would be no need for explosives. And if they missed the ambassador's residence, they could count on getting near either the Presidential Palace or the Ministry of Defense."

American land, sea and air forces were involved in the various contingency plans, making use of units already in place and facilities available to the United States scattered throughout the region. The U.S.S. *Eisenhower* had been deployed in the eastern Mediterranean since shortly after the U.S. Embassy annex in Beirut had gone up ten weeks earlier. The British airbase in Cyprus was another possible base of operations. "There was preparedness to move . . . What we did do was put units on alert and get ready for another Curacao scenario," a senior Washington official said.*

Indeed, many Americans in the Middle East almost expected U.S. action, particularly against Shi'ite targets in Lebanon. Once again, American teachers, diplomats and journalists, missionaries and bankers in Beirut kept a low profile, rarely going out at night, varying daily schedules and times of movement, letting others know where they were going—in anticipation of a raid on Shia strongholds that might, in turn, lead to retaliation by the extremists. Several living in West Beirut were so sure that the United States would retaliate that they moved to the Christian east side for the duration and the immediate aftermath. Others were ordered by their head offices to leave the country temporarily.

The mixture of American expectations and frustrations was reflected by Edwena Hegna, widow of the first hijacking casualty: "Whenever someone wants to make a statement, and they want to have the world stand up and listen, then they put Americans out front and they say, 'This one's going to get it.' And it seems like they always, even if we're not involved, somehow they find a reason why the American is to blame." She added that she did not understand why a powerful country like the United States would "let such a small country put us on hold and let us stand in limbo, and do nothing, and make us feel so helpless."

Yet the U.S. lacked real options. "There was simply no practical

* A textbook example of a successful rescue operation was carried out in Curaçao after a hijacked Venezuelan plane was flown to the Caribbean island the previous July. A special Venezuelan twelve-man unit, assisted "technically" by U.S. troops from Delta Force, stormed the DC-9 and killed the two hijackers, a Dominican and a Haitian who wanted $2 million in ransom. No hostages were wounded.

way for the U.S. to use force in this case," commented Robert Kupperman, a counterterrorism specialist at the Georgetown Center for Strategic and International Studies. "Any rescue team we sent in would have been killed along with the hostages. This case demonstrated that the Shultz Doctrine—the use of force—is at best a selective tool that does not apply in every instance."

So Americans did nothing besides mourn their dead. On December 12, 1984, a C-141 military cargo plane brought back the flag-draped coffins of Charles Hegna and William Stanford to Andrews Air Force Base outside Washington, the fifth delivery in twenty months of victims of Shia fanatics. Vice-President George Bush led the delegation of mourners at the dawn service. In a brief and angry eulogy, he offered bold words: "Wanton murder of the innocent is terrorism that no amount of incantation can disguise. So let us renew our call for all nations to uphold justice before mankind. Civilized nations can and must resist terrorism . . . We shall know their murderers with the long memories of those who believe in patient but certain justice."

But the reality was better reflected at another simple memorial service on the same day more than seven thousand miles away, at the U.S. Embassy in Kuwait, for those who had died in the embassy bombing. After a reading from the Koran, the Stars and Stripes were lowered to half staff at the compound that had been converted into a fortress. Man-sized tank traps in the shape of anchors and large concrete blocks sealed off all entrances and side roads. The gate penetrated by the suicide bomber had been bricked up. Kuwaiti troops manning .50-caliber machine guns were positioned in jeeps at strategic points. In front of a somber crowd of diplomats and employees, U.S. Ambassador C. E. Quainton observed, "The attack affected all of those who worked here. It has affected the way in which we live and work in this compound today." Then he noted dryly that the commemoration had been almost overtaken by another fatal confrontation with the terrorism of fanatics.

The two ceremonies marked completion of a full cycle, for December 12 was exactly one year since the American Embassy had been blown up. A Kuwaiti official lamented, "This tragedy is not the end, it is just the beginning."

■   ■   ■

IN EARLY 1985, the families of two of the American kidnap victims held in Lebanon, the Reverend Benjamin Weir and Father Lawrence Jenco, received letters from the victims. Both said they would not be released until the prisoners in Kuwait were freed. "As long as they are being held, I am held," wrote Jenco. "Any military intervention on my behalf will not be good for me." Families verified the hand-writing on both letters.

Then on May 16, 1985, Islamic Jihad released photos of the by then six hostages—which had risen to four Americans and two French as the result of new kidnappings—with a warning that they faced a "horrible disaster" if the jailed terrorists in Kuwait were not released. "We will not be patient for a long time but instead will act in a way that will terrify America and France forever. America and its agents understand only the language of force, and we have given her many chances before using force against her," said notes accompanying the Polaroid photos.

Several high-level sources in Washington and elsewhere suggested that the demands, eighteen months after the first kidnapping, may not have been the original intention of the kidnappers, but added as an afterthought, perhaps as a result of widespread speculation and press coverage about a connection, or because of subsequent contacts established between the Lebanese kidnappers and allies of the Kuwaiti prisoners.

Nine days after that threat, the extremists acted. As the motorcade of Sheikh Jaber, the Kuwaiti ruler, sped toward Sif Palace, a car pulled out from the curb. With split-second timing, it rammed into the royal entourage's lead vehicle. Two of the Kuwaiti ruler's body-guards, a passerby and the suicide driver were killed. Sheikh Jaber received only cuts and bruises, apparently only because the bomber drove into the first car instead of the emir's vehicle. Once again, a caller claiming to speak for Islamic Jihad phoned a Western news agency in Beirut. "The emir has received our message. We ask him again to liberate our comrades held in Kuwait jails. Otherwise," he announced, "all the thrones of the gulf will be targeted."

6 The Impact: Saudi Arabia

ISLAM DOES NOT RECOGNIZE MONARCHY AND HEREDITARY SUC-
CESSION.... ALL THE RULERS ARE AFRAID THEIR OWN PEOPLE
WILL FOLLOW THE EXAMPLE OF IRAN ...

I HOPE OTHER ISLAMIC COUNTRIES WHICH ARE BOUND BY
WORLDLY VALUES ... WILL RID THEMSELVES OF THESE BONDS
AND JOIN THEIR IRANIAN BROTHERS IN THIS GREAT CRUSADE, SO
THAT THEY CAN BECOME VICTORIOUS IN THEIR FIGHT AGAINST
THE SUPERPOWERS.

—*AYATOLLAH KHOMEINI*

THE WINDS OF PARADISE ARE BLOWING.
—*IKHWAN WAR CRY*

Although the sun had not yet peeked over the bleak Saudi
Arabian desert on November 20, 1979, more than forty thousand
Muslim pilgrims from around the world had already assembled in the
shadows of the splendidly ornate Grand Mosque in Mecca, famous
for its intricate blue-and-gold tile walls, marble pavements, and
towering minarets. The Grand Mosque is the largest Islamic shrine
on earth, off limits to any but believers.

146

A kind of awe permeated the air as the pilgrims, serious but excited about this day, waited for dawn prayers in the refreshingly cool morning temperatures. For Muslims, whose calendar began with the Prophet Mohammed's exile from Mecca to Medina to spread his revelations from God, and to launch what was to become the Islamic empire, it was the beginning of a new century—the fifteenth.

At 5:20 A.M., Sheikh Mohammed ibn Subayyal, Imam of the Grand Mosque, was just completing the first of the day's five prayers, each timed by the position of the moon. Suddenly there was a fluttering in the crowd, movement and nervous talk, questioning. Something was happening, too quickly for the pilgrims to fathom. Sheikh Subayyal had been shoved aside. Then three shots echoed through the mosque's courtyard, magnified by the microphone. A bloodied acolyte collapsed, dead. Men, lots of men, all with guns, seemed to have come out of nowhere. But they were everywhere that counted, at doors and windows and corners. Then a voice boomed over the minaret microphones, normally used only to call the faithful to prayer. To the stunned disbelief of the pilgrims, the speaker declared that the Grand Mosque had been seized.

The takeover was as shocking and unexpected to Muslims as a forcible seizure of the Vatican would be to the Catholic world. Islam dictated that blood should never be shed in the shrine that shelters the sacred black Kaaba stone marking the center of Islam, the direction in which all Muslims face in prayer. "NO, NOT IN ISLAM," bannered a Saudi paper.

Unlike the Shia, whose tradition was to defy temporal authority, the Sunni historically were not rebels against the established order. So it was almost impossible for the pilgrims to imagine who and what cause could possibly be behind such an obscene violation of Islam's oldest site.

The answers slowly unraveled over the microphone. Using flowery and pious words, the voice loudly proclaimed the arrival of the long-awaited prophet, or "Mahdi," who had come to "cleanse" Islam before the end of the world. The frightened pilgrims were ordered to join The Cause or leave. Then the band of at least two hundred heavily armed men sealed off the mosque. The proclaimed Mahdi and his followers were Sunni fundamentalists calling for a new age of Islam, one unadulterated by the corruption and deviations of the past. They could not have found a more dramatic means of publicizing their cause than seizing the Grand Mosque.

Saudi Arabian officials were as stunned and frightened as the pilgrims when the first confusing details were relayed from Mecca to Riyadh, the capital. They were also slow to react. They in effect quarantined the country, including ordering Canadian workers at the telephone company to cut all commercial communications with the outside world. Then officials unconvincingly claimed that the incident was closed, while they fumbled over ways to recapture the shrine without the use of force.

There seemed no reasonable way to end the trauma—and the deepest humiliation in the nation's history since feisty Abdel Aziz ibn Saud had overwhelmed the peninsula's warring fiefdoms forty-seven years earlier to create a single, united "Arabia of the Sauds." Initial attempts by religious scholars to use persuasion and by the military to try gentle force collapsed owing to the chaotic tactics of the untested Saudi security forces and the intransigence of the rebels.

In the end, the government turned to the Ulama (council of religious judges) for a ruling. Five days after the seizure, the clergy lifted the ban on use of weapons in the mosque. At least two thousand National Guard, army and police troops—some said the number was up to ten times higher—moved on the mosque, under direction of French military strategists flown in specially to help plot the counterattack. But it took them nine more days, fighting room to room among the 270 vaults and chambers beneath the mosque, to end the rebellion. The fundamentalists had come well prepared, complete with gas masks, food supplies, arms and a large quantity of ammunition—all driven undetected past guards at the entrance, some stored in coffins.

At least 255 pilgrims, troops and fanatics were killed in the battles, another 560 injured, according to government figures, although diplomats suggested the toll was higher. Troop casualties may offer some insight into the proficiency of the kingdom's U.S.-trained defense force: 127 dead and 451 injured.

The impact was not limited to Mecca. Ayatollah Khomeini went on Tehran Radio to comment on the seizure: "It is not beyond guessing that this is the work of criminal American imperialism and international Zionism." As unlikely as it seemed, he was not the only one with suspicions. Anti-American demonstrations followed in the Philippines, Turkey, Bangladesh, India, the United Arab Emirates and Pakistan. Mobs marched through the streets of Kuwait to the wall of the American Embassy compound. The U.S. Embassy in Islamabad was burned to the ground. The U.S. mission in Libya was raided, then set alight, by protestors chanting pro-Khomeini slogans. The anguished Saudis were horrified about what was becoming an international incident. And Washington was alarmed at how easily thousands of people in different countries were prepared to believe anything bad about the United States on the basis of a single remark by the Iranian leader.

At the time, it seemed that the situation could not get any worse. But it did. As Saudi soldiers struggled to regain control of the Grand Mosque, riots broke out on the opposite side of the country, this time involving Shi'ite fundamentalists.

Saudi Arabia's shoreline along the eastern oil-rich Gulf in Hasa province is an eerie, colorless moonscape, rocky and cratered, where it is impossible to avoid squinting even at dusk. The feeling that you are on the edge of the world is reinforced by little stickers on hotel bathroom mirrors: "Water is Gold. Don't waste it." Hasa is a bitter land of bitter people. A confrontation of some sort seemed to have been long in the pipeline. It was not just the straightforward and now familiar issue of social neglect and religious scorn felt by the Shia. As in the Shah's Iran, the demonstrations accompanying the religious festival of Ashura, the Shi'ites' holiest period, were outlawed in Saudi Arabia, for much the same reasons: the bloody self-flagellation and whipping, which occasionally led to deaths, were considered primitive by leaders trying to modernize their nations; and the feverish ten-day celebrations of Hussein's martyrdom often aroused uncomfortable sectarian passions.

But in this, the first year of Khomeini's rule across the Gulf waters, the emboldened Saudi Shia on the eastern seaboard decided to defy the ban and go ahead with the emotional celebrations of Ashura. Years later, a conflict of chicken-and-egg accounts of which side triggered the trouble still raged unresolved. Pro-government sources claimed that the violence began after demonstrators took to the streets of towns in the eastern province, shouting slogans demanding that Saudi Arabia actively aid Iran and stop selling oil to the Americans. Police were then forced to move in. Antigovernment sources claimed that nervous authorities initiated intervention in Ashura festivities, sparking a violent reaction.

Either way, the initial clashes between police and the Ashura marchers mushroomed into violence as mobs went on the rampage, burning cars, attacking banks, looting shops. At least seventeen Shia were killed. The trouble lasted for three days and was centered in Hasa's Shia-dominated town of Qatif. But four other areas nearby reportedly also experienced trouble; most notably near Ras Tanura, the vital oil refinery and export center. Unimpeded by religious strictures confining its tactics this time, the House of Saud moved swiftly and heavily against the Shi'ites, "throwing" the Sunni-dominated National Guard at the minority. The subsequent clashes were bloody, resulting in several deaths and injuries. A Lebanese paper, the only news outlet initially to report the trouble due to a news blackout from the kingdom, claimed that the Saudis rushed an additional twenty thousand troops to seal off four towns on the eastern oil coast.

Yet the Saudi Minister of Interior denied the reports. After an emergency cabinet meeting, he said that the only problem was at the Grand Mosque and that the rest of the country "enjoyed complete stability and security."

■   ■   ■

THE DUAL FUNDAMENTALIST THREAT, from both Sunni and Shia, was devastating to the Saudis—and to those in the United States who were attuned to the delicate political shifts in the region. Saudi Arabia was a key strategic ally as well as a vital source of oil; the possibility of "losing" Saudi Arabia sent shivers down the spines of many Americans who remembered the mere psychological toll on the United States when the oil price had quadrupled in 1973. American columnist Carl Rowan wrote an article that reflected the new obsession in State Department offices and Riyadh palaces entitled "Saudi Arabia: The Next Iran?" As with Iran, the fundamentalist threat had not initially been viewed as a significant concern in Saudi Arabia. But former CIA chief and Secretary of Energy James Schlesinger subsequently told reporters that instability in Saudi Arabia was "far more serious than we have been inclined to acknowledge."

The seizure of the Grand Mosque and the uprisings in the east in late 1979 happened in context of the Shah's demise and Khomeini's return to Iran nine months earlier. American diplomats at the U.S. Embassy in Tehran had been taken hostage sixteen days before the Grand Mosque was seized; the loose parallels were electrifying. Although relations had been rocky between the Pahlavis and the House of Saud, the monarchy was still terrified of the new alternative: fanatic mullahs running the Gulf's other major power. So, apparently, were average Saudis, who had shipped billions of dollars from Saudi banks to calmer climes.

Ironically, Middle East pundits had predicted throughout the 1970s that the crisis facing the kingdom was modernization. The popular scenario called for the House of Saud to accept major reforms, political and cultural, if it hoped to survive in the late twentieth century. It would be forced to shed some of the quaint but anachronistic traditions to endure. Oil wealth had provided funds for thousands of students to attend schools and universities abroad, where they were exposed to the faster-paced "real world." This group alone, it was argued, would provide a groundswell for liberalization. The ruling family would eventually *have* to introduce greater participation in government—which the King and the four thousand princes had traditionally shared only with the clergy—to satisfy the "modernized" generation.

The status of women was the best example to Westerners of how badly out-of-date the Saudi system was. As the rest of the world experienced women's liberation and the sexual revolution, Saudi women were still hidden behind black veils—even, to the perplexity of Western nations, for passport photos. They were discouraged from working and usually segregated from men when they did work; forbidden to drive or go to restaurants alone; and barred from cinemas and sporting events altogether. Most marriages were still arranged, and polygamy was the law of the land. To outsiders in either East or West, these practices were evidence of how the country had not kept up with the realities of life in the rest of the world.

The two overlapping crises at the end of the decade proved the experts wrong, or at least guilty of seeing only part of the picture. The biggest single threat to the stability and longevity of the Saudi monarchy was not from reformers, but from religious fundamental-

ists, those who felt that the strictest Muslim state in the world, at
least theoretically, had already gone too far in liberalizing and dilut-
ing Islam.

Yet the two uprisings had totally different origins.

The Grand Mosque takeover originated with Juhaiman Saif al
Otaiba, an embittered Sunni fundamentalist once described as having defiant eyes, bushy hair and a square beard. Juhaiman was a former member of the Saudi National Guard, where he had learned a
great deal about weaponry. Then, as a theological student in Medina,
Islam's second holiest city, he had learned religious militancy.

The chief original influence on Juhaiman was Sheikh Abdel Aziz al
Baz, the blind ultraconservative rector of the University of Medina,
who taught the absolutist version of "pure" Islam at the expense of
the immense inbuilt flexibility of the faith. Sheikh Baz became famous internationally during the 1969 landing on the moon. To the
embarrassment of the Saudi government, he called the U.S. space triumph a hoax. He also had once written a paper blasting the Coper-
nican "heresy," insisting that the sun orbited around the earth, and
had been quoted as declaring that the world was flat.*

During the mid-1970s, Juhaiman began openly preaching against
the House of Saud. Indeed, he had become so reactionary he even
turned against Sheikh Baz, berating him as a stooge in the pay of the
al Saud. Juhaiman now emulated the style of the old Muslim Brotherhood, the Ikhwan, growing a scraggly beard and shortening his white
thobe—the traditional men's robe—to calf length, signifying humility and poverty. And he began advocating a return to the original
ways of Islam, among other things; a repudiation of the West; an end
to education for women; abolition of the sacrilegious television; and
expulsion of non-Muslims. Oil wealth, he maintained, should be used
for Islam rather than for personal and state luxuries.

The Saud family "worship money and spend it on palaces, not
mosques," he charged. "If you accept what they say, they will make
you rich. Otherwise, they will persecute and even torture you." And
he wrote—or had written for him, since the Saudis claimed he was

* Sheikh Baz's U.S.-educated nephew later opened the first entertainment park in Saudi
Arabia, complete with a ride offering a simulated trip through space, which I visited
shortly before it opened in 1983. The giant white rocket bumped around so much that
adults and children were to be strapped into their seats as they watched the marvels of stars
and planets on a screen in front.

illiterate—a pamphlet entitled "Rules of Allegiance and Obedience: The Misconduct of Rulers." It declared:

> Our belief is that the continued rule [by the House of Saud] is a destruction of God's religion even if they pretend to uphold Islam. We ask God to relieve us of them all. . . . Anyone with eyesight can see today how they represent religion as a form of humiliation, insult and mockery. These rulers have subjected Muslims to their interests and made religion into a way of acquiring their materialistic interests. They have brought upon the Muslims all evil and corruption.

Juhaiman's following grew through the 1970s, with certain pathetic ironies. As James Buchan noted in "The House of Saud": "Juhaiman's band drew its strength from the same source as the Saudi state, from a militant piety almost as old as Islam itself. Here small communities react to the corruption of the present by puritanical behavior and violent disdain." The Saudis were sufficiently worried to haul in Juhaiman and ninety-eight of his followers for interrogation in 1978. But under pressure from the religious establishment, including Sheikh Baz, they were freed after six weeks. The release underscored the difficulty in Saudi Arabia and elsewhere of checking the fundamentalists. Whether they were judged to be misguided innocents or dangerous terrorists, popular sentiment was against punishment or persecution for Islamic belief. After all, on what grounds?

The dilemma was outlined by an American diplomat, who noted that the Iranian revolution had a deep impact on Saudi policy: "It's like the Russians being outflanked on the left, or George Wallace, in the old days, being outsegged in the South. The Saudis are accustomed to being defenders of the faith, the foremost exponents of religious purity. They can deal with secular challenges easily enough, but when they're outflanked on the religious side they're baffled and disoriented. They don't know what to do."

The Saudis were caught off guard by the Grand Mosque seizure in large part because of their preoccupation with the Shia. A long history of sporadic unrest had troubled the area—including strikes at Aramco's refineries in 1953 and 1956—since ibn Saud wrenched Hasa from rivals in 1913. The Wahhabist Sunnis of Saudi Arabia generally looked down their noses at the Shia everywhere as deviationists, while the Shia remembered the destruction of the Shi'ite holy city of Karbala in 1802—when Shia residents were massacred and the sacred tomb of Hussein, the Prophet's grandson, was left in ruins by marauding Ikhwan under the Wahhabist banner. Each side was deeply suspicious of the other.

After 1973, the potency of the Gulf Shia soared at the same rate as the price of oil. The Shia are only a small percentage of Saudi Arabia's estimated five million population, but they are roughly one-third of the residents of Hasa, where they provide the majority work force.*

Yet even after the Sunni regime became uneasy about the possible repercussions of the Iranian revolution in 1979, the Shia generally reaped only token benefits from the land they considered theirs. The billions of petrodollars were largely channeled to other parts of the country, for the glass and steel towers and eight-lane highways in Riyadh, palaces in Jeddah, development projects in the central and western provinces, fancy airports as big in area as an entire American city, and a military base up north that would house more troops than the Saudis could provide. Most of Hasa, meanwhile, remained shabby, in need of hospitals, better roads, bigger schools. Once again, the Shia felt that they suffered from injustice and were exploited by their Sunni masters.

> Underlying those disturbances was Shi'ite resentment, stimulated by the emotive rhetoric of Khomeini and the Iranian revolution. Historically, the eruptions should be seen as a reaction to neglect and suppression born of Sunni prejudice existing throughout Islam but present in the Wahhabite Kingdom in particularly primeval form. The leaders of the House of Saud should have been alerted to the dangers arising from the existence of a disaffected community long before. . . . The Shi'ite community is and will continue to be the most divisive element in the Kingdom.

Indeed, just a few weeks before the Shia demonstrations in late 1979, *The Observer* of London reported that Saudi security forces had uncovered plans for two pro-Iranian protests by Shia during the annual Hajj pilgrimage. An unspecified number of pilgrims had been deported in October after banners and political literature were found—and confiscated.

---

* Saudi Arabia does not release census figures, perhaps in part out of concern for what they indicate about Shia strength and the number of foreigners the Saudis rely on.

It was not surprising that the first major manifestations of the Shia challenge anywhere in the Arab world, after the Iranian revolution, were uprisings in Hasa.

•   •   •

AFTER THE VIOLENCE in Mecca and Hasa had ended, the embarrassed and frightened royal family responded with both carrot and stick. Sixty-three of the Sunni fundamentalists from the Grand Mosque—including Juhaiman, forty other Saudis, ten Egyptians, six South Yemenis, three Kuwaitis, one North Yemeni, one Sudanese and one Iraqi—were tried secretly, then beheaded publicly. The guilty were dispersed for their executions to eight different cities, to make a point.* Against the Shia in the eastern province, authorities launched security sweeps, detaining hundreds. The government effectively demonstrated that it was prepared to combat religious extremism.

At the same time, throughout the country, it began enforcing the Islamic code. Police cracked down on shopkeepers who did not close for the five daily calls to prayer. Newspapers were told to be more careful about photographs of women. The Interior Ministry made noises about working women, even at foreign companies. The royal family began showing up more often at tribal councils and public events, one of the few means of keeping in touch with their subjects. Traditional royal gifts to the tribal elders became more lavish. Scholarships for women to attend foreign universities dried up.

And smaller steps reflected the impact of the scare. Dog food was removed from supermarkets, since Muslims consider dogs "unclean." Many swimming pools were drained to prevent mixed bathing. Dolls and teddy bears, considered idolatrous, disappeared from shops, at least temporarily. All were steps to meet the criticisms made by the fanatics who had attacked the mosque. The reaction marked the end of calls, at least for the time being, of liberalization in Saudi Arabia.

While Saudis were appalled by the mosque seizure, it was in many cases the only aspect of the revolt they criticized. Wrote one scholar: "Many of them echoed, in milder form, the graffiti that appeared in the toilets of Riyadh University in the spring 1981: 'Juhaiman, our

* In his capacity as head of the Ulama, Sheikh Baz signed the death warrants in January 1980.

martyr, why didn't you storm the palaces? The struggle is only beginning.' "

A Saudi ambassador broke the usual bond of secrecy within government circles by telling *The New York Times*, "There's a spreading feeling of unrest and impatience with the uneven justice, with the huge commissions paid to princes, with the double standard we have to live with. The people in Mecca were asking for a change in the ruling system. They were saying that royalty is non-Islamic. Even if I don't agree with that, I tell you this movement is much bigger than its leadership suggests."

The Saudis also tried desperately to placate the Shia, perhaps less out of altruism than out of concern for their primary source of income: oil. The Grand Mosque was a catastrophe for the self-described "Guardians of Islam," but the ruling family appeared to think they could handle the Sunni fundamentalists through their own clergy. The alien Shia were a different matter. In February 1980, disturbances again broke out in Hasa despite the beefed-up security presence, confirming initial Saudi fears. This time the clashes were less spontaneous, and bloodier. A group called the Islamic Revolutionary Organization, which intelligence agencies later said worked out of Tehran, claimed responsibility.

High-ranking officials investigated Shia grievances in the east, turning up conclusions that had long been obvious to diplomats and to foreign workers at Aramco, the world's largest oil company, based in the Shia stronghold. The House of Saud responded by pouring in funds for schools, roads and housing projects. Members of the royal family toured the region to meet and try to pacify Shia delegations.

By the end of 1980, a deal had been struck: release of an estimated seven hundred Shia prisoners in return for promises of good behavior. Nevertheless, thousands of National Guard troops were added to the Hasa units, leading one U.S. official to label the security presence "overwhelming. It is large enough to handle any demonstration or outright revolt. There is no question that Saudi Arabia has the force to re-establish control." If such assertions sounded eerily similar to what the U.S. State Department had said about Iran before the fall of the Shah, few seemed to notice.

The public displays of discontent among the Shia did indeed end. But there were abundant signs that the movement was not finished.

After the 1979–80 clampdown, the dangers—as later seen in Bahrain and Kuwait—were no longer mere demonstrations, but attacks on key installations by an underground movement. The United States became concerned enough to order diplomats stationed in Hasa to do an intelligence survey of the Shia. When they concluded that there was little evidence of a threat, they were ordered to look again.

Shi'ism contains a concept known as *taqiya*. Basically, it amounts to concealment of true beliefs by a minority group in times of danger, or when living in a hostile environment. "One of the main obstacles to their receiving a positive response from us is their tenet of taqiya (deception), by the application of which, they reveal to us other than what they have in their hearts," said a Sunni writer. "The simple-minded Sunni is deceived by their pretentious display of the desire to overcome our differences." Taqiya is often cited by Shia as one of the reasons they have historically been viewed as passive. It was practiced by the Shia in Iran when they were in the minority, before their doctrine was accepted as the state religion in the sixteenth century.

Shia sources claim that after the demonstrations in Hasa, taqiya once again was the response by the majority. Only a tiny sector was daring enough to continue the crusade. "There are plenty of Dawa party members in Saudi Arabia, but it is not good to say that clearly," said Dr. Abu Asseal, Dawa's chief representative in Syria. Dawa members had been involved in the 1983 bombings in Kuwait. "Their activities are limited by the political situation." And an American official confirmed that unknown numbers of Saudi Shia fundamentalists had gone to Iran after the revolution, and returned via Bahrain. That explained in part why suspected Shia radicals were picked up and questioned with unsubtle frequency.

The Saudis are generally tight-lipped about internal unrest, even among their partners in the Gulf Cooperation Council (GCC), founded in 1981, a reaction to events in Iran and the Soviet invasion of Afghanistan. But their regional allies know the outlines of several incidents among the Shia.

One foreign envoy who served in Dhahran, where Aramco is headquartered in Hasa province, noted small incidents. Occasional pamphlets and papers critical of the government appeared. Pro-Khomeini or anti-U.S. graffiti was sprayed on walls. A Dutch ship-

per who did regular business at the oil ports noted intentional delays
and small acts of untraceable sabotage, which his sources said were
committed or organized by Shia extremists trying to discourage
Western businesses.

The small acts of sabotage began overlapping with a "regularity"
of bigger threats, involving oil rigs and government installations.
Most were either never carried out or foiled in advance. But the
threats often led to mass "precautionary" detentions anyway, in turn
deepening Shia resentment and hatred of their Saudi masters. A State
Department source conceded that Shia crusaders "could do something with a big bang and a lot of smoke against the show points" in
Hasa, such as the Ras Tanura processing plants. "It's the sheer size of
the facilities that make it difficult, impossible to protect against determined saboteurs."

■   ■   ■

IN EARLY 1980, the Iranians escalated their propaganda campaign
against the Saudis. A transmitter broadcast regular sermons and messages in the name of the Islamic Revolutionary Organization in the
Arabian peninsula. The BBC monitoring service taped one March
program from Radio Tehran which began with a verse from the
Koran: "Kings despoil a country when they enter it and make the
noblest of its people its meanest." Repeatedly, Iran had attempted to
draw comparisons between the excesses and brutality of the Shah
and the rule of the Saudi princes. This particular program dwelled
on that theme:

> When the people have self-confidence and high morale, they will
> begin to demand their rights and oppose the authorities' policy and
> conduct. Indeed, it is this which the corrupt monarchies fear most.
> This is why they always attempt to trample upon the people's dignity
> and morale, oppress them and subject them to ignominy in order to
> prevent the people from ever contemplating opposition and confron-
> tations, and to make them yield and subjugate themselves to the ruling
> authorities. This is the nature of monarchy, which is rejected by Islam.
> This is what our people in the Arabian peninsula are suffering under al
> Saud's rule.

The Saudis attempted to prevent any provocations that would lead
to open confrontation with the Iranian government. Diplomatic re-

lations continued. But in 1981, almost two years after the first Shia incidents, the kingdom's Sunni rulers became worried about the Hajj, the annual pilgrimage by Muslims from all over the world to the holy cities of Mecca and Medina. They issued warnings in advance about attempts to turn the religious event into a political demonstration. The governor of Mecca pledged that the authorities would "strike with an iron fist at whoever tries to break law and order." Notably, Iran was sending the third-largest delegation, some 75,000, to the kingdom and was reportedly also paying for Shia of other nations to make the trip.

The religious season nonetheless began with trouble. In Medina, hundreds of Iranian pilgrims staged a protest near the shrine where Mohammed is buried. They chanted, then shouted the rhetoric of the revolution: "Death to America and Zionism," and "Revolution— Khomeini is the leader." One Iranian pilgrim allegedly said it was the duty of the Iranians to "trigger the long-overdue reawakening of Muslims all over the world." Twenty Iranians were reportedly in- jured after police were called in. Tehran Radio actually boasted about the pilgrims' defiance of Saudi warnings, claiming that thou- sands then protested in a wave of violence. At least eighty Iranian pilgrims and a state television crew were refused entry after they were found carrying Khomeini posters and political pamphlets urg- ing uprisings against conservative Muslim nations.

The incidents badly marred already tense relations between Saudi Arabia and Iran. Ayatollah Khomeini wrote to King Khalid, accusing the Saudis of maltreating the pilgrims. "The ban on pilgrims inter- fering in politics is in the interests of America, Israel, and other ene- mies of Islam," he said.

The psychological warfare began to come out into the open. The Hajj trouble in the fall of 1981 was followed by public demonstra- tions in Tehran in November against the Saudis' eight-point peace plan to settle the Arab–Israeli dispute over a Palestinian homeland. Thousands marched through the streets calling for the death of Crown Prince Fahd, who had sponsored the proposals and after whom they were named. Banners declared him "an enemy of Islam," probably inspired by Ayatollah Khomeini's pronouncement that the scheme was "inconsistent with Islam." The Saudi press in turn la- beled the Khomeini regime "antireligious," with one paper using unusually strong language, calling the Iranian leadership "hellish."

The real shock developed in December, when the plans for a coup in neighboring Bahrain were uncovered. That was the final straw for the Saudis, who looked at the tiny archipelago as the gateway to their kingdom. "The Saudis went crazy," said one Western envoy stationed there in 1981. "They felt the whole Shia community had stabbed them in the back." Before dashing off to Bahrain to offer troops and any other assistance, Prince Nayef, the Saudi Interior Minister and brother of King Khalid, declared, "The sabotage plot was engineered by the Iranian government and was directed against Saudi Arabia."

The distaste and suspicion the Saudis felt about the Iranian fanatics turned to hatred. The reaction to the foiled coup just off their coast was in many ways more severe than in Bahrain itself. "There was a travel ban in the eastern province. Anyone born in the eastern province had to go through special security checks to travel. Leading businessmen in the eastern province were stopped and checked," a Western diplomat said. Saudi caution in dealing with the Iranians was abandoned. Prince Nayef said bluntly, "The Iranians, who said after their revolution that they did not want to be the policemen of the Gulf, have become the terrorists of the Gulf." And after a Gulf Cooperation Council summit of foreign ministers, the six member-states of the Saudi-dominated body declared their intention to counter "Iranian sabotage acts aimed at wrecking the stability of the Gulf region."

■   ■   ■

THE INCREASINGLY TENSE STATE of relations between Iran and Saudi Arabia was in many ways ironic. Despite their vast differences, there were many similarities. The governments in both had grown out of protest movements by religious militants. The basis of legitimacy in both is Islam, and both rule by Islamic dictates. The Sharia, which is based on the revelations to Mohammed from God through the archangel Gabriel and is thus the only code of civil law on earth not man-made, provides the framework for personal and political conduct in both nations.

The Saudis "hardly need reminding of Islam's revolutionary potential," one author explained. Fundamentalism became a powerful force in the Arabian peninsula in the eighteenth century. Indeed, Saudi Arabia was created from a host of warring tribal fiefdoms in large part because of the appeal and militancy of a particular brand of orthodoxy known as Wahhabism. A British specialist noted: "It is from the Wahhabi movement that we can date the revival of Islam as an activist and revolutionary force." One U.S. academic has gone so far as to describe Wahhabism as "probably the most extreme fundamentalist movement ever to succeed politically." And, in *The Kingdom*, Robert Lacey commented: "The renaissance of Islam did not begin with Ayatollah Khomeini. It started eighty years ago in the Arab desert when Abdel Aziz took over the leadership of a religious order." The white words on the emerald-green Saudi flag reflect the religious roots of the state: "There is no God but Allah, and Mohammed is His Prophet."

The movement's name came from Mohammed ibn Abd al Wahhab, an eighteenth-century cleric whose fundamentalist movement called for a return to the ways of the Prophet, the strict implementation of Islamic law as the only political and social basis of life. He wanted to cleanse the "corrupt" Islamic world, "to purge it and restore it to its primitive strictness"—ambitious goals that would become all too familiar in another context two hundred years later.

In 1744, to spread and consolidate the faith, Wahhab forged an alliance with the powerful tribal leader Mohammed ibn Saud. Together, the man of faith and the man of the sword built the first of three nations established over two centuries by joint Wahhab–Saud forces. It was a powerful alliance that eventually led Abdel Aziz ibn Saud, on the Wahhabi platform, to forge the current kingdom in the early twentieth century.

In 1902, with a small band of followers, ibn Saud, as he came to be known, launched his own crusade to mold the largest state in the Arabian peninsula, leading what started out as a militant reform movement against those who had strayed from the Islamic path. Like Iran's Ayatollah now, the young Saudi religious warrior was then intent on seeing his brand of Islam adopted throughout the region. He too was a militant crusader, a puritan, similar in some ways to the current Iranian regime. Ibn Saud's cadre were known as the Ikhwan, or the Brothers—the very force Juhaiman later imitated. Their life was austere and rigidly devout. Explained one Arab witness, "I have seen them hurl themselves on their enemies, utterly fearless of death, not caring how many fall, advancing rank upon rank with only one desire—the defeat and annihilation of the enemy. They normally give no quarter, sparing neither boys nor old men, veritable messengers of death from whose grasp no one escapes."

Another parallel with the Islamic Republic of Iran was the fact that other Muslims were the first targets. "From 1745 to 1934, virtually every battle the Wahhabis fought was against Muslim enemies; they justified their expansion by refusing to recognize the Islamic credentials of non-Wahhabi Muslims . . . The Wahhabis genuinely considered other Muslims untrue to the faith and therefore proper objects of jihad. Religious differences motivated these wars." It took thirty years, but by 1932 ibn Saud and his Ikhwan together had created one of only two nations in the world named after its founder, and the first modern state based strictly on Islam.

After consolidating his kingdom, ibn Saud had disbanded the feisty Ikhwan, whom he had occasionally had trouble controlling. "Islam reverted to its more familiar function, a prop to the social order, not a force to threaten it . . . In the eyes of the religious militants, it was a classic case of the ideological 'sell-out': instead of being allowed to restore the Islamic government of their dreams, the Ikhwan, like so many of their predecessors from that time of the early caliphs, had been used to further the ambitions of a worldly dynast."

By the late 1930s, the revolution in Saudi Arabia was basically over. Ibn Saud took the title "king," and made no pretensions about being a religious authority. "The Saudi state could no longer be identified with a militant reform movement determined to impose its own version of Islam on the rest of the world. It had become one Islamic state among others, with defined borders and a government prepared to temper religious zeal with worldly pragmatism."

By 1955, Harry St. John Philby, the respected English Arabist and friend of ibn Saud, noted: "The dreaded words, Ikhwan and Wahhabi, have scarce been heard in the land for twenty years, and are only remembered now with something like a blush."

In late 1984, Saudi Arabia condemned all groups and individuals who used the tenets of Islam to justify violence under the guise of being holy warriors. Abdullah Naseef, secretary general of the Muslim World League in Mecca, declared, "Islam condemns violence of any nature ... It is unthinkable that any honest [Islamic] scholar would condone crimes against humanity, destruction of installations and terrorism against innocent people committed under the pretext of jihad. Jihad in Islam was instituted to further the causes of justice, dignity and Koranic law through a formal declaration of war against forces bent on undermining these values and rights." Militant fundamentalist movements, the Saudi official said, were "abusers" of the faith.

Nonetheless, throughout the post–World War II era of enormous changes in the Arab and Islamic blocs, the Saudis have remained, in principle, loyal to their religious orthodoxy, ultimately unswayed by the various socialist, nationalist, Baathist or Nasserist ideologies that have swept the Islamic world. In 1966 King Faisal said, "A constitution? What for? The Koran is the oldest and most efficient constitution in the world."

During the same era, monarchies in Iraq, Libya and Egypt were all overthrown by revolutions, leaving only two other Arab kingdoms outside the peninsula, Jordan and distant Morocco. In light of these developments, Saudi Arabia seemed on the verge of becoming an anachronism. In some ways it had no other choice. "Without the aura of legitimacy conferred by Islam, the Saudi regime would enjoy less prestige at home and abroad," wrote William Quandt, a former member of the U.S. National Security Council staff. "It is extraordinarily difficult for Saudi leaders to ignore Islamic forces in their own country and elsewhere." Or as the Saudi Foreign Minister said on the day the Sunni fanatics were finally cleared from the Grand Mosque, "Saudi Arabia is as stable as its ties to the Islamic movement."

■   ■   ■

UNLIKE MOST SPLINTER MOVEMENTS within Christianity, the historic rivalry between Iran and Saudi Arabia—as in the basic divisions of Islam—grew out of politics as much as religion. The greatest schism in Islam developed originally not over doctrine, but over leadership after the Prophet's death. Difference in dogma developed only as a consequence of political rivalry thirteen centuries ago. Islam has always been a political force. As the Ayatollah said, "All of Islam is politics." But the approaches and the goals of the two sects differed.

"Sunni Islam is the doctrine of power and achievement. Shia Islam is the doctrine of the opposition. The starting point of Shi'ism is defeat," explained Edward Mortimer in *Faith and Power.*

Saudi Arabia and Iran are now symbols of the greatest ideological rivalry in the Islamic world. Today, Iran is a theocracy, Saudi Arabia an Islamic monarchy. In Tehran, the religious guide who intervenes between man and God is the ultimate authority. In Riyadh, the clergy do not claim divine inspiration and thus are only powerful consultants and advisors on Islamic law. They are, in effect, an agency of the state, their salaries paid for and their mosques built by the government.

Thus the House of Saud has considerable leverage over the clergy, and royal pressure has often swayed decisions by the Ulama, the council of religious elders or judges, as seen in the use of force at the Grand Mosque. King Abdel Aziz convinced the clergy that radio was acceptable because it could be used to broadcast the Koran. His son King Faisal later employed the same argument with the same success to justify television, originally banned in Islam because "no images of created things were to be allowed to seduce the mind away from the contemplative absorption of the divine word."

Saudi Arabia has managed to get around several hotly debated issues, from abolition of slavery (1962) to education for women (1960) and refusal of burials for nonbelievers in Saudi soil. Aramco employs a full-time mortician to handle the bodies of foreign workers not shipped home. A concrete liner is put into the earth, and a coffin is then lowered into it—never touching Saudi soil. The Islamic prohibition on interest from banking is circumvented by substitution of "service charges."

Religious police, the *muttawwiun* from the Public Morality Committees, patrol the streets to enforce laws, such as the prohibition on alcohol. But the home is sacrosanct. One Western ambassador said he had never had as much to drink in his career as he did in the kingdom, including at the homes of royal family members. And a U.S. colonel admitted that serious alcoholism problems had developed among the American military advisors stationed there. A standard feature of many homes in the Aramco complex, an oasis resembling a California town of the mid-1950s plopped into the middle of the Saudi desert, is a small back room with drainage for a still.

This kind of convenient "bending" is partially responsible for the charges of moral corruption and political compromise in Saudi Arabia. But it was not the only factor in Iran's escalating campaign against the House of Saud. In the eyes of Tehran, the Saudis not only abandoned the initial orthodox zeal, but also turned to a power bloc of nonbelievers to prop them up—the West. "Militarily, politically, economically and culturally dominant, the West has come to pose first a challenge and finally a threat to the Islamic world," was the succinct assessment of British author Malise Ruthven.

The West was anathema basically for three reasons. First, European colonial powers were responsible for deciding on, then freezing the boundaries that broke down the Islamic empire into modern secular states, as well as installing dynasties that were often as hostile to change as they were unpopular. From the mid-eighteenth century through the early twentieth century, Western states significantly pared down Dar al Islam in size. They also threatened the traditional Sharia as the source of law and conduct by replacing it with European codes and systems. Secondly, the West was responsible for creating and then keeping alive Israel at the expense of the Palestinians, the Arab world and Islam.

Third, Western nations "took" the oil so pivotal to their economic survival but gave little, if anything, of meaning in return. "If Saudi exports were to be discontinued, the cost to the world economy would be comparable to the Great Depression of the 1930s," explained Quandt. Yet the Saudis felt repeatedly embarrassed by their American patrons, most notably during the 1982 Israeli invasion of Lebanon and the controversy over U.S. sale of early-warning AWAC aircraft.

In the fundamentalists' eyes, Saudi dependence on the West was the same cardinal sin committed by the Shah, "selling the soul," not to mention the main resources, of a Muslim nation to infidels who only exploited the relationship by turning around to help Israel systematically against the Arabs. Saudi Arabia and its five smaller allies were deemed mere stooges of America and its allies, financially and militarily.

As one noted American expert on the Gulf wrote: "The very close linkages that many of the ruling families have with the West in general and with the United States in particular increasingly work against their legitimacy at home. The breakneck pace of modernization with its heavily Western component runs against the drive to return to Islamic roots."

In fact the barren sheikhdoms had few alternatives. Unlike Iran, they had little agriculture with which to feed themselves and no significant industry beyond oil. Nor was there a sophisticated education system to bring their people into the twentieth century. They had to go somewhere for imports and expertise.

The condemnation centered largely on the extent and blatancy of Saudi dependency. Iran frequently charged that the conservative bloc in the Organization of Petroleum Exporting Companies (OPEC) bullied its partners in order to keep oil prices and production compatible with Western economies, where those nations had invested their profits.

The kind of thing that irked the Iranians was evident in a two-page Saudi government ad in various American publications in the 1980s. It boasted that Saudi purchases from the United States averaged $9 billion annually, compared with under $1 billion a dozen years earlier. That meant the Saudis spent roughly $1,300 in American markets in a single year for each Saudi man, woman and child—buying more per capita than any other nation. But the tone of the ad was even more telling: the Saudis were advertising to improve their image to the Americans. Militant Muslims felt it should have been the other way around. And militarily it was no secret that two thousand U.S. military advisors were stationed in the kingdom as chief consultants on development of Saudi Arabia's fledgling military. The United States was also the main source of arms. As in the Shah's day, this arrangement was seen by the Iranians as another means of milking and controlling Muslims and their resources.

The grateful words of Dr. Ghazi Algosaibi, Saudi Minister of Industry and Electricity, were just the kind of thing that seemed justification for Iranian vitriol and internal opposition. Of the U.S.–Saudi relationship he said, "No interdependence could be more complete. . . . The independence of the Arab countries in the face of expanding communism cannot be maintained without your [U.S.] strength and resolve."

The high visibility of Saudi–U.S. relations was softened somewhat in the aftermath of the Grand Mosque seizure, as the Saudi royal family realized that the criticism was not just from Iran. The connection was seen at home, by Sunni and Shia, as a dependence inconsistent with Islam. In 1981, outsiders noticed that "Saudi Arabia is paying a domestic price for maintaining high production to win western influence." Oil Minister Sheikh Yamani, "who in the past defended Saudi oil pricing to the west, now apparently has been given a new task: defending oil policy to informed Saudi Arabia opinion. In essence, this policy appears to envisage continued high oil production and no real price increases for the foreseeable future." In short, the Saudis would continue their old policies under new guises. But they would pay dearly for not addressing the sources of fundamentalist ire.

■   ■   ■

THE 1982 HAJJ SEASON, six months after the Tehran seminar, marked a distinct change in Iran's aggressive posture. The Ayatollah reportedly had exhorted, "Revive the great divine political tradition of the Hajj. Acquaint Muslims with what is taking place in dear Lebanon, in crusading Iran, and oppressed Afghanistan. Inform them of their great duties in confronting aggressors and international plunderers."

The Hajj trouble reflected another tactic of the crusade. As Iranian President Ali Khamenei said shortly after the seminar, "Our support for the [Gulf and other] liberation movements is first of all spiritual. . . . We aim at conveying to the people of the world our ideology, our experiences and our recognition of the affairs pertaining to the revolution." Words were far more important than weapons in spreading the message of militant Islam.

In 1982, several incidents involving thousands of Iranians in both Mecca and Medina marred the pilgrimage. Saudi security forces broke up political rallies where the fundamentalists were exhorting Muslims of other nations to join their crusade. Some of the pilgrims were found with arms. At least once, tear gas was used to stop the demonstrators. Again, many were injured.

Saudi state radio charged that Ayatollah Khomeini's personal representative had instigated the riots. He was Hojatoleslam Mohammed Hossein Musawi Khoeiny, who had earlier gained notoriety as an advisor to the students occupying the U.S. Embassy in Tehran.

According to one account, prominent Saudi officials had tried to convince the influential cleric to call off the demonstrators. He replied, "Do slogans such as 'Death to Israel' and 'Death to the U.S.' create disorder? Do such slogans bring discomfort to Muslims? . . . We do not intend to violate security, rather we intend to invite Muslims to unite against the U.S., Israel and the Soviet Union. We are surprised that you opposed this action, as we expect you to lead the way." Hojatoleslam Khoeiny was among dozens detained and then deported from the kingdom.

The use of the Hajj for politics underlined a basic difference between the Sunni and Shia sects. For the Sunni, the pilgrimage was strictly religious, the ultimate personal homage to God, the most holy time of the year or, indeed, a lifetime. It amounted to a celebration of the brotherhood of Muslims. Reverence for the occasion was absolute. With an average of two million men and women all shrouded identically in the ihram, a white seamless robe, the symbolism of the multifaceted ceremonies was sufficient to make the point that Islam stood for universal justice and equality.

To the Shia, the occasion had become, in practice, secondary to Ashura, a commemoration that has been compared to Good Friday in Christianity and Yom Kippur in Judaism. More importantly, "the Iranians saw things differently: since Islam made no distinction between religious and political activity, the Hajj was inherently political and those who had tried to make it a purely spiritual occasion had deviated from the true path laid down by the Prophet." It was not just a matter of demonstrating good faith; action was required to enact Islam's principles.

The difference was reflected in the diatribes exchanged between the Saudis' Sunni royals and Iran's Shia theocrats. Before the 1984 Hajj, Iranian President Ali Khamenei told a meeting of clergy and pilgrimage supervisors, "Today the people expect to be taught by Iranian pilgrims. Those in the world who accuse our struggling and self-sacrificing Muslims of making the Hajj the scene for taking political advantage do not permit their people to understand the Hajj properly."

At a separate but similar session, Ayatollah Hussein Ali Montazeri, the leading contender to succeed Ayatollah Khomeini, exhorted: "During the Hajj ceremonies, Iranian pilgrims ought to inform the

oppressed nations of the secret of the victory of the Islamic revolution in Iran. If, as we have seen, the Saudi officials usually make arrangements to prevent Iranian pilgrims from contacting brothers and
sisters in other countries, it is because they fear this. By exporting the
revolution, we mean putting the experiences and fruits of our revolution at the disposal of the oppressed and the deprived people of the
world. . . . The leaders of Islamic countries should know that,
whether they are in favor of it or not, nations are awakening . . . If
they wish to remain in power and to rule over their countries, they
should rely on Islam and their own people, not America and the
U.S.S.R."

In 1984, Iran sent the largest delegation of any nation, 154,000
pilgrims, to Mecca and Medina, tripling its presence in three years.
The wary Saudis had cleverly started the year before to segregate the
Iranians from others. "We put them up with the West Africans," a
Ministry of Information official explained with a grin. "They can't
talk to each other." There was only one minor incident involving the
Iranians and, by most accounts, not at their instigation. Iraqis carrying posters of their President, Saddam Hussein, marched on the Iranian tents in Medina. With the two nations into the by then
four-year-old debilitating Gulf war, it was not surprising that fighting ensued. One Iranian was killed, several were injured. Special
Saudi security forces had to step in to prevent further trouble.

But in the context of the now deep-seated animosity between Iran
and Saudi Arabia, that was enough to re-ignite tempers. Iran implied
Saudi complicity or that Saudi troops had initially turned a blind eye
to the aggressive Iraqis. On its Arabic-language service beamed
across the Gulf, Radio Tehran reacted swiftly with a warning from
Mohammed Khatami, Minister of Islamic Guidance: "We draw the
attention of the Saudi government to the fact that just as attacks, assaults and imprisonment by the Saudi government in recent years
failed to foil the Muslims' endeavors to carry out their divine mission—that is, liberating themselves of duplicitous and arrogant people—the new ploy by colonialist lackeys will not only fail to stop this
gigantic movement, but will instead increase the anger of the awakened."

The Saudis, through Prince Nayef, responded brusquely: "What
has happened was a frank and clear message to anyone who wanted

to play with or exploit this sacred religious occasion, confirming that the kingdom would allow no political celebration or the raising of any nonreligious banner during the Hajj season." Several hundred pilgrims had tried to demonstrate, but the security forces were able to block them, he added.

As a British author commented: "For the Iranian revolutionaries and other Muslim activists who sympathize with them, the annual gathering of Muslims in the cradle of Islam is a symbolic re-enactment of its beginnings that must lead on to the creation of a true Islamic order, a world free from injustice and oppression." But for the Saudis, their Islamic "credentials" now on the line, it remained the most nerve-wracking time of the year.

■   ■   ■

WHEN THE HEADS of the six states that made up the Gulf Cooperation Council met for their fifth annual summit in November 1984, they faced a glum lesson in practical options. Their armies and air forces had just completed the second joint military maneuvers at enormous expense, drilling for almost a full month at the Saudis' expansive Hafr al Baten base for a simple three-hour live-ammunition exercise at the end. Collectively, the GCC states were spending an estimated $40 billion a year on defense and related matters. But the exercises were somewhere between comic and disastrous.

To make matters worse, the six leaders could then not agree at the summit about the two most important issues of joint survival: first, an internal-security pact, stalled already for two years, that would allow them to swap information on subversion as well as pursue operatives across their joint borders; second, the formation of their own rapid deployment force, a two-brigade force to be based at military complexes in Saudi Arabia and the United Arab Emirates. Although widely heralded in advance of the summit, the final agreement bordered on nothing at all: any of the six nations facing a threat could summon the forces of another member state. No joint unit would be on constant alert and no common bases prepared in advance. "The time lag makes it useless," said a Western envoy who had hoped for more.

The internal disagreement was almost unbelievable in light of various scares each nation had faced. Shortly after the Kuwaiti bombings in late 1983, the Saudis had a narrow escape from disaster. At Ras Tanura, the biggest single oil facility in the world, someone had stolen a series of blank security passes needed to get into the drilling, refinery and export center. Suspicion centered on the Shia who dominated the local work force. Large concrete blocks went up in front of both the oil installations and the homes of the Americans working there.* Parking was banned. Saudi troops were deployed throughout the enormous compound. "Everywhere you went, people were talking about when 'it' was going to happen," said an American who had been resident at Ras Tanura for eight years. "It used to be such a sleepy little place. It's been awful."

The day after the Kuwaiti bombings, two British bankers, both blond and dressed in pinstripe suits, were hauled in at the Saudi airport near the oil fields by nervous security guards. After their passports were confiscated and their belongings searched, they were interrogated for more than an hour because one of them had a map with a cross marked near the capital's airport. The soldiers apparently thought the X marked the spot of a bombing target, when in fact it represented a chunk of land one of their clients was about to buy. The bankers subsequently learned the Saudis had received a warning that a major oil installation was going to be bombed. Many others who also did not fit the "terrorist profile" were also questioned.

"The internal social and political problems that plague the traditional patrimonial Gulf countries do not exist in a political vacuum, but rather continue to fester in an explosive regional context where the seeds of revolution blow in the winds from the Iranian north," explained James Bill, an Iranian specialist at the University of Texas. "The social and political challenges to the traditional regimes in the Gulf will surely magnify with time. The ability of the Gulf leaders to meet these challenges remains to be seen. If this ability should be lacking, then we may expect a great deal of political upheaval and revolutionary violence in the Gulf in the later 1980s."

* More American civilians lived in the Aramco complex than anywhere else outside the U.S., according to Gulf specialist John Duke Anthony.

The lesson of the contrasting events was that for the foreseeable future Saudi Arabia and its closest allies would still be dependent on the West—and therefore exposed to the suspicions and wrath of the force it most feared. And whatever happened in Saudi Arabia was likely to affect all the little sheikhdoms nestled along its borders.

7 The Scope: Egypt and North Africa

WE ARE GOING TO CHANGE THE FACE OF THE WORLD
BY ISLAM, AND RULE BY THE KORAN.
—*BANNER WAVED BY DEFENDANTS AT THE CAIRO TRIAL OF
302 MUSLIM FUNDAMENTALISTS, 1984*

THE REASONS WHICH LED MUSLIMS AT ONE TIME TO BECOME
SUNNIS AND SHI'ITES DO NOT EXIST ANY LONGER. . . . WE ARE ALL
MUSLIMS . . . THIS IS AN ISLAMIC REVOLUTION . . . WE ARE ALL
BROTHERS IN ISLAM.

—*AYATOLLAH KHOMEINI*

President Anwar Sadat always reveled in the pomp and polish of a military parade. His favorite was the annual pageantry of October 6, the anniversary of Egypt's surprise attack across the Suez Canal against Israel during the 1973 war. On October 6, 1981, Sadat hosted two thousand dignitaries—ambassadors, cabinet ministers, military leaders and others—at the martial spectacle of the eighth celebrations, held across from Egypt's pyramid-shaped Tomb of the Unknown Soldier on the outskirts of dusty Cairo, and broadcast live throughout the nation.

173

Sitting on a wooden café chair in the front row of the massive con-
crete-and-brick reviewing stand, Sadat took in the display of his
army, the largest and one of the best equipped in North Africa and
the Arab world. In a change from recent fits of temper in public over
a spate of new troubles in Egypt, he seemed relaxed, alternately
puffing on his pipe, chatting with his Vice-President and Defense
Minister, and mopping his sweating brow in the humid noon heat.
The two-hour display of his odd combination of American and East
bloc weapons was going well: Squadrons of fighter planes performed
finely timed aerobatics, then streaked low and noisily over the
parade ground, leaving trails of red, blue, white and yellow smoke.
Hundreds of miniature Egyptian flags and portraits of the Egyptian
leader, attached to tiny parachutes, were shot high into the air from
cannons and cascaded down in waves. Dressed in his gold-braided
blue field marshal's uniform and bedecked with the medals of his
long military career, Sadat also stood to salute the regally turbaned
members of the Hagganah Camel Corps, a holdover from the past
which still patrolled the desert border.

Most spectators were still riveted by the daring flight formations of
French-made warplanes overhead when Sadat next stood up. He was
apparently preparing to salute a young lieutenant who approached
from the ground show, a slow-moving procession of seventy-two
shiny Soviet trucks, each towing large pieces of North Korean artillery. Then a loud explosion near the stand drowned out even the
roaring aircraft. "At first, I thought it was more fireworks for the
parade," said David Ottaway of *The Washington Post,* who watched
dumbfounded as men at the rear of one truck started firing their automatic rifles in staccato bursts—*at* the reviewing stand. Foreign and
Egyptian guests began screaming in several languages and scrambling in a panic for exits.

The attack was so stunning—after three days of meticulous security to ensure that no live ammunition was allowed on the parade
grounds—that surprised bodyguards and troops did not open fire at
the four approaching assailants for at least a full minute. The implications dawned slowly too as, Ottaway recalled, "the mad, ghastly
recognition that I was watching the assassination of the most important American ally in the Arab world took shape in my mind."

Struck by at least five bullets and pieces of shrapnel in his chest,

thigh, forearm and neck, Sadat had no pulse by the time aides transferred his blood-soaked body by helicopter to Maadi Military Hospital. Doctors worked desperately for more than an hour before one
went to the first floor and made the announcement with a simple line
from the Koran: "Only God can live forever."

■   ■   ■

"I AM DEALING WITH FANATICISM," President Sadat had said less than
a month before his murder. But even he did not realize to just what
degree. Egypt, often referred to as the "soul" of the Arab world because of its long tradition of leadership and scholarship, had a long
history of sporadic fundamentalist fervor. Yet in 1981, a visible esca-
lation in religious zealotry was deemed so threatening that Sadat had
ordered a purge. In the weeks before his death, a security sweep net-
ted almost 1,600 religious militants—Sunni Muslims and minority
Coptic Christians—teachers and students, journalists, lawyers, doctors, engineers, merchants and others. The charges ranged from fo-
menting sectarian sedition to violating the so-called "Law of
Shame," which outlawed rumors damaging to the state.

The main targets, however, were the Muslim extremists, as reflected in the outlawing of fifteen Islamic societies, nationalization of
forty thousand "independent" mosques not under government juris-
diction, and the banning of radical Muslim publications. Whereas
Pope Shenouda III, head of the Coptic Church, was exiled to a desert
monastery, Omar Telmissani, chief of the Muslim Brotherhood, was
locked away in one of Cairo's prisons. The Egyptian leader justified
the dramatic and traumatic moves in a rambling three-hour speech,
charging, "This is not religion. This is obscenity. These are lies, the
criminal use of religious power to misguide people." He declared
angrily that a sophisticated conspiracy was attempting to destroy his
authority.

In a session with foreign correspondents, Sadat revealed a stronger
motive for the politically risky crackdown: "Don't fear that we will
have a Khomeini here." But his declaration only served to underline
the strong religious current resurging in Egypt. The familiar fundamentalist trademarks were surfacing in both urban and rural centers—a variety of drab scarves or veils for women, robes replacing
Western dress for men. On campuses, the breeding ground for funda-

mentalist passions, Islamic societies known as Al Jamaa al Islamiya were gradually becoming the dominant social and political forces. Mosques were overflowing again on Fridays.

The trend had swept far beyond the so-called "Arab heartland" of Southwest Asia into the Sunni strongholds of North Africa. "Although the revolutionary rhetoric of Iran's Shi'ite Muslims doesn't carry much weight in Sunni Muslim countries like Egypt, the Iranian example clearly has raised the hopes of Islamic fundamentalists throughout the Middle East," David Ignatius wrote in *The Wall Street Journal* three days after the assassination. Another U.S. analyst remarked, "After the Iranian revolution in 1979, most militant Islamic groups were no longer content to serve as a diversionary opposition." Without lifting a finger, Iran had an impact, serving as a model for the already simmering fundamentalist movement in Egypt. The potential was evident two years before Sadat's death: seven of the sixty-three executed for seizing the Grand Mosque in Saudi Arabia in 1979 had been Egyptians.

Sadat's state of mind in the months before his death was reflected when he complained bitterly about *The Guardian's* David Hirst, a British journalist who had been expelled from Egypt in 1977 after predicting Sadat's downfall. In 1981, the widely respected journalist had gone even further by comparing Sadat to the Shah of Iran. The Egyptian leader complained to foreign correspondents, "They are saying, Don't deal with Sadat, he is Shah Number Two."

Indeed, some similarities made comparisons tempting, uncomfortably emphasized by the presence in Egypt in 1981 of the Shah's widow and heir, ensconced under heavy Egyptian guard at a palace on the outskirts of Cairo. The Shah had passed the last days of his wandering exile in Cairo, unwelcome almost everywhere else, finally dying on July 27, 1980, of cancer—at the same hospital where Sadat was taken fourteen months later.

Sadat's unwavering loyalty to the Shah—which included walking the full length of his funeral procession—provided a symbolic rallying point for the fundamentalists' campaign. "He is my friend. Of course I will give him sanctuary," the Egyptian leader told British Foreign Secretary Lord Carrington. But more basic was the fanatics' resentment of other parallels, such as the growing bond with the United States—the inflow of American arms and advisers, joint military exercises, and joint political strategies which had more of an American than an Egyptian flavor—and with Sadat's anxiously advertised eagerness to bring Western business into Egypt, sometimes at the expense of local entrepreneurs. Sadat had made the latest of his many trips to Washington just two months earlier.

In the eyes of militants, the defiantly proud Egyptians, who once ruled the Mediterranean, were becoming another satellite of the United States. Indeed, several Middle East papers and politicians later commented that the real assassin of Sadat had been the U.S., which had forced him to compromise Egypt, the soul of the Islamic world.

Widening economic inequalities, comparable to the gap between the opulently wealthy elite and the staggering poverty of the majority in Iran, were also turning even Sadat's supporters into questioners. Cairenes were often bitterly atwitter with the latest gossip about the jewels of Sadat's wife, his brother's thriving businesses and Sadat's own resplendent palaces, when thousands of destitute were forced to turn Cairo's cemetery into a squatters' village. The mass crackdown in September 1981 also seemed all too similar to—if not on the same scale as—the Shah's use of SAVAK and army force against his religious and leftist opponents. Iran's crackdown had provided a common cause for a highly effective alliance between unlikely factions, who eventually forced him into exile. The same strategy in Egypt carried similar potential consequences. And, finally, growing restrictions on opposition groups left the mosques as one of the last forums for mobilizing dissent.

There were at least two crucial differences, however, between Egypt and Iran. The North African state is predominantly Sunni, without the highly organized and independent clerical organization of the Shia to whip up mass demonstrations. Egypt has some leverage to rein in the religious establishments. Nor is there a "bazaar class" in Cairo to mobilize economic discontent.

Yet within hours after Sadat's death, officials in Cairo and Washington confirmed that Islamic fundamentalists, at least some of them from within the Egyptian Army, were responsible. Authorities in both capitals attempted to minimize the fundamentalists' strength, pointing out that only a small band had been involved. But two days later Asyut, a city 250 miles south of Cairo in Upper Egypt with a long history of religious militancy, erupted. At least fifty men attacked a police station in the first stage of an uprising that led to major clashes between fundamentalists and security forces. When the conflict grew more violent the next day, security reinforcements were sent into the troubled area. The final death toll was eighty-seven, including sixty-six police.

The fundamentalists were not just an odd group of ragtag militants. In less than a week, they had twice displayed cunning, strength, organization—and secrecy so efficient that not a single intelligence agency inside or outside Egypt had realized their full potential.

■   ■   ■

AFTER THE GUN and grenade smoke had cleared, Sadat was buried next to the Tomb of the Unknown Soldier—with more homage paid by Western leaders, including three former U.S. Presidents, than by the usually effusive Egyptians. Vice-President Hosni Mubarak was quickly installed as his replacement. In the Middle East, many Muslims, both moderate and militant, did not mourn Sadat's passing, since popular feeling backed a fresh start for Egypt. But sorting out the organization behind the assassins, many of whom had been arrested shortly after the murder, was more difficult than rearranging the nation's leadership. Early reports about just which fundamentalist group the assassins belonged to were conflicting and confusing, for a host of movements operated both openly and clandestinely in Egypt.

Modern fundamentalism in Egypt can be traced as far back as 1928, when the fiery Hassan al Banna formed the original Muslim Brotherhood, which later spawned branches of varying form and strength throughout the Middle East. A schoolteacher by training, Banna was deeply concerned with the religious and moral laxity in Egyptian society. In mosques, schools and private homes, he preached a return to Islam in both government and society by whatever means available, including militancy. "My brothers," he said in 1943, "you are a new soul in the heart of this nation to give it life by means of the Koran."

It was "the first mass-supported and organized, essentially urban-oriented effort to cope with the plight of Islam in the modern world," according to scholar Richard Mitchell. Indeed, it varied from all other established Egyptian organizations of the time, for the Brotherhood sought to change a nation's politics as well as each individual's life. Like the tenets of Islam, the movement covered everything.

From 1928 through 1981, the Muslim Brotherhood went through alternating waves of acceptance and persecution under different Egyptian governments as it grew ever more powerful. By 1949, it had an estimated 2,000 branches and 500,000 members or sympathizers, a size sufficiently worrying that Banna was assassinated that year, purportedly by King Farouk's secret security guards.

The movement evolved increasingly into militancy. The early "athletic" training became arms and military drilling for various jihads, notably against British colonialists and alongside Palestinians against the new Israelis in 1948. A network grew as members were divided into small "families," a euphemism for cells. Twice, in 1954 and 1965, former President Gamal Abdel Nasser ordered mass arrests after assassination attempts were tied to Brotherhood members disillusioned with his secular nationalism.*

A former Egyptian Interior Minister, Ahmed Mortada al Maraghi, wrote about how the young militants were recruited:

> A small room lit with candle light and smoky with incense is chosen. . . . Once the likely young man is selected, he is brought to this room ... where he will find a sheikh repeating verses from the Koran. . . . The Sheikh with eyes like magnets stares at the young man who is paralyzed with awe ... They will then pray, and the sheikh will recite verses from the Koran about those fighting for the sake of Allah and are therefore promised to go to heaven. "Are you ready for martyrdom?" the young man is asked. "Yes, yes," he repeats. He is then given the oath on the Koran. These young men leave the meeting with one determination: to kill.

Taking over after Nasser's unexpected death in 1970, Sadat at first got on well with the Brotherhood. He released many of those who had been incarcerated, and encouraged the renewal of Muslim practices through Islamic Societies to counter leftist and Marxist trends.

---

* Ironically, before coming to power, Nasser was an admirer of the Brotherhood, to which his Free Officers' Movement gave backup roles in the 1952 coup against King Farouk.

Early in his political career he had declared, "In the face of a world in conflict, our answer must be to return to our Islamic revolution proclaimed by the Prophet in 622, to inspire us by its scientific, moral and spiritual import." Sadat began incurring their opposition, however, after opening up to the West and expelling Soviet advisors in 1972. The inflow of the West and its money exacerbated the economic gap, which in turn played into the hands of the Brotherhood.

Sadat's historic trip to Jerusalem to promote Arab–Israeli peace in 1977, followed by the U.S.-orchestrated Camp David Treaty in 1979, was the ultimate sacrilege in the eyes of the militant fundamentalists. The young proselytizers did not consider the retrieval of the Sinai Peninsula, lost to Israel in the 1967 War, sufficient reward for recognition of the Jewish state, among other complaints.

More importantly, Sadat, who frequently declared and demonstrated his Muslim faith, had committed one of the ultimate violations of Islam. He had gone against the *ijima*, the unity of Muslims. In fanatics' eyes, this made him a Kharijite, a seceder from the ranks of the faithful. His peace with Israel may have won him respect and credibility in the eyes of the West, but he had betrayed the umma, the greater Muslim community.

"Throughout the 1970s and early 1980s, the Muslim Brotherhood remained the principal vehicle for Sunni political activism," wrote Malise Ruthven in *Islam in the World*. Yet in many ways the Brotherhood had become a conservative body. While its platform called for constitutional changes that would erase alien European codes in favor of Islamic laws, it never advocated a pure Islamic republic.

As a result, in the fertile atmosphere of the 1970s, other groups sprouted. Members of Al Taqfir Wal Higrah, or "Repentance and Flight from Sin," made their mark in 1977 by going on a rampage against nightclubs during Cairo's food riots. A few months later, the group abducted Sheikh Mohammed al Dhahabi, a moderate and the Minister of Religious Endowment, then murdered him in a grisly ritual—first strangulation, then a bullet fired into his left eye. The leader of the group, Shukry Mustafa, was among at least four hundred who were subsequently detained. Mustafa, who was executed for his role in the murder, was known as the "prince of princes," for the movement was broken into cells each headed by a "prince." The princes preached, in effect, a permanent jihad. The blood of heretics must be spilled if they did not repent and return to Islam. One State Department official described the group as "a Moral Majority with AK-47s." Despite the government crackdown, membership in a reorganized Al Taqfir Wal Higrah was estimated within a year to be as high as four thousand. At first, this movement was the prime suspect for Sadat's death.

The Islamic Liberation Organization made headlines in 1974 by attacking the Military Technical Academy near Cairo, killing at least a dozen, in the first stage of an attempted coup. Two leaders were later executed and thirty others imprisoned. At first, the various Islamic Societies were considered social rather than political groups, operating fairly openly on campuses, mainly Cairo University, Alexandria University and the University of Asyut. Members had clashed with Christian Copts, whom they suspected of arming in preparation for a new crusade against Muslims. The young fundamentalists had also staged a strike and sit-in at Asyut University on the day Sadat signed the peace treaty with Israel.

Among a host of smaller, seemingly harmless groups was Al Jihad, or Holy War. Before Sadat's death, it had been heard from only once, in 1980, when it claimed responsibility for planting small bombs at Coptic churches in Cairo. But among Al Jihad's members was First Lieutenant Khaled Islambouli, the brazen young officer who dared, in front of the two thousand eyewitnesses at the parade, to approach Sadat with a grenade in his hand. If two of the three grenades thrown at the reviewing stand had not been duds—one landing at the feet of Egypt's Defense Minister and the other bouncing off the face of the Army Chief of Staff—Islambouli's little hand-picked band might have wiped out most of Egypt's top tier of government. Islambouli, from this little-known movement, was the ringleader of the assassination.

The quick capture of the attackers offered no reassurance. Instead, two worrisome questions arose: First, how had such committed fanatics managed to escape official attention, especially since Islambouli's brother, allegedly a member of Al Taqfir Wal Higrah, had been among those rounded up in the September dragnet? A subsequent disclosure from Defense Minister Abdel Halim Abu Ghazala made this question more pressing still: Islambouli had been under observation because of suspected militant tendencies—then cleared.

Indeed, military intelligence had said he "was known for his loyalty and discipline." The case was eerily similar to the story of Juhaiman in Saudi Arabia.

Second, to what degree had the military, on whose power and loyalty Sadat and so many other Middle East leaders ultimately relied, been penetrated by extremists? A military observer in contact with Egypt's high command told *The Washington Post*, "The reason Sadat's assassination came as such a surprise to us was, up to this time, we had been told that his crackdown had found very few suspects in the Army. We were told that they had cleaned out the dangerous Islamic factions from the military." As he conceded, "Apparently, the measures were not enough." Even more unsettling was the unofficial report that two hundred other military personnel were quickly and quietly purged after Sadat's death because of their religious views—at first glance an insignificant number out of 367,000 members in the Egyptian armed forces. But in light of the few it took to kill Sadat, the continuing potential was enough to shake the confidence of even the most entrenched and well-guarded leaders in the Middle East.

■   ■   ■

WITHIN TWO MONTHS, Islambouli, his three accomplices and twenty others were put on trial for the assassination. A well-built man with a ruddy complexion, Islambouli defiantly bragged of his guilt when called upon to enter a plea. "I am guilty of killing Sadat and I admit that. I am proud of it because the cause of religion was at stake." His lawyer, however, hastily intervened to plead his client's innocence, arguing that the outburst did not constitute a confession. The chief assassin also shouted to his mother and his heavily veiled wife during a recess, "Do not be sad, because I will be joining my God. We are free and you are the prisoners . . . I am at the peak of joy." Although all but the opening and closing sessions were held in secret, news leaked daily into the Arabic press. The plotters reportedly admitted freely that their ultimate objective had been a "popular Islamic revolution" and the creation of an Islamic state.

A fifty-four-page booklet entitled "The Missing Pillar," reportedly introduced as evidence, reflected the depth of Al Jihad's belief in "sacred terror": "If we cannot form an Islamic nation except by fighting, we have to fight . . . The first battlefield in our jihad is to uproot the infidel leadership. . . . The tyrants of this earth will only vanish by the power of the sword . . . The way to get rid of a ruler imposed on one is by revolt."

Jihad was to become the sixth pillar of Islam, after the established five: spoken testimony that "there is no god but God, and Mohammed is His Prophet"; praying; fasting; alms-giving; and the Mecca pilgrimage. "Today's leaders have become apostates of Islam, bred in the ways of imperialism, whether it be crusader or communist or Zionist," the booklet charged, adding that dialogue and other legal channels were insufficient means of changing the system. "The peak of worship is jihad. . . . We are asked to do God's bidding and not worry about the results."

At least one of the two key questions was answered in court. The group apparently had no intention of attempting a military coup, since they felt that the armed forces were not yet "prepared." One of the accused reportedly said that most of the ringleaders were convinced they would need at least another two years before conditions were right for a full-scale revolution. Their decision to kill Sadat was based in part on their access to the parade site, and on hopes that the regime and the government machinery might collapse. The assassination was to be followed by calls for an uprising from loudspeakers in mosques and street corners in Cairo and Upper Egypt cities, mainly Asyut and Al Menia.

Perhaps the most intriguing evidence concerned the assassins' obsession with obeying Islamic dictates, to the point of seeking religious "clearance" at every stage of their planning. When the plotters sought funds to finance arms purchases, they went to Dr. Omar Abdel Rahman, a blind theologian at the University of Asyut, for advice. They proposed robbing a Christian jeweler in a Cairo suburb. Dr. Abdel Rahman allegedly ruled in a *fatwa*, or religious edict, that taking gold from a Christian shop was not considered theft—that a Christian who used wealth or arms against Muslims would have his blood and property forfeit. The loot could be considered "spoils of war." During later consultations, Dr. Abdel Rahman ruled that it would be a sacrilege if Egyptian soldiers were murdered as part of plans to ensure access to the parade. He suggested instead the use of drugs to put soldiers to sleep. Drugs were actually sought, and a pharmacist was later arrested by police.

At the sentencing of the twenty-four conspirators on March 6, 1982, none showed remorse, instead disrupting the High Military Court convened in a converted barracks on the edge of the capital. Pandemonium broke out as the defendants, more in control of events than were their guards, shouted political and Islamic slogans, waved banners made from sheets, and climbed up the iron bars of their specially constructed cage. The signs labeled Sadat a "pharaoh," a "dictator" and, predictably, a "shah." Others warned, "The Muslims are coming," and "Islamic Jerusalem shall return," emphasized by a picture of an Israeli Star of David dripping with blood. One defendant spotted Anis Mansour, editor of Cairo's *Mayo* magazine and a close confidant of Sadat, and shouted through the bars, "You shall have the same fate as Sadat however long it might take." Another screamed at diplomats and journalists, "Sadat was the biggest Zionist agent" and "[Israeli Prime Minister Menachem] Begin shall die at the hands of the Muslims."

When the court session finally got under way, the judge sentenced five, including Islambouli, to death. Five others were given life at hard labor, while twelve received terms ranging from five to fifteen years. Two were acquitted. A high government official had originally called for public executions in front of the Egyptian Army, since four of the assassins had been or were officers. But by the time of the judgment that seemed unwise, for the case had become a rallying point for fundamentalists and others. Islambouli and his cohorts had become popular heroes in some quarters. A "Save Islambouli" campaign was launched in Egypt and other Middle East capitals to save the men from being "martyred." Sympathizers said that the twenty-four had not murdered Sadat, but had justifiably executed him for treason. One of the two acquitted was Dr. Abdel Rahman.

■   ■   ■

THE UNITED STATES, which by 1981 had its largest embassy in the world in Cairo, was left stunned by the turn of events. Just ten days before the assassination, the U.S. ambassador had told an American reporter that Sadat had a firm grip on the situation, and that fundamentalism was not a threat to his regime. The reporter concluded that "the U.S. had no handle on the domestic situation and did not understand the breadth or depth of the fundamentalist movement." When the news of Sadat's death was finally confirmed, President Reagan, who just six days earlier had declared that the U.S. would not allow Saudi Arabia to become "an Iran," found himself instead mourning the death of a different "close friend" at the hands of Muslim extremists.

At the time of the assassination, Egypt was the U.S.'s main ally and investment in the Arab world, evident in aid of almost $2 billion annually. The level of trust was reflected in the joint U.S.–Egyptian military maneuvers, and the fact that U.S. military planes had refueled in Egypt en route to the aborted rescue mission of the U.S. hostages in Iran eighteen months earlier.

Egypt's new President, Hosni Mubarak, quickly reaffirmed Cairo's commitment to all treaties with the United States, Israel and other allies. But equally important to Mubarak's intentions were the intentions and strength of the opposition, for the United States once again had failed to foresee what was bubbling below the surface in a pivotal land. And initial indications were ominous.

The depth of the fundamentalist appeal was evident in a new wave of mass arrests after the Sadat murder. By December 1981, as the assassins' trial was under way, Egyptian Interior Minister Mohammed Nabawi Ismail announced to the People's Assembly that 2,500 had been detained in a crackdown on extremists—on top of the majority of the 1,600 who were still in jail from Sadat's last security swoop. Ismail noted that the arrests were not excessive "compared to the plan they had in mind, which aimed at turning Egypt into another Lebanon or Iran."

Many of the 2,500 were subsequently, if slowly, released. But in December 1982, a full year after the crackdown, one group of 302 was finally taken to court on charges of plotting to overthrow the Egyptian government and participating in the Asyut uprising. It was the largest mass trial in Egyptian history, conducted in a huge Cairo exhibition hall where, this time, twelve massive steel cages had to be built to contain all the defendants. Outside, sandbags and freshly dug foxholes provided protection for troops armed with machine guns and automatic rifles.

Once again, the bearded and robed prisoners managed to overwhelm the court from behind their barred cages. Several waved the Koran or pulled up shirts to show scars they claimed were the work of prison interrogators. Others chanted, "Muslim blood is not for sacrifice on the altar of Jews and Americans." As had been true in the Kuwaiti trial, there seemed no question of their guilt in trying to create an Islamic republic in Egypt. "It's no charge," one prisoner proudly yelled. "It is an honor."

The bill of indictment against the "Jihad 302," as they became known during the trial, indicated that the movement was highly organized and, more importantly, that they had learned from the mistakes and misfortunes of earlier Muslim underground movements in Egypt. Al Jihad's planning was intensive and comprehensive, including rigorous arms and explosives training, studies of the behavior and routines of key government figures, and research of the layout of strategic installations. Other evidence indicated support and funding from sympathizers outside Egypt.

The scope of Al Jihad's membership was alarming. More than half were students or teachers from vocational centers and at least eight universities. But infiltration had been successful in more crucial quarters, for other defendants were members of the Air Force, military intelligence, Army central headquarters, the Central Security Services and, in one case, the Presidential Guard. In addition, the defendants included employees at strategic jobs in the broadcasting building, the telephone exchange and municipal services. All the evidence indicated that Al Jihad was the most thorough and extreme of the many fundamentalist groups to grow up in Egypt during the twentieth century. Indeed, at the trial, one of the ringleaders condemned all the other movements for only preaching the call to Islam, rather than undertaking an armed struggle to establish an Islamic state.

After 142 court sessions and forty thousand pages of evidence over twenty-two months, the verdicts at the subversion trial finally came in on September 30, 1984—just one week short of three years since Sadat's death. Anticipating trouble, police were put on alert and hundreds of special security forces surrounded the makeshift courtroom; relatives and supporters also waited outside for the verdicts. The day before, the Egyptian parliament had extended the state of emergency originally imposed after Sadat's assassination, for another nineteen months, allowing police searches without warrants and detention without trial, as well as outlawing demonstrations and strikes.

The prisoners ended the trial as it had begun, shouting slogans such as "Egyptians wake up!" and "No to America. No to Israel." Banners declared, "God is our only judge," and "Holy war against lackeys, Jews, Christians and atheists." The T-shirt of one defendant labeled him an "Islamic martyr." But his assumption was premature, for the sentences were considerably milder than expected, especially since the prosecution had demanded the death sentence for all but three of the 302. No one was sentenced to die on the gallows, and 174 were totally acquitted.*

Most notable among those freed was, again, Dr. Abdel Rahman, Al Jihad's blind spiritual advisor, who had delivered an impromptu sermon on "martyrdom for Islam" before the verdicts were read. Of the 107 sentenced to prison, only sixteen received life terms, which means about twenty-five years in Egypt. (Of the remaining twenty-one, nineteen had never been apprehended and the other two had died during incarceration.) The stiffest sentence went to Aboub al Zomor, a former military intelligence officer who the prosecutor said had masterminded the Asyut riot. From his cage, Zomor cried, "We refused to be tried except under the Sharia. . . . We tell the Egyptian leaders to let the past be a lesson. Learn from Sadat's destiny."

The crackdown did not seem to be working. After the Sadat assassination, beards and conservative Muslim dress had almost disappeared, as young people especially were aware of the plainclothed security police who had been added to college campuses to prevent disorder and sniff out extremists. But in 1984 the physical symbols of fundamentalism were reappearing. Students again campaigned for student unions on fundamentalist platforms, and won in growing numbers. The Islamic incantation, "There is no god but God, and Mohammed is His Prophet," became a common sight on the rear windows of cars.

The trouble started when a police car struck and killed a student at Al Azhar University, the most famous and prestigious theological

---

* The chief judge later explained to an Egyptian paper that the lenient sentences were due to his conviction that the defendants had indeed been tortured in order to force confessions.

institution in the Islamic world, which first opened more than a thousand years ago. Rioting broke out as protesting students confronted thousands of baton-wielding police. The initial flashpoint rapidly grew to include issues at the heart of the fundamentalist crusade: Islamic dress and moral codes of conduct, and implementation of the Sharia as basic law of the land. At least two hundred students took to the streets shouting Islamic slogans and carrying homemade banners with their demands. The skirmishes dragged on for four days.

Officials tried both carrot and stick approaches to end the violence. The government pledged that the police driver would be put on trial. And police sealed off the university's two campuses, where 120,000 students were enrolled, then used generous doses of tear gas to stop the demonstrators. Both tactics were insufficient to end the trouble. Finally, after dozens of injuries, the government was forced to close down the university temporarily.

On January 18, 1985, some 1,500 fundamentalists assembled in one of their old gathering places, the half-completed Mesgid Ennur Mosque in Cairo. The speaker charged the government with persecution of the most devout Muslims; that fundamentalists who had been charged with extremism and subversion, then found innocent, were suppressed by the government, their groups and meetings banned. Yet the Coptic Pope, freed from desert exile before the 1984 Christmas, was quickly allowed to preach again. Indeed, he had been publicly embraced by Sadat's successor, President Hosni Mubarak, a Muslim!

The speaker drawing such a crowd was Dr. Abdel Rahman. And the mosque meeting was not an isolated event, for it ooincided with U.S. Embassy reports—never mentioned by the government—of Egyptian security convoys hauling in newly arrested Muslim militants, whom diplomats heard shouting through the bars the familiar *"Allahu Akbar!"*

By April 1985, the Egyptian national assembly was also facing mounting pressure to accept the Islamic strictures of the Sharia as the sole law of the land. The rector of Al Azhar reportedly stressed the need for immediate application, since the Sharia was the only means "to check the cultural invasion of Egypt." And a poll carried out by the National Center for Social and Criminal Research revealed that 96 percent of Muslim Egyptians favored application of the Sharia. The National Assembly later voted against the resolution, but in a concession to the militants, it agreed to review the nation's legal code "gradually and scientifically" to revise provisions that contradicted the Islamic code. It also voted for a proposal to expand and improve religious education.

Meanwhile, government officials, again apparently bending to the pressures, said television ads "which deviate from the religious values or contradict the Sharia" would be banned, and more emphasis would be placed on religious programming. Among the first to be removed were ads for birth control devices. The government also charged three booksellers with violations of pornography laws by printing, importing and distributing the unexpurgated version of *Thousand and One Nights*, a Middle East classic and, according to some accounts, the best-read book in the region after the Koran. An Egyptian intellectual commented: "My fear is that if we continue to confiscate obscene words from our literature, it will not stop there. It will move to poetry, swimming suits, alcohol, and step by step it will lead us to become another fundamentalist state."

Since the end of the Egyptian monarchy in 1952, fundamentalists had been the main threat to the established order, disrupting campuses and entire cities, attempting to assassinate Nasser and succeeding with Sadat. The series of events in the early 1980s led the prestigious *Middle East Reporter* to conclude: "However much any regime in Egypt may try, Islamic passion will continue to guide political life in that predominantly Sunni Muslim country." The question neither the Egyptian leadership nor its worried allies could answer was: To just what degree?

TUNISIA AND MOROCCO

Crackling flames leapt from the small single-story shops in the Tunisian village of Nefzaoua on Friday, December 30, 1983. Fumes almost overtook the throngs who had stood back to watch. Then what had begun as a protest march turned into a full-scale riot. Women and children joined the men in the melee along the narrow streets and alleys. Outnumbered and inexperienced police in Tunisia's semidesert Saharan south scrambled to contain the sudden violence, but eventually had to call for Army reinforcements. The military presence only escalated the tension, symbols of the state offering new targets for crowds that pelted troops with rocks and bricks, the only available weapons.

The "revolution of the loaf" was what Tunisians called their explosive reaction to a government announcement abruptly ending subsidies of bread and cereals. The ailing economy of the tiny North African state could no longer afford the annual $246 million— roughly $37 per head—to help feed the nation's 6.6 million people. That translated into a 110 percent increase in the price of the staple food of Tunisia's hundreds of thousands classified as living in absolute poverty.

The "revolution" quickly spread over the following days from village to town. Demonstrations and fiery attacks moved north until the capital itself finally erupted on January 3, 1984. In Tunis, large gangs chanting antigovernment slogans ruled the streets, setting cars alight, stoning government buildings and looting shops. Again, the Army was called in, and soon the rumbling of military vehicles and the spat of automatic weapons echoed along the capital's palm-fringed boulevards as troops attempted to quell the rioters. Finally, on what became known as "Black Tuesday," the government declared a state of emergency, including a dusk-to-dawn curfew and a ban on gatherings of more than three people. Tanks and armored personnel carriers closed off strategic government installations. Commercial centers shut down in fear. Schools were ordered to close.

In the end, eighty-nine people were killed and 938 injured by official reckoning during the bloody five-day episode, although diplomatic counts claimed that the death toll exceeded 150. At least one thousand were arrested on charges ranging from murder and arson to stealing shoes from a looted shop. Since the winning of independence in 1956, Tunisia had never witnessed such violence. And it ended only after President-for-life Habib Bourguiba, nicknamed the Great Mujahed, "Great Warrior," for his role in the struggle for independence from France, in effect admitted government defeat at the hands of the protestors in a nationwide broadcast: he canceled all price increases.

The ordeal in Tunisia might have been recorded as simply a troubling but isolated domestic incident, but a mere two weeks later, on January 19, violence erupted in nearby Morocco. This time, schoolchildren and university students in the ancient and cosmopolitan city of Marrakesh stormed into the streets to protest rumored increases in education fees. The rumors and the rioting then spread rapidly to the north, a repeat of the Tunisian chaos. Thousands of unemployed workers and students who had graduated but could not find jobs reinforced the youths and the housewives to demonstrate their wrath over threatened additional hikes in food and fuel costs.

The crisis broke out just as Morocco's King Hassan II was playing host to the heads of state of the forty-five-nation Islamic Conference Organization, an important public relations boost to his ailing nation. Aware of the impact of press reports during Tunisia's ordeal, the monarch immediately ordered a news blackout and dispatched troops to set up cordons around all towns that succumbed to "the Troubles," as Moroccans euphemistically later referred to the violence. The wily monarch, who was earlier thought by Arab and Western allies to be in firm control of his tradition-bound nation after twenty-three years on the throne, then ordered the Army to "use all force necessary." The command was heeded to the letter as soldiers, inexperienced in crowd control, repeatedly fired into rampaging mobs in several cities.

Few details ever emerged about exactly what happened behind the army cordons during those three days, except the government-released figures of twenty-nine dead. But the casualty estimates from diplomats reflected the level of violence: up to 150 killed, more than 1,000 injured, and so many detained at overflowing town jails that hundreds reportedly had to be transferred to military bases.

The back-to-back incidents in Tunisia and Morocco were stunning, at least temporarily shattering the countries' images as two of the few stable nations in both the African and Arab worlds.

■   ■   ■

AFTER MOROCCO HAD CALMED DOWN, a grim-faced King Hassan went on television to address his subjects. The monarch, known as something of a fast-paced playboy in his youth, held up a large glossy pamphlet with a color photograph of Ayatollah Khomeini on the cover. This, he angrily told the nation, was one of the main factors behind the riots. The leaflet castigated King Hassan as a *tahouti*, or "corrupt agent of Satan," a favorite Iranian epithet, and condemned the Islamic Conference—which Iran had boycotted. Islamic fundamentalists and agents of the Iranian leader, King Hassan charged, had distributed the inflammatory literature all over the country in order to spark unrest and break up the Islamic summit. Outside intervention by "Khomeinists" in league with Communists and Israeli agents, and not internal discontent, had triggered the wave of unrest, he stated flatly.

In Tunisia, authorities also claimed that young Islamic fundamentalists were guilty, mainly of turning the initial protests into large-scale riots. Officials in the Prime Minister's office hinted that Iran, directly or indirectly, had played a role. In a nationwide television address, the Premier blamed the bread riots on elements "attempting to overthrow the regime ... Let these individuals or small groups who think it will be easy to topple the regime know that all their efforts are doomed to fail." Tunisia's ambassador to Paris told French television that the price hike had "very little to do with" the violence.

Both governments preferred to implicate foreign meddlers rather than face the facts: demands for change were growing, and the medium of expressing discontent was increasingly Islam. Fundamentalism had become a major new factor in Tunisia and a growing trend in Morocco in the early 1980s. By 1984, the trend was gaining control over a small but active part of the populations in both nations. The nearly simultaneous riots served to prove how conditions in impoverished nations helped to promote militancy.

No one ever suggested conspiracy theories linking the almost identical waves of violence in the two Maghreb (Arabic for Western) states. But strong evidence suggested that common circumstances, and the common force of Islamic militancy, were at play. The riots demonstrated the breadth of the fundamentalist appeal, and how even relatively balanced, tolerant nations were far more susceptible than anyone had realized. As the crusade spread into the farthest corners of the Muslim world, the ordeals also demonstrated that terror was in fact but a small element in the broader campaign.

Richard B. Parker, a former U.S. ambassador to Morocco, Algeria and Lebanon, explained: "In both cases the upheavals can be linked

to deeper dissatisfaction among young people drawn to Islamic fundamentalism . . . Because their ideology is the official religion of the
state and has very deep roots in the society, it is impossible to suppress them effectively. They can perhaps be coopted, or assuaged
and corrupted, but not rooted out."

■   ■   ■

WITH ITS HIGH-RISE BUILDINGS and bright neon signs, Tunis resembles
neither an African nor an Arab city. The Mediterranean architecture
and the European lifestyle, even the weather, are more reminiscent
of France, its former ruler. Squeezed between militant Libya and socialist Algeria, little Tunisia has been an island of pro-Western moderation. It has a sunny atmosphere that attracts thousands of
Scandinavian, German and British tourists for inexpensive beach-
front holidays. No banners of revolutionary rhetoric greet visitors
at its tiny international airport, where stalls peddle quaint white
bulbous-domed bird cages instead of the militant literature found in
Algiers and Tripoli. In Tunisian cities, French is more common than
Arabic. A predominantly Sunni Muslim nation with a Christian minority and no significant Shia population, Tunisia seemed an unlikely
place for avid fundamentalism to erupt.

President Bourguiba also had a record of political moderation and
religious tolerance. He had passed antipolygamy laws, allowed birth
control education, recognized women's rights, and announced that
observance of Ramadan, the Muslim holy month of fasting and sacrifice, was optional.

Nevertheless, fundamentalism became a visible political factor in
1981—three years before the riots—when fundamentalists launched
intense political activities in schools, factories and mosques. Government concern led to a wave of arrests of the young fanatics, including
eighty-seven who were eventually jailed after confronting authorities
over control of the mosques. As the crackdown widened, several activists fled to France.

In 1982, violence erupted at the University of Tunisia when fundamentalists and leftists fought out their ideological differences, injuring dozens. The Islamic Tendency Movement (ITM) was the leading
group, one of scores in Muslim states that grew up alongside the Iranian revolution. Its most visible following was on the campus, al-

though youth from all over the nation reportedly were either members or sympathizers. Tunisian officials openly labeled ITM "Khomeinist." The youths later admitted they admired Iran, but claimed they had no direct ties with the Tehran theocracy. "The Iranian revolution is popular and Islamic, although the government has committed political errors," one ITM official explained in 1984. They did, however, support the 1979 takeover of the U.S. Embassy in Tehran. "It was not an embassy, but a spy center," he added.

The group's goals sounded similar to Iran's. "We want to build a new society based on equality between the classes and our specific Islamic identity," one member told *The New York Times*. "We want to organize all public life on the basis of Islam. We oppose cultural colonization of our Islamic world by Westernization and by American or Russian imperialism." So did their complaints: "Our economy is based on producing things that we don't need, with cheap labor, for the West, and on tourism," one ITM official said. "We must first modernize our agriculture to meet our own needs and then start industries to produce for us. We must stop exporting our phosphate cheaply and export it as fertilizer at twenty times the price," said another.

ITM readily acknowledged playing a major role in the riots. One ringleader, who had served a prison term for earlier activities, boasted, "The people acted spontaneously. At the beginning they were not organized. But then we, as the people's movement, joined in. We organized demonstrations . . . What happened this week is a triumph for us. We struggled for bread, and it takes the Army to keep us down. The economic struggle, the political struggle, it begins now." Another, who had also done time, added, "We are the main opposition. That is why the Communists are legal and we are banned." A resident British correspondent confirmed: "ITM is the single most threatening opposition force in Tunis. One word from the fundamentalists will close down the campus or start a demonstration."

In late 1984, a former Tunisian Interior Minister, Driss Guiga, provided a candid assessment of fundamentalism's strength and goals: "The Muslim Brotherhood represents a substantial trend in Tunisia . . . in view of the attraction of the Islamic message, both morally and socially. The Islamic ranks in our country, however, are split, with some calling for the violent seizure of power in order to impose an Islamic constitution on the country, while others are closer to the political realities and work within the constitutional context."

■   ■   ■

POORER BUT MORE ROMANTICALLY SCENIC than Tunisia, Morocco also had a relaxed atmosphere. A few coup attempts had been quickly, if brutally, put down; earlier troubles were considered strictly internal. King Hassan is unusual among both African and Arab leaders. The scion of an old dynastic family that has ruled the nation for more than three hundred years, he is also Morocco's religious chieftain, with the title "Amir al Moumineen," or Commander of the Faithful. He claims to descend from the Prophet Mohammed, with a genealogical chart dating back thirty-seven generations to prove it.

Bordering the Atlantic as well as the Mediterranean, Morocco is the westernmost Arab state geographically and, under King Hassan, also arguably the most Westernized politically. The United States, always skeptical about the longevity of its Third World allies, felt enough confidence to establish a permanent Voice of America transmitter in Morocco, powerful enough to reach the Kremlin, as well as to seek agreement for use of Moroccan military bases on a "standby basis" in case of emergencies. The King's credentials as a solid ally were reflected in a 1982 picture of him at President Reagan's California ranch—that invitation alone being a rare treat for a foreign dignitary. In the photograph, both leaders are relaxing on horseback.

The new brand of fundamentalism in Morocco was considered placid and controllable in the 1970s. But it too grew assertive if somewhat less threatening than in Tunisia, in the early 1980s. Among the early signs were student demonstrations against the Shah's brief residence in Morocco after he left Iran in 1979. In 1982 and 1983, several reports leaked about incidents in mosques after Friday sermons, which the authorities had considered "subversive." And just six months before the 1984 riots, dozens had been arrested for urging Moroccans to take up arms to undermine national institutions. At the trial, the prosecution charged that seventy-one defendants were members of the clandestine "Jihad Squad," an organization using Islam as a means of promoting the overthrow of King Hassan. The group had also established contacts with unspecified "foreign quarters."

As the new year began in 1984, the Islamic purists from at least five major groups, the latest being followers of Ayatollah Khomeini, had become one of the main forces opposing King Hassan. The changing mood was evident during a walk through the labyrinthine alleys of the ancient quarter in Fez or the wide highways of industrial Casablanca. The chic of foreign jeans on men and short skirts for girls were increasingly being replaced by the enveloping modesty of the jellabah robe. Government officials and diplomats scoffed, perhaps rightly, at suggestions that King Hassan could ever go the way of the Shah. At the same time they conceded that religious militancy was the most vocal and active force in this strategically located nation at the entrance to the Mediterranean.

Ambassador Parker wrote shortly after the 1984 riots: "The fundamentalists in Tunisia and Morocco may admire the Ayatollah Ruhollah Khomeini, and the Iranian revolution has obviously been a great stimulus to their movements, but there is no evidence of an organizational connection between them and the Iranian leader. The link is one of similar motivation—a drive for a return to traditional Islam and a rejection of imported Western values that can now be found throughout the Muslim world."

The tremors were also felt across the Mediterranean. Spanish Foreign Minister Fernando Moran warned that Europe's biggest problem was the emergence in North Africa of Islamic fundamentalism. He predicted, "If the instability becomes more or less permanent in North Africa, it will not only affect Spanish politics in the area, but also all of Europe."

■   ■   ■

THE EXPLOSIONS OF VIOLENCE actually had many seeds, for the pattern of fundamentalist growth has traditionally coincided with other basic problems. What happened in the two Maghreb states in some ways resembled the Iranian model, as religion became the chief outlet for expressing political opposition. The two cases also demonstrated how side issues, unrelated to Islam, could be exploited by fanatics.

As elsewhere in the region, general discontent about the lack of major progress since 1956—the year of independence from French rule in both states—was the starting point. Disillusionment with adopted Western systems, as well as the West's perceived lack of respect for the Arab world in general, had spawned a resurgence of Islamic feeling and a desire for change, particularly among the youth, who dominated the population. More than half the population in both Tunisia and Morocco was under twenty-one. This first generation to grow up after independence was suspicious of their leaders' close alliance with the United States. "The kids feel the country has become a colonized American state," said one foreign resident in Tunis.

Other issues and parties were also behind the bread riots. In Tunisia, an atmosphere of general uncertainty about aging and ailing President Bourguiba was aggravated by 25 percent unemployment. If things were this bad now, what of a future without the man who had led the nation since it was born? Palace rivalries over the unnamed successor added to the unease, as did disputes over reforms being debated in government—and in public. In the aftermath of the riots, the President actually charged Guiga, his own Interior Minister, with high treason for exploiting the price issue in order to undermine the Prime Minister and further his own political ambitions. It was easier to find a scapegoat and simply cancel price hikes than to deal with the deeper causes of unrest.

In Morocco, food prices had already soared by an estimated 70 percent in 1983, a major blow to an essentially agricultural nation suffering from many years of severe drought and industrial depression. Much of the aid for development from wealthy Gulf allies was absorbed by Morocco's million-dollar-a-day war with Polisario guerrillas who wanted independence in the neighboring Spanish Sahara, over which Morocco claimed an historic mandate. Education had become a luxury in a nation where more than 75 percent of the 21 million population is illiterate, and roughly one-half of the nation lives below the poverty line. More than one million workers had gone abroad in search of jobs paying better than the average $850 per capita annual income.

Extensive corruption and the ostentatiously opulent lifestyle of the tiny wealthy class further enraged the poor. The King's enormous and ornate palace in Fez, just one of many, had one anteroom with twenty crystal chandeliers, no two the same. Twelve men were employed full time just to prepare flower arrangements. And during television coverage showing the King in his gardens, it was widely noted that his fountains splayed magnificently—in a nation suffering a severe water shortage. So it took only rumors to ignite the Moroccans, for they had had enough. Desperate conditions in both nations had led Tunisians and Moroccans to look for extreme solutions or alternatives.

But the movement did have a boost from outside as well. Iran provided more than just inspiration. In Europe, notably France, Iranian diplomatic and religious representatives had been working among the millions of North African exiles and temporary laborers at mosques and cultural centers, laying the groundwork of militant Islam in preparation for the emigrés' eventual return home. Their message had wide appeal. In effect they were saying: "Your leaders have not used their long years in power to solve either ideological or economic problems. Their unimaginative policies modeled on Western systems have only benefited themselves while your suffering has increased. Islam offers the answers, and justice for all." The impact was almost visible.

The French became so concerned about an Iranian cultural center in Paris that they closed it down shortly after the bombing of their peacekeeping contingent in Beirut. French diplomats in the Middle East claimed that Iranians were forming cells among foreign workers from Islamic states at industrial centers that employed large numbers of Muslims. They were also allegedly going door to door at Muslim homes in Paris and elsewhere to urge families, children and adults, to enroll in Islamic education classes at the center. Officials' concern began when they realized that the lessons centered on revolutionary doctrine that might affect the stability of former colonies, as well as other Arab allies in the region. "They were clear-cut bases of operation," one French envoy said. After the center was ordered closed in 1983, several Iranians were quietly asked to leave the country. But Western envoys do believe that loose and informal links continued between the Sunni movements in both states and Shi'ite Iran.

Indeed, one Iranian diplomat boasted of the connection. "The food riots in Tunisia and Morocco were examples of what was preached at the [1982 Tehran] seminar," boasted Abbass Shekouhi, the Iranian chargé d'affaires in Bahrain. "Leaders went back and aroused their followers to achieve the same thing as in Iran. This was an important step from the seminar."

                    ▪   ▪   ▪

THE FIERCE GOVERNMENT REACTION to the riots in both states reflected the unprecedented nervousness about the new trend. Tunisian officials may have realized the depth and danger of the sentiment behind the "revolution of the loaf," for the sentences handed out during a long spring of trials of an estimated three hundred rioters were unusually severe. Two youths were given ten years for stealing shoes. Three were sentenced to twenty years' hard labor for looting a bakery, throwing rocks at official buildings and stealing a bus. Death sentences passed on ten men, aged eighteen to twenty-two, for the murder of two motorists killed by rock-throwing crowds sparked an unprecedented clash between lawyers and the judiciary.

Citing "irregularities," legal circles charged that the government pressured judges to hand down stiff punishment even if guilt remained in doubt. The opposition Movement of Socialist Democrats warned: "Intimidation and exemplary punishment, far from resolving the grave crisis through which the country is passing, risk aggravating a situation which is already worrying." President Bourguiba eventually commuted the sentences to life at hard labor and, as a conciliatory gesture on his birthday, released several fundamentalists jailed since 1981 shortly before their terms were up.

But on the first anniversary of the riots, January 3, 1985, tension still crackled in Tunis. More than one thousand university students held a commemoration to honor the "Black Tuesday martyrs." A military helicopter circling overhead and riot police stationed outside the campus grounds underlined the vulnerability of the existing systems, and the fact that it would take only a small spark to ignite the opposition again. Politically and economically, the underlying problems had still not been resolved. The situation remained ripe for exploitation.

It came as little surprise when the Islamic Tendency Movement's official appeal to the Tunisian government to recognize it as a political party was turned down. An ITM spokesman claimed in 1984 that the movement would prefer working as a legal party in Tunisia, but added, "If the government continues to outlaw us, arrest us, torture and beat us in prison, there's nothing we will not do. We refuse to die."

In Morocco, King Hassan responded to the extremists by fighting fire with fire. He launched a campaign to fortify the nation's Sunni faith against "destructive heresies" propagated by the Islamic radicals. At a meeting with leading clerics, he urged a program to promote the Sunni sect as an "Islam of tolerance and coexistence" as the main means of fighting the "heresy cancer." A television and radio campaign would be initiated, with programs "concise and not boring," to explain the Sunni version of the Koran.

Among other things, the monarch said the series would explain that it was not sinful for women to beautify their faces and hair—a none-too-subtle response to the fundamentalists' successful campaign against women wearing makeup, going to hair salons and wearing Western dress. But in the spring following the riots, the government was still arresting alleged extremists.

Ambassador Parker concluded that "for the moment, the genie has been put back into the bottle in Tunisia and Morocco. Yet there will be no keeping it there unless some progress is made on the serious social, economic and political problems facing both countries. . . . Time is running out for Morocco and Tunisia."

The two men who had spent most of their reigns—among the longest of all leaders in Africa or the Middle East—struggling to bring their people into the twentieth century suddenly were being challenged by those who wanted to revert to ways of life dating back to the seventh.

SUDAN

Kober Prison is a tightly guarded quadrangle of dull sun-baked bricks stretching along the banks of the Blue Nile, which dissects scorching Khartoum. The building still serves as a constant reminder of Britain's colonial past. And, until April 1985, the inmates served as symbols of the erratic political temperament of Sudan's longest-ruling leader, President Jafaar Nimeiri. Prisoners rotated in and out of Kober with such regularity that Sudanese nicknamed it "the National Hotel."

Dr. Hassan Turabi did time at Kober. The urbane British- and French-trained lawyer was sentenced to seven years at Kober shortly after Nimeiri took over in 1969. Turabi never committed a felony, in the Western sense. Sudanese authorities wanted him locked away because of his connections: Turabi was the leader of Sudan's Muslim Brotherhood, the organization of Sunni fundamentalists opposed to secular rule and to dependence on the West.

Promoting sectarianism had particular dangers in Africa's largest state, which had barely survived a seventeen-year civil war between Christians and Muslims that finally ended in 1972. Indeed, since a coup brought him to power, Nimeiri's biggest single achievement had been agreeing to a formula allowing the five million minority Christians in southern Sudan a degree of autonomy from the Muslim-controlled government, ending their grievances and the bitter fighting. Peace seemed to have been permanently restored by the man who brought together Sudan's past and hopes for the future: Nimeiri's face still bore the scars of tribal ritual, yet he received his military training at Fort Leavenworth, Kansas.

Suddenly, in 1983, Nimeiri became a born-again Muslim—some say due to a stroke he survived, others claim as penance for past excesses. In a swift and stunning move that September, the man considered a key U.S. ally flabbergasted even his Muslim allies by announcing on nationwide television that Islam would immediately be instituted as the law of the land. Sudan thus became the first Arab nation in the aftermath of the Iranian revolution to revert to its Islamic roots.

Nimeiri then installed Turabi, who had been released in an earlier amnesty, in an executive office in the People's Palace and appointed him chief presidential foreign policy advisor. The swift transformation was not an isolated case. As Islamization swept through the government in late 1983, other Muslim Brothers were placed in the cabinet, the judiciary and the parliament. Long-serving presidential aides were dropped in favor of mystics, youths and clerics with solid Islamic credentials. Some of those who lost their jobs—including a former Prime Minister—also lost their freedom and were confined behind Kober's walls.

The constitution was amended, and the Islamic code known as the Sharia was applied with grisly frequency in Kober's large courtyard.

Strapped to a chair in front of a concrete table positioned next to the gallows, the guilty—such as one man who stole a taxi, and another who robbed parts from a truck—had their right hands tied to the table and then, with one swift blow of a machete, sliced off. Prison orderlies often waved the severed bloodied limbs in front of the hundreds, sometimes thousands, who responded to "amputation day" advertisements in newspapers and on radio and television. The crowds responded with frenzied chants of *"Allahu Akbar"* and other Islamic slogans, the enthusiasm reminding one eyewitness of "the mobs who witnessed the guillotine at work during the French Revolution." For stealing electrical cables, the right hands and left legs of two thieves were amputated. Other forms of punishment included stoning to death for adulterers, and whipping for possession or consumption of alcohol.

Liquor, like Western-style dancing and mixed bathing in public places, had been abruptly banned in the desert state, troops raiding bars and dumping bottles into the Nile waters. Despite an earlier Nimeiri pledge that Christians would be exempt from the rigors of the Sharia, the Islamic strictures were indeed brutally applied also to Christians and animists—and foreigners. The public flogging of three Italians, including a Roman Catholic priest who was in possession of sacramental wine, created a diplomatic furor in which even the Vatican became involved.

The potential impact was not limited to Sudan; Islamization threatened more than sensibilities in the West. The strategic land borders eight African states, as well as the vital Red Sea, with the oil-rich Arabian Peninsula just across the narrow shipping route. Whatever happened in Sudan could in turn affect trends on two continents.

■   ■   ■

THE SEQUENCE OF EVENTS in Sudan was so startling because the country was among the least likely candidates for Islamization. At the time of the bloodless coup that brought him to power, Nimeiri was considered one of the most left-leaning nationalists within the Army, and was rumored to enjoy alcohol. His subsequent reign was marked by a wandering search for identity—including one flirtation with communism as a means of helping reunite and rebuild his disparate and desperate nation. Some diplomats, notably from the West, argued that the Islamization was merely an attempt to try another approach and to hold off the many factions increasingly questioning the meager results of his fifteen-year rule. Yet militant fundamentalism was making genuine headway in Sudan, particularly among the intelligentsia and youth. The trend led Turabi to predict confidently, "No future government in Sudan can afford to dispense with or ignore us."

In a 1984 interview with *The Wall Street Journal*, six months after the implementation of the Sharia, Turabi defended the fundamentalist revival as a response to the disillusionment with institutions left behind by colonial powers that had become corrupt and incapable of fostering economic development. "So people have fallen back on their own original values," he explained. "They are more conscious of their own identity and history."

"Until last year, the penal code was based on British law," said the slight, smartly dressed man in another interview in 1984. "Now we are not British, we are Arabs. So why should we govern ourselves through alien laws?" The harsh and uncompromising system of justice "is a strong deterrent against crime, and robberies have become less and less frequent. The West should perhaps think more of the victims than of criminals. Look at the United States or Europe. The law is so weighted in favor of a criminal that murder, rape and robbery are all too common. If the harshness of our laws deters people from committing these crimes, then society is a better place." Police statistics did indicate that crime was lower: murders fell by 71 percent, robbery by 59 percent, and cases of grievous bodily harm by 55 percent in the first year of Islamic law.

Yet the criteria of the Sudanese justice sometimes seemed uneven. Mahmoud Taha was another former inmate of Kober. He was also a fundamentalist, allegedly a member of the outlawed Republican Brothers, a nonviolent movement that advocated a modern and moderate reinterpretation of Islam. In January 1985 the seventy-six-year-old Muslim was convicted of being a heretic. The specific charges were "heresy, opposing application of Islamic law, disturbing public security, provoking opposition against the government, and reestablishing a banned political party."

Taha and four others had "provoked opposition" by preparing

leaflets demanding abolition of the Sharia, on the grounds that it "distorted Islam in the eyes of intelligent members of our people and in the eyes of the world, and degraded the reputation of our country." At the two-hour trial of the five, the main evidence involved confessions that each was still opposed to Sudan's interpretation of Islamic law. In effect, the five were found guilty of not being sufficiently fundamentalist. As the ringleader, Taha was sentenced to death.

Just hours before Taha was scheduled to be hanged at Kober on January 18, 1985—following Muslim tradition, after noon prayers on Friday, the Muslim Sabbath—security police launched a sweep in Khartoum. At least four hundred people were rounded up. "They started first with those who might have been able to take effective action" in protest, said a source at Khartoum University, where many students were hauled away. "It was a very effective sweep. Security services knew whom to pick up." The campus had become a focal point for verbal confrontations between differing fundamentalist groups, primarily the Republican Brothers and the Muslim Brotherhood, which had put up signs supporting the hanging.

The divisions among Muslim groups indicated that not everyone was happy with the rigors of Islamic militancy. That was evident again at Kober, after a judge read the charges against Taha over a loudspeaker: "The Prophet said that those who change religion would be punished, and those who come with false ideas should be killed and killed and killed." Thousands outside the prison walls shouted support for Taha, demonstrating with such passion that police on horseback used bullwhips to drive back the crowd.

But inside the courtyard, as the trapdoor of the red steel scaffolding swung open and Taha's neck snapped in the noose, another large crowd of spectators leapt to their feet, applauding and shouting, "Death to the enemy of God!" Death was not Taha's final punishment. The court also ruled that no Muslim prayers could be said over his body, nor could he be buried in a Muslim cemetery. The U.S. State Department publicly condemned the hanging as "a clear violation of human rights," and Egyptian officials privately expressed their horror. The Sudanese situation had sparked a major dispute within Islam, as well as a wave of anxiety among its friends.

Taha's four co-defendants had also been ordered to the gallows, although an appeals court judge said they would be granted a brief delay, for consultations with Islamic scholars, to "repent." All four recanted publicly two days after being forced to witness Taha's execution and a day before their own scheduled deaths. Under the watchful supervision of six religious sheikhs gathered in a dirty prison room, each of the men, his feet in heavy chains, signed a confession that he had strayed from the true path of Islam. They also denounced Taha, at least one reluctantly. Television cameras recorded the event for nationwide broadcast that night, leading a Sudanese professor to comment, "If Fellini had wanted to film a modern Spanish Inquisition, he could hardly have found a more suitable event." All four were pardoned and released.

After the hanging and the TV broadcast, a European diplomat told *The New York Times*, "President Nimeiri may have intended this as a warning to opponents. He may have wished to show that he is still in charge, still to be feared and obeyed. But the hanging and recantations were morally repugnant to his people, even to his dwindling supporters. We may look back and say that it signaled the beginning of the end for him."

■   ■   ■

IN DECEMBER 1984, a crackling radio broadcast monitored in Kenya declared that Sudanese rebels had captured Boing, killing seventy-three Sudanese troops in intense fighting. The insurrection by the Sudan People's Liberation Army (SPLA) was led by John Garang, a former Sudanese Army colonel who had earned a doctorate in economics at Iowa State University. During the broadcast, Garang totally rejected all appeals for reconciliation with the Nimeiri government, instead pledging to overthrow it. Boing was hardly a strategic loss. A nothing little Sudanese village 516 miles southeast of Khartoum and close to the Ethiopian border, Boing does not even show up on most maps of North Africa.

Yet Boing represented the second impact of imposing Islamic law in a nation of many sects. Unlike the trouble elsewhere in Sudan or the Muslim world, the SPLA rebellion was not launched by fundamentalists. The issue, however, was religion: the guerrillas based in Sudan's arid south were Christians and animists. Their campaign was a protest *against* the byproducts of the Islamic revival, and represented the kind of instability that extremist policies provoked.

The Islamic renaissance had once again ignited sectarian strife and alienated the non-Muslims, who accounted for roughly a third of Sudan's 22 million population. And the southern region they dominated was almost the size of France.

After implementing the Sharia in 1983, Nimeiri had also in effect scrapped the most important aspects of the 1972 peace treaty ending Muslim–Christian strife. The first round of small but effective new attacks by Christian and animist guerrillas had begun again in 1984. The twelve-year peace was over. Army strength in the south collapsed after a mutiny and defection by key officers to the antigovernment factions.

This was just what Sudan's closest allies, including Saudi Arabia and Egypt, had most feared. Saudi Arabia employed the same code of law, but its government was deeply worried about the impact of strict Islamization in a land of mixed religions and traditions. Sudan's geographic proximity across the Red Sea made the House of Saud shiver over the possibilities for trouble across from its western border—and the Saudis' alternative oil pipeline at Yanbu. Fundamentalist influences from Iran were already squeezing its oil-rich eastern shores. And Egypt, which had a defense pact with Sudan, feared instability on its southern flank, as well as the precedent that Islamic rule in Sudan might set for its own population.

By April 1984—only seven months after the Muslim code was adopted—Nimeiri was forced to declare a nationwide state of emergency, giving the government sweeping powers of arrest, search and seizure, press censorship, and "swift justice" with penalties of up to ten years in jail. It did little to end the crisis. In one attack alone, southern guerrillas claimed to have killed 274 of 390 soldiers being ferried north on a Nile steamer. Diplomats estimated that the SPLA was up to ten thousand strong. By early spring 1985, the rebels had virtually severed steamer traffic and road links between southern provinces and the north, the main routes for fuel, spare parts and certain vital foods. A string of other villages was overtaken, and Juba, the capital of Equatoria province, was threatened.

More important perhaps for Sudan's tattered economy, the southern rebellion closed down oil exploration by Chevron. The first oil production was scheduled to have begun in 1985, a major boost to a nation so barren that the per capita annual income was a pitiful $364. Construction of a pipeline also shut down. Foreign workers, including French and American contractors, fled when they too came under attack, abandoning other vital projects, such as a scheme to divert Nile waters to the arid interior.

■   ■   ■

THERE WAS NEVER even the slightest suggestion from Sudanese or Iranians that Tehran's mullahs played a role in Sudan's dramatic change. Indeed, Nimeiri repeatedly declared, often with a touch of scorn in his voice, that the reversion to Islam would *not* lead his nation to follow in the footsteps of Iran's Islamic republic. Minister of Information Ali Mohammed Shoumo conceded, "There is some support for the Iranian revolution among the Muslim Brotherhood in Sudan. But it is a corrupt regime and despotic. The Islamic image suffered as a result of the Iranian revolution. We don't believe in violence as a means of solving problems." And Turabi claimed, "We don't want a [Islamic] revolution. It would unleash so much energy that we couldn't control." Of Iran, he added, "They are destroying themselves. Religious energy is breathtaking. If it is liberated without having a constructive program, it is capable of destroying everything, including us."

Indeed, Sudan had already been through an Islamic revolution during a period of fundamentalist zeal a century earlier. In the mid-1800s Sudan was the setting of the most significant era of Mahdi—or "Leader of the Faithful"—cultism and one of the most successful holy wars in modern history. The self-proclaimed Mahdi, Mohammed Ahmed Abdullah, was a religious rebel who preached Islamic reformation and opposition to the Turks and the British in Sudan. Originally scoffed at, the Mahdi's call for jihad resulted in the fall of Khartoum in 1885, the death of Britain's famed General Charles "Chinese" Gordon, and the first rule of Sudan by Sudanese in centuries. It lasted fourteen years.

Now the Sudanese were fighting not outsiders, but each other. Under mounting pressure, both domestic and foreign, Nimeiri tried various appeals to end the renewed civil conflict, including a general amnesty so that all Sudanese "could return home and participate in the reconstruction of a unified Sudan." And, coinciding with Taha's trial, he pardoned 209 men—mainly Christians, and including 127 military men—charged with "crimes of iniquity" and plotting to overthrow the government.

But the Battle of Boing reflected Christian rejection of Nimeiri's offers, as well as the depth of discontent and dissent. The bulky, tenacious Sudanese leader, who had earlier survived at least a half-dozen coup attempts, had taken an extreme course; the danger was that the Christians and moderate Muslims he had provoked would respond in kind.

Washington began to worry. "Nimeiri has gone crazy," a member of the Reagan administration said about one of the United States's closest African allies. Its strategic location—as the gateway to the Gulf as well as to the belly of Africa—made the otherwise barren state an attractive property.

The United States—which was doling out roughly $250 million a year in economic and military aid, the largest American aid package to any black African state—fretted about the future of the North African nation, its leader as well as its financial status. The switchover to Islam was not just an issue of law. Pure Islam forbids usury, so the whole Sudanese economic system had to be overhauled. Income tax was replaced by religious levy. That, in turn, led to questions about whether Sudan's economy, already on the brink of bankruptcy, would be able to repay its hefty $9 billion foreign debt.

In late 1984, Washington suspended its aid package, a devastating blow at a time when tens of thousands of drought-stricken Ethiopians were streaming into Sudan in search of food, yet another burden for one of the poorest nations in the world. The United States, the International Monetary Fund, the Saudis and others urged sweeping reforms as a precondition for releasing the funds. Implicit in the pressure was a suggestion that Nimeiri lighten the strict Islamic format of government, which might in turn help reconciliation with the southern rebels.

■   ■   ■

IN MARCH 1985—a mere eighteen months after the abrupt Islamization—the Sudanese President once again reversed his course, with two dramatic moves. To comply with austerity measures suggested by the United States and the World Bank, he withdrew government subsidies, leading to price increases of between 30 to 60 percent on food and gasoline. And with no advance warning, he purged the Muslim Brothers who dominated his government, and ordered a review of all sentences issued by Islamic courts over the previous year.

Calling them "brothers of the devil," Nimeiri said in a March 1985 radio broadcast that the fundamentalists were trying to usurp his powers. He said militants had smuggled in arms for use by new fundamentalist militias to topple the government. They had been responsible, he alleged, for arming students involved in recent clashes at the University of Khartoum, forcing its closure. "This devilish scheme was aimed at undermining the achievement of the revolution and paving the way for a takeover of power," he charged. Diplomats said Nimeiri feared he would meet the same fate as Sadat at the hands of Sunni extremists. More than 120 prominent figures were arrested, including judges, officials of the ruling party and members of the People's Assembly. Among those to go back to prison in March 1985 was Hassan Turabi.

Either overconfident or oblivious to the national reaction, Nimeiri set off in late March for the United States for a medical checkup and to renegotiate aid, leaving behind a country in an uproar. In response to the price hikes and the fundamentalist purge, demonstrators took to the streets of Khartoum. The pent-up frustration and anger of thousands then erupted into riots, as troops loyal to Nimeiri tried to quell the trouble. Each new day brought more onto the streets.

The breaking point came when doctors called for a nationwide strike, initially to protest alleged police brutality against the demonstrators. So many sectors joined in—including normally quiescent lawyers, bankers, engineers, professors, businessmen—that Khartoum literally closed down. Almost nothing worked: the airport shut down, and all telephone and other communication systems with the outside world were cut off. Public transportation came to a standstill. Electricity was on in only one suburb, apparently because it had a hospital.

The strikers then boldly began calling for Nimeiri's resignation. The doctors' union drafted a "Dear Mr. President" letter. "We address you today while the country is going through a serious political turn which will define the destiny of this nation. The regime has failed utterly," it said bluntly. "It is our patriotic duty to ask you to step down from the leadership of the Sudanese people and leave the national and democratic popular movements to make their destiny." On the streets, the protestors were less diplomatic. "We won't be governed by the dictator!" they shouted. Others chanted, "We won't be ruled by an American spy."

One demonstrator commented to *The Washington Post*, "Blaming the communists and the Muslim Brothers for all the country's troubles may go down fine when Nimeiri talks to President Reagan in Washington, but here we know better. It sounds like the Shah blaming his troubles on the same kind of opposites just before he fell." During that crucial week, government newspapers reported that more than 2,600 had been arrested, at least 850 summarily tried. But still the trouble did not stop.

In Washington, the Sudanese leader did manage to win back $67 million of U.S. aid, as well as fresh endorsement for his beleaguered regime. Indeed, one longtime Middle East analyst likened the praise dished out by the Reagan administration for Nimeiri to the toast to the Shah given by President Jimmy Carter on the eve of the Iranian revolution.

The ongoing unrest at home led Nimeiri to cut short his U.S. trip. But it was already too late. The Sudanese had grown tired of waiting for his response. As his presidential jet landed in Cairo on April 6, 1985, for a brief stopover en route home, Nimeiri was handed the text of a communiqué broadcast in Khartoum. "In order to save the country and its independence, to avoid bloodshed and support the people and its choice," the Sudanese Army announced, Nimeiri had been overthrown.

Among the first people to benefit from the coup d'état were those in Kober Prison. All prisoners and detainees picked up during the purge and the riots were freed, so hastily that many of them left the compound still in chains. One report likened the operation to the storming of the Bastille during the French Revolution.

But initial signals from the new military regime indicated that the Sharia would remain the basis for law in Sudan, and reaction from the Sudanese showed that the Muslim Brotherhood still had a large following. As Turabi, who was among those freed that day, later explained, the reaction was not against Islamic law, but to the way Nimeiri had applied it. Others seemed to agree. At evening street rallies to celebrate the coup, crowds numbering in the thousands chanted, "Islam has come. We shall follow the rules of the Prophet Mohammed, or we shall die for it. There is no alternative to God's Sharia."

■ ■ ■

WHEREVER FUNDAMENTALISM SPROUTED, trouble seemed to follow. Yet what happened in Sudan, Egypt, Tunisia and Morocco—all Sunni Muslim nations—also demonstrated a "legitimate" side to Islamic fervor. In its varying forms, fundamentalism was genuinely perceived in many parts of the Muslim world as offering an attractive alternative for millions of troubled lives, both Sunni and Shia. The impact was too broad to be written off, as many in Washington tried to do, as a product *solely* of Iranian mischief. Sometimes the impetus was external, but, as evidence in almost every Middle East state indicated, the base was usually indigenous. By 1985, the distinction had become academic.

JORDAN

In May 1984, Jordan's Prime Minister Ahmed Obeidat, a former intelligence chief, told Parliament that the kingdom faced a "national threat" from Islamic radicals. With rare candor, he disclosed that pro-Iranian religious groups had been secretly recruiting students, soldiers and civilians in mosques and schools. "Some" had been involved in acts of sabotage and terrorism both at home and abroad. A recent security sweep had hauled in members of more than one clandestine pro-Iranian group, uncovering weapons and explosives in the process. "Hardly a week passes without the security forces finding weapons or explosives that have been smuggled into Jordan for use against government and public institutions," the Prime Minister said. Leaders of one movement which, to avoid detection, had not given itself a name had visited Iran twice. Saboteurs had been in touch with "religious and nonreligious parties and groups . . . and with Iran for the purpose of coordination."

At the same time, diplomats noted that fundamentalism had a growing following in Jordan. "At least fifty percent of the women at the university now wear scarves. Four years ago it was rare to see anyone dressed conservatively," said one who has monitored the movement. "And these people are not terrorists." A trend which had originated with the young was growing even faster among adults. "Originally the kids were the most radical. But that peaked eighteen months ago," the diplomat said in late 1984. "Now you see it among the adults. Mosque attendance continues to go up." For the first time in living memory, the 1984 Ramadan, a month of strict fasting and sacrifice, was rigorously enforced by the government, which ordered restaurants and bars to close during the day. Any social appearance by King Hussein had to wait until after dusk. "This has always been a loose, tolerant environment," the envoy commented. "But now you feel the Islamic pressure, and no one dares fight it. It is very real."

ALGERIA

In April 1984, an estimated fifteen thousand men, most of them clad in white Islamic robes, turned out at Kouba Cemetery outside sprawling Algiers for the funeral of fundamentalist leader Sheikh Abdel Latif Ali Soltani—a surprising crowd, since no obituary had run in local papers and no official word of his death had been released. Indeed, Sheikh Soltani had died while under house arrest, virtually incommunicado from friends and colleagues. He was one of many—the numbers were never disclosed—either detained or banned during a security clampdown in 1982 in response to growing fundamentalism. "We consider him a martyr," said one mourner. The funeral crowd was, in effect, the first mass Islamic demonstration in Algeria since 1982.

Religious fervor had erupted that year when fundamentalists issued one of the most serious challenges to any government in Algeria's twenty years of independence. It began with the stabbing deaths, by Islamic militants, of two students as they put up posters for campus elections. When the murderers and several of their contacts were arrested, Muslim Brotherhood leaders apparently decided it was time for a showdown with the government. Pamphlets declaring the formation of the "Islamic Republic of Algeria" circulated throughout the capital. Large demonstrations followed after Friday prayer services and on campuses. Before the situation got out of control, security police moved swiftly, picking up an estimated two thousand Muslim fundamentalists.

President Chadli Benjadid, a socialist but also a pragmatist who was turning gradually to the West for modernization, warned that the Algerian revolution would not be swept away "by a wind of reactionary mysticism." He urged his colleagues in government to stop "those elements trying to set up obstacles between our country and progress." The government told diplomats in 1983 that fanaticism had been checked. But Sheikh Soltani's funeral a year later indicated otherwise.

Indeed, like governments throughout the region, Algeria was visibly trying to "accommodate" the new religious mood. About the same time as the funeral, Reuters reported: "An ultra-modern Islamic university and what will be one of Africa's biggest mosques are going up in eastern Algeria—as part of the Algerian authorities' answer to what they see as the challenge of Islamic fundamentalism." Cynics preferred to label the moves "concessions," yet another reflection of the fear sweeping the Middle East about the potential of militant Islam.

A French ambassador serving in the region once explained the potency of fundamentalism in Sunni states by telling the story of a teacher he knew in Algeria. In her English language classes, usually chosen by the most Westernized youths, she asked her students to write an essay on the nation they most admired. More than 70 percent wrote about Iran.

LIBYA

Although U.S. officials have frequently mentioned Libya as a propagator, along with Iran and Syria, of "state-sponsored terrorism," Colonel Moammar Qaddafi has had his own troubles with Islamic extremists. Ironically, Qaddafi considers himself to be an ardent fundamentalist, although he has his own version of interpreting the Koran and Islamic traditions, as outlined in his "little green books"—teachings which many other Muslims dispute.

On May 8, 1984, fifteen gunmen attacked Aziziya military barracks in Tripoli—where the Libyan leader both worked and had quarters—in an apparent assassination attempt. The Libyans later disclosed that the assassins were members of the outlawed Muslim Brotherhood. Eight were reportedly killed in a fire fight with police. Within a month, five of the remaining seven had been hanged.

THE PALESTINIANS

Even the Palestine Liberation Organization has felt the squeeze. On October 19, 1984, the BBC monitoring service picked up a new radio station at 9855 kHz that began, "In the name of God, the merciful and compassionate . . . This is the Voice of the Palestinian Islamic Revolution." In subsequent days, commentaries attacked the United States, Israel, the Soviet Union and PLO chief Yasir Arafat for "moving closer daily to Arab reactionary policies." The new station closed with "We shall meet again tomorrow and every day until the usurped Islamic lands are liberated."

"Fundamentalism is a widespread phenomenon on the [Israeli-occupied] West Bank, as it is throughout the Arab world," explained Dr. Hanna Nasr, a member of the PLO executive committee and president-in-exile of Bir Zeit University. "The trend has been growing for about five years among young people who feel that no answer to the occupation of their land has been found by traditional nationalist groups." The young radicals were as opposed to the PLO's vision of a democratic, secular Palestinian state as they were to Israeli control of their land. Nasr conceded that Islamic militancy had begun to undercut the PLO's strength, especially among the young. Nasr may have reflected the feeling of secular leaders throughout the Middle East when he conceded that he found the trend "frankly scary."

8 The Hydra: Israel

BETTER TO DIE ON ONE'S FEET THAN TO LIVE ON ONE'S KNEES.
                                                          —*CAMUS*

IF ONE COMES TO KILL YOU, MAKE HASTE AND KILL HIM FIRST.
                                          —*TALMUDIC INJUNCTION*

Allon Tsur never got to take his honeymoon. The thirty-year-old Israeli farmer, so distinctive because of his bushy red mustache, married in September 1984 and planned to take his bride, Niva, to the Far East. But, like all Israeli men under fifty-five, he still had a 40-to-55-day annual tour of duty with the army reserve ahead of him. He was assigned to Lebanon, where the Israeli Army had been entrenched in the aftermath of "Operation Peace for Galilee."

Tsur, a reserve corporal, was used to danger. He had already served one tour of duty in Lebanon. He lived on Kibbutz Shamir in Israel's northern Galilee, a settlement of only three hundred people just five miles from the Lebanese border, one of many rural villages sporadically pounded by Palestinian guns since 1968. In 1974, four Palestinian guerrillas had slipped across the Lebanese border and infiltrated Kibbutz Shamir, where they killed two women, one a pregnant Israeli and the other a New Zealand volunteer. The 1982 invasion, which finally swept the PLO out of south Lebanon, initially had strong support from the war-weary northern Israelis.

Yet Tsur had some doubts about going back. He discussed his feelings with his friend Ran Barnur shortly before he left. "He didn't want to go, but he felt it was his duty to do it. He thought we shouldn't be there," Barnur recalled, then added, "Most of the people who serve there do not like to be there. The percentage of people who don't like to be there is going up every day." By 1984, a lot had changed for Israel since the original euphoria about the potential for peace in the vulnerable Galilee.

Tsur had been in Lebanon, where he escorted military convoys, only three weeks when a rocket-propelled grenade hit his vehicle. On October 21, 1984, his coffin, draped with the blue-and-white Israeli flag, was lowered in silence into a hillside overlooking the farm where he had raised cattle. Tsur would go down in Israeli history. He was the six hundredth Israeli soldier to die in Lebanon.

"No one here wants us to stay in Lebanon long enough for the death toll to reach seven hundred," commented an angry Ofer Bolshi, another friend and co-worker at the kibbutz. "If it depended on me, all the soldiers would be back inside Israel right now." In a eulogy for Tsur, a kibbutz leader was angrier: "This Lebanon is eating our children. How long will we sit there? Allon was the six hundredth killed, and thousands have been hurt. We are a settlement that suffered from [Palestinian] infiltrators and we say today, Take us out of Lebanon."

The same week, in Lebanon, Raef Noureddin, also thirty, had set out from Beirut with a small band of Shi'ite commandos for the south, walking hours in the night through the lush but tricky mountain terrain. Near the town of Jezzine, the dark-haired youth and his gang found what they wanted: Israelis. "We sought a confrontation," one of the fighters boasted later. "Everyone wanted to fight on the soil of the south. The battle took place at thirty meters and lasted thirty minutes." One Israeli was killed, another injured. Noureddin was also hit, and he bled to death on the journey home.

Hundreds of Muslim mourners turned out at the Garden of Two Martyrs' Cemetery in Beirut to bury the Shi'ite guerrilla. Women wailed and comrades fired volleys into the air as his coffin was lowered to frenzied shouts of "God is great." Said his eulogist, "Our martyr Raef is one of the resistance heroes. We promise to continue our march. Every day we are ready to give new martyrs. We will accept only the full liberation of south Lebanon."

■   ■   ■

A DEATH TOLL of six hundred was a price the Israelis could not afford to pay. Israel's loss in just two and a half years in Lebanon was proportionately equivalent to half of the United States death toll in a full decade in Vietnam. The six hundredth Israeli death, relative to the country's population, was equivalent to the thirty thousandth American fatality. And the number of Israelis wounded at that stage, an even 3,600, was already higher, proportionately, than what the United States suffered in all of the Vietnam war. And now Israel was fighting a force with an apparently limitless enthusiasm for martyrdom. The Shia never tallied their losses, boasting instead of the numbers *eager* to die to drive out the Israelis.

Less than three months after the funerals of Tsur and Noureddin, on January 14, 1985, Israeli Prime Minister Shimon Peres acknowledged, "The time has come," as he prepared for a heated debate in cabinet over Israel's presence in Lebanon, by then costing an estimated $1.2 million a day. Peres, who had won a mid-1984 election on a platform of withdrawal, was finally going to do something about it.

One of the reasons the Israelis had stayed so long was that Peres's predecessors had been preoccupied with security guarantees. They wanted some deal or device to ensure that the Galilee would remain peaceful. During their first two years of occupation, the Israelis had offered withdrawal only if the Syrian Army and the Palestinian guerrillas in northern and eastern Lebanon also withdrew. Otherwise, they feared, the PLO would simply move back to the south, and the invasion would have been for naught. But the guarantees proved elusive. The Syrians argued that the Arab League had dispatched them to Lebanon as peacekeepers in 1976, and that their presence was on far different terms from the invading Israelis'.

Hopes of a security pact with the Lebanese appeared negligible. A 1983 U.S.-orchestrated deal between Lebanon and Israel had been abrogated by Lebanon, under Syrian pressure. More recent talks under United Nations auspices were deadlocked. And Israeli casualties in southern Lebanon, which ran higher than those in the Galilee before the invasion, continued to mount.

So, after hours of debate on January 14, 1985, Peres called for a vote. The coalition cabinet decided 16–6 to withdraw. The three-phase pullback would begin in February and was originally scheduled to end by September. It was an historic moment, the first time in the Jewish state's thirty-seven-year history that a government had decided voluntarily to retreat under pressure from an Arab foe. Israel had obtained not a single guarantee about the estimated 30,000 Syrian or 8,000 Palestinian troops still in Lebanon, nor a promise that the weak Lebanese Army would patrol the south. Some commentaries even suggested that Israel, considered by many to have the fourth most powerful military in the world, had "lost" its first conflict. South Lebanon had become, in effect, Israel's Vietnam.

■   ■   ■

BETWEEN 6 AND 7 A.M. on Saturday, February 16, 1985, officers under the command of Army Chief of Staff Moshe Levy made three telephone calls, to the U.S. Embassy in Tel Aviv, to the United Nations headquarters in Jerusalem, and to the Lebanese government. The message was brief: Israel would immediately begin the first part of its three-phase withdrawal, two days ahead of schedule.

The Israelis were so nervous about intelligence reports indicating the Shi'ites would attack their withdrawing convoys that they moved out of Sidon, their northern base, on the Jewish Sabbath, a day when Talmudic law forbids travel except in life-threatening situations. With surprise and speed on their side, they hoped the revised pullback plan would avert trouble. By 8 A.M., troops throughout the two-hundred-square-mile area had received their orders. They would have known of the pullback anyway. The Israeli Army radio station had begun its programming that day with undisguised delight: "Good morning. It's a very good morning. We are going home."

The last Israeli convoy to leave the port city of Sidon consisted of thirty-eight tanks and armored personnel carriers, three hundred troops and two dogs, Vodka and Esther, strays adopted as mascots. As the column rumbled south, war planes screamed low over the route for reconnaissance and protection. One group of jittery troops, their eyes peeled and their guns cocked, nonetheless fired volley after volley into banana groves, just in case. But by 3 P.M. the convoy had crossed the new Israeli defense line farther south, the flag of the last armored personnel carrier flapping in the wind, as if waving goodbye. Some went all the way home, others deployed behind a temporary line until the final withdrawal later.

The Israelis retreated almost as rapidly as they had advanced thirty-two months earlier, when their lightning invasion on June 6, 1982, swept through south Lebanon. Within seven days, the Israeli Defense Force (IDF) had surrounded Beirut. Almost twenty thousand Lebanese deaths and seventy days later, "Operation Peace for Galilee" accomplished its goal: the PLO had lost all its front-line bases in south Lebanon and the operational headquarters in Beirut. More than seven thousand guerrillas had sailed off by September 1, 1982, to scattered exile in eight Arab states under a U.S.-negotiated truce. PLO guns firing on the Biblical Galilee had been silenced. What the Israelis did not realize was that the war was far from over.

The withdrawal was an odd and totally unexpected ending to "Operation Peace for Galilee," one that the vast majority of Israelis and Lebanese would probably never have believed possible at the outset. Israel had effectively and painfully been forced out by the bravest and most cunning opponent it had ever faced.

As his troops pulled back, Brigadier General Ori Orr, Israeli Commander of Operations, tried to deny that it was a retreat. "Nonsense. This area is not important for the security of Israel. If the area were important, we would not be leaving. Why should I pay the price in people and money to stay here? This country is not ours." And a captain in the elite Golani Brigade, the last to leave Sidon, offered, "The important thing is we are not leaving with our tails between our legs but with our heads held high. We are leaving only because of the government's decision to withdraw. Militarily, we could stay here as long as we like." But it sounded oddly similar to the U.S. Marines' rationale when they "redeployed" from Beirut to ships offshore a year earlier, and eventually sailed home.

Other indicators may have better reflected Israeli public opinion. At the time of the first withdrawal, more than 140 soldiers had been sentenced to prison for refusing to serve in Lebanon, a staggering figure in a fiercely patriotic country. And shortly after the cabinet vote, one poll showed that almost half the Israeli population favored a total troop withdrawal from Lebanon, with only 5.5 percent opposed to any pullback in the near future. An editorial in the right-wing mass-circulation *Yediot Aharonot* concluded: "We are tired. We've been worn out. The fact is we wanted to end it. And at any price."

·   ·   ·

MAARAKEH IS A MISERABLE PLACE, an isolated hilltop village of stark cinder-block homes and rutted dirt streets, located through the spring of 1985 deep in the heart of Israel's Lebanese holdings. Its thirteen thousand residents, mostly farmers and small traders, are dismally poor and devoutly religious. Life revolves around the market and the mosque, although it is hardly a docile community.

In the late 1970s, Maarakeh became a center of resistance against Palestinian guerrillas trying to usurp the Shia territory because of its proximity to the Israeli border. Dozens in Maarakeh died in the bloody clashes, outgunned and outmanned by their Muslim brethren. Indeed, when the Israelis invaded in 1982, the men, women and children of Maarakeh threw rose water and rice, the traditional signs of welcome, at the "liberators." They too were delighted that the Palestinians were gone, and that their land was free of harassment. Unlike Israel's other three neighbors—Egypt, Syria and Jordan—the southern Lebanese had basically been at peace with Israel until the Palestinians moved in. The Shia had a long record of de-facto acceptance of the Jewish state.

But in 1983 Maarakeh became an unofficial capital of resistance against the Israelis, a symbol of the reaction of an estimated 800,000 Shia to occupation in the southern third of Lebanon. The change happened slowly, as the Shia realized that the IDF was in no hurry to return home after the Palestinians had fled. Instead, their liberators planned to stay long enough to build an infrastructure to ensure that the PLO would not return, that Galilee was permanently secure.

"For seven or eight months, there was no resistance against the Israelis because people thought they had come for peace," said Sheikh Ali Ibrahim, a Shi'ite mullah in the south. "Israel said it was to provide protection for the Galilee. But people here were deceived. They began to believe that they were facing a bigger nightmare than that of the Palestinians." The liberators had become occupiers. Initially, the reaction was small-scale: boycotts of Israeli products that flooded the Lebanese markets, attacks on the homes of collaborators, small bombs of five to ten pounds buried on roadsides to await Israeli patrols. Then real trouble erupted.

In the Shi'ites' view, the Israelis' first major offense was the campaign to pressure them into active long-term support, political and military. In early 1983, the IDF launched the "Organization for a Unified South" (OUS), based loosely on the controversial village league system in the West Bank. The Israelis wanted to establish new "village committees" of five to eight men to administer each of the roughly two hundred hamlets spread through the craggy hills and wadis of the south. They would be backed up by new "National Guard" militias, armed and trained by the Israelis, of up to sixty men per community. Residents started calling their area the "North Bank" in the belief that Israel had the same ultimate designs on south Lebanon as it had on Jordan's West Bank, captured during the 1967 war.

The Israelis promoted the plan with both carrot and stick. Those with relatives held at the Israelis' makeshift Ansar Prison in south Lebanon (some by then for up to six months) were told that release might be expedited if they joined the OUS. And the IDF subtly hinted at reprisals against prisoners if family members did not sign up. Israel also promised economic and social assistance—badly needed after the invasion's devastation—to any new village committee. But those villages that refused to participate in the OUS scheme would have militias made up of outsiders imposed on them.

Israel reportedly hoped to build the National Guard into a 5,000-man force to patrol the south, an area one-fifth the size of Connecticut, against both returning Palestinians and local opponents. At that stage, in early 1983, Israel was already taking an average of one casualty a day from small-scale attacks. Israel did have a Christian-led militia of about 2,300, led by renegade Lebanese Army Major Saad Haddad, operating in the south. But it clearly did not have popular local backing, nor was it sufficiently effective to protect the Israelis.

The name of the plan changed several times, including once to "the United South Assembly" (USA). But the village committee concept failed to attract followers, and only a few hundred joined the National Guard, often merely for extra pay in the poor region, according to United Nations sources. The Israeli tactic backfired in large part because it challenged the centuries-old power structure and fierce independence of the southerners.

Coexistence with the Israelis was one thing; working as their surrogates was another. "A deal was possible, but it had to be quiet," said one former U.N. observer in the south. Trespassing on their lives and their land, followed by the attempt to dominate them—as the majority of Shia saw the Israeli presence—triggered an enormous increase in the resistance. A tiny core of active opponents grew into a popular movement.

The second turning point was the Israeli violation of the Shi'ites' most sacred rite, Ashura, marking the death of Hussein thirteen centuries ago. On October 16, 1983, the annual Ashura procession was in progress in Nabatiyeh, the gathering point for villagers from Maarakeh and neighboring towns, when an Israeli military convoy arrived. The officer in charge insisted on driving through the crowd, estimated at fifty thousand, which had worked itself into a frenzied mood during the ceremony of self-flagellation by men and chanting and wailing by women.

A confrontation was inevitable, since neither side was in a mood to concede. As Israeli trucks and jeeps forced their way through the commemoration, the Shia celebrants struck back at the intrusion, screaming, throwing stones, and setting roadside tires alight in an attempt to block the column. In the melee, an Israeli truck was set on fire. The Israelis called in reinforcements and started shooting. Two Shia were killed and fifteen wounded. The soldiers were subsequently disciplined, but the damage had been done. Thousands were embittered. The infuriated head of Lebanon's Higher Shi'ite Council, based in Beirut, issued a *fatwa*, or religious edict, later that day calling for "civil resistance" against the Israelis. The clergy made it an act of sacrilege to collaborate with Israeli troops—which amounted to an official declaration of war.

Nineteen days later, on November 4, a green Chevrolet truck driving down the scenic Mediterranean highway swerved suddenly toward the iron gate in front of one of the IDF headquarters in Tyre, eight miles from Maarakeh.* A sentry shot at the driver, and later

---

* The Tyre bombing happened less than two weeks after the attacks on the U.S. and French Multi-National Force installations in Beirut.

claimed that he fell over. Its tires deflated and water rushing from the radiator, the truck nonetheless continued until, fifteen feet from the two-story building, it blew up.

The final count of bodies dug from under the heap of rubble was sixty-one: twenty-nine Israelis and thirty-two Palestinian and Lebanese prisoners. It was the largest single toll Israel had incurred since the invasion. A lone Shi'ite suicide bomber had killed more in one day than the PLO had claimed in the five years leading up to the invasion. "The terrorist looked like a boy of twenty—maybe twenty-two," said the sentry. "He looked like a nice boy." Once again, an anonymous voice from Islamic Jihad phoned a news agency in Beirut claiming responsibility.

As one of the most hard-line Shia mullahs explained, "Israel could have won the southerners' hearts and minds, but instead its warlike style has turned people against it. Staying on will only increase hostility and hatred toward it." A Tyre merchant said later, "Had the Israelis left after three months, we would still think they were giants. But now it is open season on them, and even old men want to become martyrs." A Shi'ite leader in the south concluded, "This is the first time Israel is facing a people's war. They are stronger in tanks and planes, but our faith is stronger."

■   ■   ■

THE CLATTERING ROAR of forty-eight tanks, armored personnel carriers and trucks awakened almost everyone in Maarakeh at 4:30 A.M. on June 28, 1984, as the Israeli column surrounded and sealed off the village. Those few who did not hear them were awakened by intimidation shots fired into the air, followed by shouting through a bullhorn. An Israeli officer demanded that all male residents report to the schoolyard—immediately. Before many had time to dress, a house-to-house search began. A bulletin from the United Nations Interim Force in Lebanon (UNIFIL), based in the south since the 1978 Israeli invasion, reported that the Israelis had launched the largest raid ever conducted during their occupation. (It was not, however, the first raid on Maarakeh; in an earlier episode, the Israelis had opened fire, killing two and wounding thirty-five.)

"The old and the young were separated at the school," said Ibrahim Saad, son of a man who doubled as the town elder and chief butcher, in an interview four days later. "They called the men forward in groups of ten and asked each things like 'Why are you against us? Why do you throw stones?' They warned everyone that if anyone did not tell the truth he would be detained. Everyone had their arms marked. They were sorted into three groups, dangerous, less dangerous and then the other category, the ones they took away. They took one hundred and nineteen, some as young as thirteen, fourteen, and some fifty or sixty. One old man who went to ask why his thirty-year-old son was being taken away was told to hold out his arms. They put handcuffs on him and took him away, too."

As an afterthought Saad added, "I don't think they were sure about what they were doing. They had a list of names, but names are pretty common in the south. If there were several people with the same name as one they were looking for, they took them all." Saad's story was later confirmed by U.N. observers who witnessed the search. "It was the hardest day during my stay in Lebanon," said one observer who had served for sixteen months.

The raid became typical of the Israelis' response in 1984 to Shia ambushes of their patrols, which were increasing in both frequency and effect. Due to fears of Israeli sieges, nearby villagers stopped going to Maarakeh's regular Thursday market, their main source of income. The IDF also virtually closed off the south, limiting passage from Beirut to a single crossing through tortuous mountain roads that could take days to pass, and only after thorough searches. A queue of 750 cars and trucks was not unusual. The south's economy stagnated, as oranges, bananas and other produce could not reach northern markets before rotting. The tactic amounted to economic sanctions.

The Israelis also began to deport key religious leaders. One was murdered. Sheikh Ragheb Harb was shot in the head three times by gunmen as he returned from watching television news at a neighbor's home. Sheikh Harb had become a major power in the south, and Israeli intelligence reportedly considered him the "inspiration," a militant religious guide if not a planner, for a number of attacks, notably against youths who were prepared to join the National Guard. The cleric had recently returned from a "spiritual journey" to Iran, which many of the Shia leaders made regularly. A U.N. source said of him, "When religious leaders like the late Sheikh Harb walk in south Lebanon today, the earth trembles under their feet. They have filled a leadership vacuum . . . and are now a power the Israelis have to reckon with." Local Shia were convinced he was gunned down by Lebanese militiamen loyal to the Israelis, a widely accepted conclusion. The assassination triggered nationwide strikes in protest.

But the Shia—from the south as well as commandos who infiltrated from Beirut and the Bekaa valley—also launched their own ruthless attacks. Bilal Fahs, a seventeen-year-old bodyguard to Amal leader Nabih Berri and a former Boy Scout in a troop led by Hamza akl Hamieh, took leave from his job and went to the Tomb of Zeinab, a Shia shrine outside Damascus, to pray for guidance. He came back and went to each of his friends to ask forgiveness for past offenses, then headed for south Lebanon. He was last seen by friends sitting in a Mercedes by the roadside, whistling. Minutes later he drove the car into an Israeli convoy, detonating a bomb estimated at more than two hundred pounds. The force of the blast picked up a giant armored personnel carrier and blew it twenty yards across the road and through the wall of an orchard. Miraculously, only five Israelis were wounded.

With each new Israeli clampdown, the Shia resistance became more visible. In Maarakeh, pictures of Ayatollah Khomeini and Imam Musa al Sadr, the missing Shi'ite cleric, which once were displayed only in the privacy of homes, suddenly appeared on walls, shop fronts and around the mosque and the husseiniyeh. Large white squares were painted on fences and street corners with bold black Arabic calligraphy issuing declarations such as "Islam has given us strength for martyrdom."

The Maarakeh husseiniyeh was a simple two-story building of cinder blocks, so rawly constructed that it looked unfinished, in the middle of town. Covered with bright posters, banners of Islamic graffiti, and painted signs pledging "Victory or Martyrdom," the Shia study center and mourning house was also the headquarters of the resistance, and the Israelis knew it.

Whenever the Israelis approached, the husseiniyeh's muezzins—the loudspeakers that issued the five daily calls to prayer—blared what became known as the *Allahu Akbar* early-warning system. "God is great" echoing through the village signaled that the IDF was on the outskirts. It was also the cue for women and children to ignite tires on the roads to slow the column and to collect stones to throw at

the convoys—signs of protest as well as a diversion while the commandos fled into the surrounding hills. During the June raid, the six
blue-and-gray loudspeakers were riddled with bullets by the Israelis,
then smashed. "That's the fifth time," said one Shi'ite fighter. "Each
time we just get new ones."

From a dirty pale-yellow back room on the second floor, the Shia
coordinated activities against the Israelis. Khalil Jaradi ran the operations for Maarakeh and six surrounding villages, known by mid-1984
as "the arc of resistance" because the Israelis no longer dared to
enter except in force and during daylight. Deathly pale and thin,
with a scrawny pointed beard, he hardly looked like a leader. In fact,
he was a theology teacher at a local secondary school. Jaradi was
technically an official of Amal, the most moderate of Shia groups in
Lebanon. However, the southern branches were more radical than
Beirut headquarters, which had little communication with and even
less power over the southerners.

"Israel thinks Maarakeh is responsible whenever anything hap-
pens. They have been coming since January," he said in an interview
a few days after the June raid. "Every time they come it gets bigger.
They think that we should be happy when they come. They say they
want good relations. How is this possible?"

Sitting at his desk, under a gilt-framed picture of Ayatollah Khomeini, Jaradi explained, "We fight Israel not because our religion is
Islam, but because they are occupying our country, the same as we
fought the [Christian] Phalange and we fought the PLO. Our religion
gives us a good means and strength to fight back at the Israelis when
we are treated in an unjust way and feel we must do something."
Many of the commandos likened themselves to their militant brethren in Afghanistan fighting off an occupying power that they felt had
no reason to be there.

Jaradi had escaped detention during the raid by hiding in town. At
one point in our interview, he held up a miniature book with sayings
from the Koran. "I saw the boots of soldiers. They were right in front
of my eyes. I kept reading this, over and over. They didn't find me."
The twenty-five-year-old's growing militancy was typical of what
happened in south Lebanon as the cycle of violence—Shia ambushes,
Israeli crackdowns, and further attacks—escalated.

Seven months later, in early 1985, he boasted to a Beirut paper,

"We are proud to say that Maarakeh is a confrontation village, and we are also proud to say that many resistance fighters take refuge in this village. We challenge the Israelis to try and come into Maarakeh or any of the seven villages. Of course, they can do it with four thousand soldiers or helicopters, but never with a small unit. . . . They have not been able to arrest any of the resistance fighters they want to. . . . We have a firm belief in our land. It is rightfully ours and we have the right to defend and liberate it from the occupiers."

The frail youth, along with Mohammed Saad, a major guerrilla coordinator in the south, also claimed to have had a role in the massive truck bombing against the Israelis in Tyre which had been claimed by Islamic Jihad. Jaradi and other southern Shia were among those who were angered by Islamic Jihad's boasts. "Some statements issued in Beirut are untrue. . . . The resistance is not led by commanders, by a Mr. X or a Mr. Y, as the media say. It is directed by the ideas of Islam."

He said of his involvement, "In my case, there are no secrets. The Israelis know all about me, and their intelligence officers are working to arrest me. . . . If they want me, let them come and get me. Now I can proudly say I am responsible for dozens of attacks against the Israelis and their agents." Indeed, he had become the object of numerous interrogations. After one arrest of twenty men in October 1984, the detainees claimed that the main topic of Israeli questions was Jaradi: where he slept, what instructions he gave villagers about Israel, who his colleagues were.

Jaradi told reporters that he was not impressed with the Israelis' first pullback in February 1985. He, like many southerners, was suspicious that the IDF might not pull out all the way—which had effectively happened after the 1978 invasion when a pro-Israeli enclave controlled by Christian allies and open to Israeli patrols was established inside south Lebanon. "We will change our attacks from quantity to quality. Our war against the Israelis is one of attrition. The biggest attack is carried out by three fighters, because we don't need more. We have vowed to fight until the end, and we will, even if [Israelis] stay at the border area. We will clear this land of all [Israel's local] collaborators and agents."

One of his colleagues explained the Shia tactics: "We observe the target for more than a week. Then we plan and hit. What we notice

about the Israelis as a general rule is that they are scared. I remember during one attack, they got so confused they shot each other.
People might not believe that, but we have it on film.* Up to now
it has been easy. But if they don't withdraw from all our land, we
will turn to suicide attacks." Chimed in Jaradi, "They are not as
strong as the people think they are. They lack a belief in what they
are doing."

Jaradi expected the Israelis to come back soon, mainly to look for
him. He did not seem worried about his ability to continue escaping
their dragnet. He bragged that he would leave a note on his desk in
the husseiniyeh addressed to the Israelis, warning, "Your practices
will not succeed. It is better for you to leave."

■   ■   ■

THE REACTION AMONG SHIA in the area north of Maarakeh evacuated
by the Israelis was electric. As the IDF moved out, the Shia militants
quickly moved in. Two days after the withdrawal, an estimated three
hundred trucks and crowded buses from Beirut carrying members of
Hizbollah, the Party of God, roared through the boulevards of Sidon.
Honking horns and chanting the now familiar *"Allahu Akbar,"*
young men in jeans and fatigues, many raising their rifles in rhythm,
took temporary control of the Mediterranean city from the Lebanese
Army, which had moved in only twenty-four hours earlier. The frenzied crowd marched through the streets, five or ten abreast, carrying
posters of Ayatollah Khomeini and various Lebanese "martyrs." "We
want a Muslim city and an Islamic republic," they shouted over and
over, louder and louder, during a two-hour demonstration, frightening the predominantly Sunni Muslim and Christian residents.

The demonstrators set at least three bars on fire, smashed bottles of
liquor in shops or shot them from shelves like wooden ducks at a carnival stand. They tore down and trampled national flags and pictures
of President Amin Gemayel that had been put up for his visit the day
before to celebrate the recovery of another small chunk of territory.
The Party of God put up new banners denouncing Gemayel as the
"Shah of Lebanon."

The demonstration coincided with the publication of Hizbollah's

---

* His claim to have film may be true, for Lebanese TV at least once showed footage allegedly shot by the commandos in an ambush against the Israelis.

first "political manifesto," which finally admitted what many people had feared about the extremists: "We do not hide our commitment to Islamic rule, and we call on all people to chase this [Christian-led] regime." The forty-eight-page manifesto, issued by a militant young mullah expelled from the south by the Israelis in 1984, called on all Christians to embrace Islam, and for Lebanese to adopt Iran's religious principles and systems. The manifesto declared that an Islamic Lebanon would come under the influence of Iran: "This vanguard has laid the foundation of a pan-Islamic state under the wise guidance of the fully qualified spiritual judge Ayatollah Khomeini." The fanatics returned to Beirut that night, leaving a trail of doubt and discomfort about Lebanon's future in their wake.

As the Party of God paraded in Sidon, separate but nearby roadside bombs killed Israeli Sergeant Shlomo Avrumov and Major Shaul Zehavi. Colonel Avraham Hido died when an ambush hit his patrol with small arms and a rocket-propelled grenade. In the less than five weeks between the Israeli cabinet approval and the first withdrawal, five Israeli troops were killed, 104 injured.

The retreat not only failed to temper the Shia antagonism, but, at least short term, the perceived victory actually fanned their passions. Israel's new defense perimeter thus offered no guarantee of safety. Israel still held nine hundred square miles of Lebanese territory, populated by 400,000 people—the same number as in the area it gave up. More importantly, this southernmost sector had the longest history of militant resistance, for it is the Shia heartland of Lebanon. Only about 10 percent of attacks on Israel had emanated from the Sidon area. Indeed, on the day of the first pullback, the Israeli Defense Minister conceded, "The area is infested with terrorists and terrorism. There will be an increased number of terrorist attempts." He was more prescient than he realized.

Israel's response was an "iron fist." Ten days after the first retreat, Israeli helicopters dropped clouds of leaflets addressed to "the dear citizens south of the Litani [River]" announcing new regulations: all vehicles had to have at least one passenger or Israeli troops would fire at it—a precaution against the lone suicide driver. All motorcycles were banned. Unattended cars would be blown up. An indefinite curfew would prevail between sundown and sunrise. Troops would shoot violators on sight. The IDF also launched massive simultaneous raids on other towns, which resulted in several deaths, hundreds of arrests and the deportation of suspected dissidents.

An Israeli officer told *The Jerusalem Post:* "This has become an all-out war and we have to protect ourselves. The argument that we will only create more enemies has become irrelevant. There are no more enemies to make." On the same day, Jaradi issued a statement: "If the Israeli Defense Ministry says it will use a fist of iron against us, then the resistance villages around Tyre will respond with a fist of faith."

As dawn broke on March 2, 1985, an estimated eight hundred troops—in 150 armored personnel carriers, five tanks, thirty trucks and jeeps and two bulldozers—converged again on Maarakeh from three directions as helicopters swooped low overhead. About 350 men were rounded up and questioned, according to the United Nations. Israeli officials said the troops blew up three houses and a car after discovering large quantities of weapons and ammunition.

"It is working," commented one Israeli officer. "Our feeling is that the population today is beginning to build a rejection towards these radical elements that live among them." And Defense Minister Rabin had earlier told a Knesset committee, "We are now dictating events in the area and are no longer sitting ducks for guerrilla attacks. We have taken the initiative . . . making clear to the Shi'ites they won't enjoy quiet if we don't. . . . I don't claim we have found the answer to terror. There is no absolute answer . . . but we have succeeded in limiting the guerrillas' freedom of action."

The raid came just six days after Jaradi had told reporters he would leave a message on his desk for the next Israeli "visit." The Maarakeh husseiniyeh was searched thoroughly, while villagers were kept outside. Eyewitnesses later said an Israeli truck was backed up at the main entrance, blocking the view. Several copies of the Koran were later found with pages ripped out and lying on the floor, the grid of bootprints stamped over the words, according to residents and United Nations sources. Police dogs, considered unclean by Muslims, nosed through the Islamic center. The Israelis mixed together winter supplies of different grains, making them unusable; they did the same with kerosene and cooking oil, international relief agency workers reported. They took at least seventeen men from Maarakeh, although Jaradi and other key figures once again escaped. There were similar scenes all over the south.

On March 4, less than thirty hours after the Israelis pulled out of Maarakeh, a thirty-pound bomb, planted in a support column directly below the husseiniyeh's back upstairs room, blew out the side of the building, killing twelve and injuring thirty-four. U.N. sources said a remote-control device triggered the explosive, which detonated just as a meeting was convened to discuss food relief and distribution. Everyone in the room, including a Tyre doctor and the head of the government social relief agency in the south, was killed. Mohammed Saad and Khalil Jaradi, who had returned to Maarakeh from hiding, were chairing the meeting. Both were buried under rubble in Jaradi's office.

The Lebanese government immediately cabled the United Nations to charge that Israel was responsible, an accusation the Israelis vehemently denied. "We are witnessing a bloody internal conflict," said Uri Lubrani, the coordinator of Israeli affairs in Lebanon. "I have no doubt we are talking about an internal power struggle within the Shi'ite Amal movement that is finding expression through means foreign to us." Whatever the truth, the story had little credibility among the southerners.

At the mass funeral for Jaradi, Saad and others, as women wept and prayed and Jaradi's old speeches were played over the mosque loudspeaker, an Amal fighter warned, "The martyr said a word just two days ago, that Israel got into trouble with the people, that it does not know the depth of the trouble, just as the Shah in Iran didn't." He added, "Just like the Shah, Israel will be overturned in south Lebanon. The views of Khalil Jaradi will be in every attack on Israel until liberation." Another said chillingly, "We used to fight to liberate our land, but now we will fight to avenge their deaths."

Yet visible rage was missing as thousands stood solemnly at the side of the communal grave. A British reporter who had spent a decade in the region commented from Maarakeh, "The crowd possessed a lack of anger, perhaps a confidence, in their mourning that was curiously similar to the street scenes in Tehran that followed the Iranian revolution." In Beirut, the cleric who had earlier issued an edict that cooperation with the Israelis was a sacrilege now called for an all-out jihad by the Shia against Israel. Something new was brewing among the Shia. The campaign against Israel had begun as a nationalist issue simply to get the foreigners off Lebanese soil, but now the crusade in southern Lebanon appeared to be evolving into a broader movement with long-term implications for Israel even after its final withdrawal.

Six days after the Maarakeh bomb, a pickup truck approached an Israeli convoy bringing fresh troops up across the border at Metulla. The atmosphere was relaxed along this line tightly controlled by the IDF and the small Christian militia, even though two IDF soldiers had been killed at this doorstep to Israel just a month earlier. The driver of the lead jeep tried to wave the truck aside. Instead, the truck detonated. Another two-hundred-pound bomb had killed another twelve and injured fourteen. On the other side of the border, the shock waves blew windows and doors out of their frames.

In Beirut, two groups claimed responsibility. Islamic Jihad boasted: "The car bomb was originally prepared to blow up the Israeli village of Metulla. A tactical mistake by one of our colleagues forced us to blow it up near an Israeli military post." Another group, as yet unheard of, the "Holy Warriors," claimed: "We affirm to our enemy [Prime Minister] Shimon Peres that we shall reply to his use of the iron fist against our people with a victorious and faithful fist of Hussein."

But by this stage the names of groups were almost irrelevant. Everyone knew who was doing what to whom. There was no formal structure and little coordination beyond the village level among the Shia, just an overpowering determination and will. As the cleric who issued the Hizbollah manifesto had earlier explained, "That's the beauty of the thing. In the south there is no leader. Every Muslim has a leader who is not a man. His orders come directly from God."

Iran had little to do specifically with what was happening in south Lebanon. "While the Iranian revolution had an influence on the nature of the political mobilization of the Shia community, the revolution was only one of several factors which shaped political action," wrote an American academic who did extensive field work in the south. "Extremism is not a permanent characteristic of the Shia, it is a reaction." Explained Sheikh Fadlallah, "The same phenomenon that revived Islam in Iran is true here too."

The nightmare for both sides escalated. Every day, the Israelis raided at least three and sometimes up to seven villages. And many days, the Shia hit the Israelis and their local allies seven to eight times—about nine hundred times in all of 1984. In the first four weeks of their 1985 pullback, the tally had risen to more than two hundred. As Timur Goksel, the U.N. spokesman in the south, lamented, "We are in an area with a hysterical population and a hysterical occupying army."

The spiraling violence led to renewed pressure inside Israel to hasten the withdrawal. But as yet only a few people had noted the larger potential for tragedy. Israeli Defense Minister Yitzak Rabin commented wearily,

> I believe that among the many surprises, and most of them not for the good, that came out of the war in Lebanon, the most dangerous is that the war let the Shi'ites out of the bottle. No one predicted it; I couldn't find it in any intelligence report . . . Lebanon will remain a center of terror. Terror cannot be finished by one war. It's total nonsense; it was an illusion . . .
>
> If as a result of the war in Lebanon, we replace PLO terrorism in southern Lebanon with Shi'ite terrorism, we have done the worst [thing] in our struggle against terrorism. In twenty years of PLO terrorism, no one PLO terrorist [ever] made himself [into] a live bomb. . . . In my opinion, the Shi'ites have the potential for a kind of terrorism that we have not yet experienced.

■   ■   ■

QIRYAT SHEMONA is a sprawling Israeli town in the verdant northern hills of Galilee, slightly bigger than Maarakeh, and more prosperous. Most of the residents are sephardic Jews, many, ironically, from Iran. By spartan living and long hours of work, the sun-toughened farmers, men and women, have made it a symbol of what Israel has always hoped to do with the land. Since 1968, Qiryat Shemona has also become a symbol of Israel's relationship with Lebanon. The town of fourteen thousand abuts the Lebanese border.

The first PLO Katyusha rockets fired into Israel landed here, and in 1974 Palestinian guerrillas killed nine residents in a surprise attack. A rocket once plunged into the middle of a classroom. Although the students had already rushed to an underground shelter, it still would have been a disaster had the shell not been a dud. By mid-1981, a small-scale shelling war had driven an estimated ten thousand civilians from the town and neighboring cities and farm collectives, many permanently. "Qiryat Shemona became a ghost town. At least 50 percent of the population packed their bags and left," recalled Hirsh Goodman, military correspondent of *The Jerusalem Post.*

Tension in the north was tangible. "When a door slammed in school, the class was halfway downstairs to the bomb shelter before they realized what had happened. . . . The situation became intolerable. We spent so much time in underground shelters," said Eric Jacobs, who emigrated from the United States in 1971. Jacobs lived in what became known as "the last house in Israel," for his backyard stopped at the rusty barbed-wire fence marking the border. Palestinian shells had often landed nearby.

At the time of the Lebanon invasion, then Prime Minister Menachem Begin roared pledges at public rallies that Soviet-made "Katyushas will never again fall on Qiryat Shemona. Never. Never again." And, indeed, the lush agricultural lands of the north thrived after the PLO was forced out of south Lebanon and during the thirty-two-month occupation. Mothers no longer worried about children playing outdoors. Farmers took quiet siestas in the scorching afternoon heat, and did not worry about laying clothes out in case of nighttime assaults. Vandals were the only ones to use the bunkers.

But six hundred deaths was a price even the northerners were unprepared to pay. As Eli Geva, a dissident army colonel, noted with some bitterness, "I just can't grasp how you can take a fellow from Qiryat Shemona or a kibbutz in the Galilee, call him up for reserve duty, send him out to be killed in Sidon or on the road to Bhamdoun—and face the television cameras and without blinking say, 'Not a single Jew has been killed in the Galilee for over two years.' No, no one has been killed. But tell me, where did this soldier come from?"

Geva gained fame in Israel as the youngest army brigade commander, a full colonel by the age of thirty-one. His tanks spearheaded the land thrust of the 1982 invasion. But, five weeks later, as the war still raged, he asked to be relieved of his command; he recognized that the cost in Israeli lives was going to be high. Geva was the original military war protestor. But he was not the last.

By February 1985, the endangered northerners seemed resigned to the pullout as the lesser of two evils, according to random interviews by the foreign press. A rally called to protest the government's vote on withdrawal drew only 250 people. "I really don't think our army belongs in Lebanon. . . . My feeling is that we have to get out," said Jacobs, who has an antitank fortification next to his house. "This particular situation was not working, and another direction has to be tried. To go forward, we need first to back ourselves out of a blind alley." Yet he admitted, "We are very worried about what is going to happen once the army moves back to the border. . . . I don't know what the answer is."

But northerners understood the implications. Shortly after Peres' narrow victory in mid-1984, the mayor of Qiryat Shemona called in his security chief and ordered him to refurbish the city's 140 public bomb shelters. They would be needed again, he had decided, to protect the residents from the possibility of rockets falling across the border. The city spent roughly $3 million to repair the shelters, and the Army promised to build twenty-five new bunkers. On his own initiative, a high-school principal began bomb drills for students again. "I knew it was coming," he said of the withdrawal and its implications. Said the town's deputy mayor, Yoel Avraham, "I pray that people will not move out in droves if the rocket attacks resume."

The cost to Israel was not only in soldiers killed during the occupation, but possibly also in civilian deaths after the withdrawal. The danger of Shi'ite militants carrying their anger across the border, and perhaps even to Jerusalem, grew almost daily. Originally, the Shia had merely wanted to rid Lebanon of Israelis. "If Israel withdraws from our land, we are willing to live as one neighbor with another," a prominent Shi'ite clergyman had said in early 1984. But the intervening tension and the final "iron fist" crackdown had changed the tone of the Shi'ite crusade.

Said an Amal official in south Lebanon, "If the razing of houses and killing of innocents continue, we are obliged to transfer it . . . We are able to threaten the houses and population outside Lebanon's borders, inside the Israeli settlements. We are able to reach the Galilee. The more arbitrary practices that Israel takes, the more energetic our action will get." Added a young fighter after twenty-four people were killed and thirty-seven injured during an Israeli search operation on another village close to Maarakeh, "Tell them we are going to get them. Someday we will watch Israeli mothers cry like our mothers."

Nabih Berri, the leading Shi'ite in the Lebanese cabinet and head of the Amal movement, responded angrily to Israel's "iron fist" crackdown, "From now on, whenever a southern village is attacked, a Galilean village will be hit." A few months earlier, he had renamed his Ministry of the South the "Ministry of the Resistance," promising to pay the guerrillas with government funds as well as to provide explosives and other weaponry. In effect, that gave the Shia resistance the appearance of a government seal of approval—even though it seemed doubtful they would actually receive money or equipment from government stocks.

Berri has never been as militant as many, maybe even most, of his followers. During the first two years of the occupation, he had been reluctantly willing to negotiate a peaceful end to the Israeli presence. In the early stages, he appeared to quietly condone, though not actively plan, suicide missions like the one undertaken by his former bodyguard. But the mid-1984 raids and the early 1985 "iron fist" crackdown were the last straws for him. Berri's advocacy of an offensive against the Israelis reflected the change in many traditionally moderate Shia, although in Berri's case it appeared to some of the militants that he was jumping on their bandwagon rather late in the day. Unlike Syria, Egypt or Jordan, the Lebanese government had also never before declared open hostility against Israel. Indeed, the Christian party that dominated government had been Israel's only secure ally in the region. But during the two-and-a-half-year occupation, Shia fanatics in Lebanon had become the most active force in the Middle East against Israel. And after the first withdrawal, the Lebanese Army even had brief skirmishes with the IDF south of Sidon.

Several tangential developments had contributed to the activist stance: Christian–Israeli relations had soured. The Christians were in disarray, divided between, on the one hand, hard-liners who basically wanted partition of Lebanon into sectarian fiefdoms and, on the other, moderates, including President Gemayel, who still wanted a strong national government. Syria had replaced the United States as the main mediator of various internal crises, which in turn deeply affected the Lebanese position on Israel's presence.

But both Berri and the government still looked moderate by comparison with other quarters. Hizbollah, the secretive Party of God radicals, wanted more than just revenge on Galilee. The day after the first withdrawal, their manifesto pledged to continue the struggle against Israel until the whole land was freed "from the claws of Zionism." The cry became "On to Jerusalem," appealing to Arabs in other occupied territories to join Hizbollah's new jihad.

A massive painting on the exterior wall of Hizbollah offices in the Beirut suburb of Hay Madi showed throngs of rifle-toting troops and chador-clad women marching in unison toward Jerusalem's Al Aqsa Mosque, the third-holiest site in Islam. In the bottom left corner, a blazing fire leaped around the Israeli, U.S., British and French flags. At the top, a stern Ayatollah Khomeini looked on. It was just one of many paintings or posters with similar themes. Israel's presence had helped unleash a force more lethal than the PLO, and the cost could only get higher. The risks became so great that Israel moved up its third and final withdrawal. Instead of waiting until September, the IDF was out of Lebanon on June 6, 1985—the third anniversary of its invasion. That morning, CBS reported that a poll taken in Israel showed that 75 percent of the population viewed the war in Lebanon as a failure, and that 80 percent approved of the withdrawal.

General Orr admitted that the dangers were more than possibilities: "The extremist wing of Shi'ite terrorism will come looking for us . . . We will be involved with terrorism in the north of Israel for a long time to come, for years." Another defense official offered, "Some of the Shi'ite actions will diminish when we leave, but there are other extremists who draw their inspiration from the mystique of the Iranian revolution and could continue to present a threat." And the head of Israeli military intelligence was quoted by Radio Israel as saying, "We are raising the deadliest enemy, and the least predictable."

On a visit to fourteen soldiers wounded during the border bombing, Prime Minister Peres promised, "The terrorist will not determine our plans. We will determine them ourselves." But developments in Lebanon indicated otherwise. Shortly after the pullback began, Katyusha rockets were fired for the first time against Israeli forces inside Lebanon. And nothing would prevent their firing into the Galilee.

Israel's experience in Lebanon also had broader implications for its other crucial occupied territories, mainly the West Bank and the

Gaza Strip. Moshe Maoz, chairman of Middle East studies at Jerusalem's Hebrew University, said, "The Lebanon war gives proof for the first time that Israel can be forced to retreat from Arab territory through guerrilla warfare. This has far-reaching implications for the West Bank, Gaza and the Arab–Israeli conflict in general."

In the thirty-seven-year Arab–Israeli dispute, the Shia of south Lebanon were the first Arabs to make real headway against the stubborn Israelis, forcing a voluntary retreat. Boasted a key southern leader, "The Israelis were famous for their intelligence coups—stealing the gunboats from Cherbourg under the nose of the French, kidnapping Adolf Eichmann, the Entebbe raid freeing the airline passengers, stealing the radar from Egyptians. But they have failed here. We have destroyed the myth that Israel is the world's fourth military power. We have done it ourselves, without being paid like the Palestinians and without being helped by other Arabs. In all the Arab world, no one has resisted like us."

The issue was not just the vulnerability of the Israeli military, but the strength of the opposition. The Shia had set an example, a precedent under the banner of militant Islam, which had the potential to attract others. The rhetoric of distant and Persian Iran may have been an inspiration to fundamentalist radicals closer to Israel in Lebanon. But this "victory" by *Arab* Shia served as concrete proof that militant Islam could be the path of success. "One of the important lessons learned in this war is that terror got the IDF out," said Hirsh Goodman, the defense correspondent of *The Jerusalem Post.* "Terror works against Israel. That is a lesson that is going to permeate other groups, like the Palestinians, and affect us later." Indeed, in 1984 one Palestinian group warned Israel that it too would use suicide bombs in the occupied territories, although it appeared a rather hollow threat at the time.

Israel's officials responded to the threats of cross-border attacks by suggesting it would brutally strike back. Rabin pledged, "We'll see what the Shi'ites do. If there is a problem, we'll bomb them, we'll shell them. If there is a need, we'll send an armored column in to cope with the area from which they come."

But Israel's alternatives were also hazardous long-term. As one member of the Knesset, former Brigadier General Binyamin Ben-Eliezer, told an American news magazine, "All our options are bad.

We would make clear that if there is any border terrorism, we will return in force and strongly retaliate. But the risk of terror attacks is less than the risk of irreparably antagonizing the Shi'ites by staying. . . . Lebanon is in the throes of a historic change. The Christians are losing their hegemony, and the Shi'ites are beginning to establish their own. Two decades from now, our neighbor to the north will be dominated by the Shi'ites and it will be vital for us to get along with them."

More important than Israeli ability to retaliate was the question of will. Perhaps the biggest casualty of the confrontation with the Shi'ites was Israel's self-confidence and self-esteem, among both soldiers and civilians. Israel's national ego had been devastated. A headline in Beirut's *Daily Star* summed it up: "Israeli Goliath Learns Costly Lesson from the Shi'ite David."

The Israeli press was also scathingly critical, in unprecedented quantity and boldness, of its own government and military strategy. Several papers defied military censors in articles about the low morale of troops, and about long-term plans. As the casualties mounted, Israeli television pointedly began its nightly broadcast—whatever else was going on in Israel or the world—with the funeral services of the latest victims in Lebanon. Among the biggest doubters were Israel Army officers. "Brigadier generals refused to serve in Lebanon," Goodman said. "Pilots returned with bombs undropped. . . . The Army really showed it was separate, and different, from the political echelons."

The feelings among troops were reflected by a sign on an armored personnel carrier April 24, 1985, the day Israel began the second phase of its withdrawal. In large spidery script, the sign read: "When I die I will go to heaven, because I have already been to hell." Dov Tamari, author and a reserve brigadier who fought in every Israeli conflict since 1956, said of the overall impact, "The Israeli government has to realize that if any war in the future is not a direct war initiated by Arab armies on Israel, there will be no consensus here."

In March 1985, a member of the editorial board of the prestigious *Ha'aretz* newspaper wrote movingly of the trauma of having his son serve in Lebanon and of living in fear of the telephone, the television, the intercom buzzer and the doorbell because of the bad news they might bring him about new attacks against the IDF. "Then you

start to hear the reactions and the babble about a 'heinous deed' and
'the war against terrorism.' You wonder: what are they talking
about?" he wrote in a piece later reprinted by *The Times* of London.
"The Shia Muslims are fighting for their land the only way they know
how and according to the norms prevailing there."

Such public questioning of government policy, not to mention the
understanding attitude toward the perceived enemy, was unprecedented during a period of conflict in Israel. The unnamed editor
went on to hold various government officials responsible: "My son
. . . is required to stay there for months longer because of our dema-
gogues."

The mood had also changed within the military. Ze'ev Schiff, military columnist for *Ha'aretz* and co-author of *Israel's Lebanon War*,
wrote of his "astonishing and painful" findings during a visit to Lebanon after a nineteen-month absence:

> You can see the change first of all in the eyes of the soldiers . . . It is
> the look in their eyes that had the greatest effect on me in Lebanon in
> February, 1985. It is a look that reminded me of the look in the eyes of
> the American soldiers I saw in the final stages in Vietnam. It is the
> look of soldiers and officers who know that their chances of winning
> are less than negligible.
>
> In Lebanon, you can see an army [that] has experienced first hand
> how military might is rendered impotent; how an army that was con-
> sidered a winner cannot realize its military strength.

Schiff pointed out that Israel, like the United States in Vietnam,
could have wiped out the resistance, but only by "wholesale executions, the expulsion of large numbers of Shi'ites from dozens of villages and turning southern Lebanon into a wasteland." In other
words, an Israeli victory could be achieved only by destroying south
Lebanon—and, perhaps along with it, the moral foundations of the
Jewish state.

A few politicians also dared to condemn the Lebanon episode.
Former Israeli Foreign Minister Abba Eban noted, "If we compromise our Jewish particularity and our democratic nature to maintain
territorial aggrandisement, we will only destroy our own vision of Israel." He concluded, "The gap between the goals that were sought
and the results that ensued is so vast that the Lebanese war would

compete for the first prize in history for political and military miscalculation."

Some of the damage may be lasting. Esther Koenigsberg Bengigi is an American-born psychologist married to an Israeli paratrooper. "The war changed my feelings toward Israel more than toward Lebanon," she said. "It was always very important for me to feel that Israel was right, was smart and that it always did things the right way, especially after having grown up during the whole Vietnam period in America and really feeling worked over by the government. I was taught that Israel wants peace more than others and just wants to be left alone. After Lebanon, everything wasn't so clear. I really felt anger."

As Goodman said, "This war has caused profound soul-searching. It caused a lot of internalizing. There has been a lot of questioning, not of the Army, but of the morality of the leadership [of the Begin government, which launched the war]. The Peace Now movement drew hundreds of thousands at demonstrations *while the war was going on.* I don't think you'll find any sane person, or actually anybody in Israel today, who can justify the war. We learned that you can't achieve political goals by armed force. You can't kill Shi'ite terrorism or Palestinian nationalism with the gun. Not a single goal of the war was attained."

The euphoric mood of Israeli invincibility and rightness, both "proven" during the 1967 war against the combined forces of Egypt, Syria and Jordan, had slowly but painfully dissolved. "The early naiveté of the pioneers, all that is gone now," commented Rabbi David Hartman, one of Israel's leading philosophers. "Now all those grandiose dreams of what is possible are gone. We will be much more sober about what we can and can't achieve. We will be far more cautious."

The American-born rabbi, whose son-in-law was killed in Lebanon, also said the dangers for Israel were worse than for the United States in Vietnam. "The U.S. went home. For us, there's no leaving the problem, there's no returning to normalcy here. The disease is not going to go away. We will live with perpetual uncertainty about when the next bomb will go off." Rabbi Hartman, like many Israelis, seemed convinced that the Shi'ite crusade would not end with the Israeli withdrawal, that Jerusalem had become its goal.

Ran Barnur, the friend of Israel's six hundredth fatality and a

northerner who served three tours in Lebanon, said of Israel's experience in Lebanon, "At first, I was convinced that the invasion was
something good. But then it continued and we went further and further. I felt something was wrong. It was a false judgment to do what
we did there." And of the possibility of future face-offs with the Shia
that would hurt Kibbutz Shamir and other northern settlements, he
said only, "I am afraid others will die."

9 The Options: The United States

THERE ARE BUT TWO POWERS IN THE WORLD, THE SWORD AND
THE MIND. IN THE LONG RUN, THE SWORD IS ALWAYS BEATEN BY
THE MIND.

—*NAPOLEON IN EXILE*

MEN FREELY BELIEVE THAT WHICH THEY DESIRE.

—*CAESAR*

Just inside the Capitol parking lot in Washington, D.C., near the identification checkpoint, a police officer sat in his car "whistling softly and watching the blowing leaves" in late 1984, according to a wire service report. He was on what Washington police called the "bomb watch." His job was to prevent a terrorist attack by ramming any vehicle speeding toward the Capitol building, an idea hatched after the second U.S. Embassy was bombed in Lebanon. Then the department decided "that was a bad idea as far as wear and tear on the car and the buildup of carbon monoxide. It's cost ineffective to keep the car running all the time." But the cost efficiency also meant that a policeman could probably do little but watch any terrorist speed by as he reached for the starter. "No, obviously it wouldn't work," explained a deputy chief. "It's an enhancing of our

243

security. We realize it's not perfect. But we continue to explore and try new ideas."

The gravity of this farcical situation was best reflected by the warning of an Irish Republican Army official after a bomb shattered the Grand Hotel in Brighton, England, where Prime Minister Margaret Thatcher and Britain's ruling Conservative Party were holding their annual conference in 1984: "We have only to be lucky once. You have to be lucky always."

After the second U.S. Embassy bombing in Lebanon in 1984, Congress passed legislation creating a $10 million fund for information on planned terrorist attacks against American citizens or property, authorizing rewards up to $500,000 to individual informers. Congress also approved $110 million for emergency improvement of security at American missions abroad, with another $356 million allotted for 1985 to improve security—by new walls and barriers, better lighting, and guard booths—at seventy of the most threatened United States posts. President Reagan stated that the bill provided funds "essential in countering the insidious threat terrorism poses to those who cherish freedom and democracy. This act is an important step in our multi-year effort to counter the pervasive threat international terrorism poses to our diplomatic personnel and facilities overseas."

But even those funds proved insufficient. In early 1985, the State Department discovered that 139 diplomatic posts, more than half of the 262 U.S. facilities abroad, did not meet new minimum security standards established after the second embassy bombing in Lebanon. A study revealed that the United States would have to undertake the biggest embassy rebuilding program in its history to ensure basic safety either by "significantly overhauling" or by replacing the structures. The cost was estimated at $3.3 billion, almost two-thirds of which would be spent in the Middle East. As a State Department official told the *New York Times*, "It's sad to see a bunker mentality. But how can you complain when we're so naked everywhere?"

In early 1985, the United States had 55,165 diplomats and federal civilian employees living abroad—not including thousands of American military personnel at bases around the world. The State Department unofficially estimated that 1,756,808 American civilians lived overseas. The United States also maintains 10,000 buildings abroad where American officials and dependents live and work. The cost to protect those lives and buildings was soaring. Yet it is unlikely that any amount of money or any number of security guards can offer fully adequate protection. Broader steps are required to cope with a major conflict threatening a growing number of American lives.

■   ■   ■

ON JANUARY 27, 1981, the day the fifty-two American hostages at the embassy in Tehran finally flew home, President Reagan set the tone of his administration by declaring the U.S. would not tolerate another assault on American honor. "Our policy will be one of swift and effective retribution," he warned.

More than 260 Americans died in the Middle East, all believed to be victims of Shia commandos, during Reagan's first term. Brian Jenkins, the Rand Corporation's terrorism specialist, predicted in late 1984 that U.S. foreign installations would come under "several hundred" attacks by the end of the decade. He also predicted, based on the odds, that four to eight incidents would have major diplomatic consequences for the United States. "We may be on the threshold of an era in which limited conventional war, classic guerrilla warfare and international terrorism will coexist with both governments and subnational entities employing them individually, interchangeably, sequentially or simultaneously. As a result, the United States will be compelled to maintain capabilities for defending against and, with the exception of terrorism, waging all three modes of conflict." Robert Lamb, an assistant Secretary of State in charge of security, conceded that "U.S. embassies and U.S. diplomats abroad are on the front line of a new kind of warfare."

In the Middle East, the bloodiness of the past attacks and dire predictions about the future were sufficient evidence of the crusade's ominous intent and growing extent. The bombings, hijackings and kidnappings were not flukes. Yet, despite the painful exposure, the exhaustive studies and the copious intelligence analyses, the United States still did not seem to understand the basic reasons behind the trend and, in the opinion of many analysts, therefore misjudged how to handle it.

A journalist who covered the annex blast commented: "I fear we have only begun to witness the fruits of their passionate intensity. And blaming what they do on terrorist cliques plotting in cellars be-

neath bare lightbulbs, or imagining them to be some Levantine in-
carnation of immature Weathermen simply evades the problem."

Tom Friedman, who won a Pulitzer Prize for *The New York Times*
while in Beirut, explained the scope of the growing crusade:

> Although political moderates probably remain a majority in the
> Middle East, they are finding it increasingly difficult to defend their
> values . . . Moderates are on the run.
>
> Extremists are not an aberration confined to the fringe. People who
> resort to extremist violence are often acting on feelings widely shared
> by their compatriots. Sometimes the only difference between the ex-
> tremists and the average citizen is that the extremist takes the frustra-
> tions and anger of the people around him and plays them out to their
> limits and beyond. . . .
>
> Perhaps what is most worrisome about such developments in the
> Middle East is not the rise of the extremist fringe but the rise of an
> extremist center. As extremist violence engulfs more and more peo-
> ple's lives, it gains more and more recruits. Behind every extremist
> act, one can usually find an amorphous body of feelings and attitudes
> that supports it to a significant degree.

Despite thoughtful warnings by many who had firsthand exposure,
the United States approached the crusade basically from the stand-
point of mere violence, without examining its roots, or its implicit
politics. The administration did not fully appreciate that the outcome of the conflict with Muslim extremists depended as much on
U.S. political initiative as on the success of Iranian propaganda or en-
rollment at the martyrs' training centers. Looking at the trend sim-
plistically, officials came up with simplistic responses.

At a press conference shortly after his second inauguration, President Reagan described the crusaders as "criminals committing the
worst and most despicable kind of crimes. Now you have the same
kind of problem that you have with crime. They act surreptitiously,
they come out of hiding, they're anonymous, they disappear again,
you have to track them down, you've got to find them. You try to
prevent their crimes by crime prevention measures, defensive measures the best you can . . . Then you hope that you can punish."

Prevention, as the president implied, is one thing—and of course
all possible defensive or preventive measures must be implemented
wherever they might protect American lives. Even the most severe

critics of U.S. foreign policy in the Middle East agree that Washington should stand firm in refusing to concede to the demands of specific hijackers or kidnappers, since concessions might alleviate the immediate problem, but not the broader phenomenon and conflict. There is, however, a crucial difference between the U.S. defending itself and American operatives going on the *offensive* in the name of self-defense. And, increasingly, the Reagan administration has focused on the "punishment"—offensive moves either preemptive or retaliatory—mentioned in the President's last sentence.

On April 3, 1984, the President signed a directive approving preemptive, preventive and retaliatory action against individuals, groups or nations sponsoring terrorism. And throughout 1984, Secretary of State George Shultz repeatedly advocated reprisals. Otherwise, the United States would become the "Hamlet of nations, endlessly wringing its hands over whether and how to respond. . . . We cannot opt out of every context. If we do, the world's future will be determined by others—most likely by those who are the most brutal, the most unscrupulous and the most hostile to our deeply held principles. . . . Terrorism is a contagious disease that will inevitably spread if it goes untreated. We need a strategy to cope with terrorism in all its varied manifestations. We need to summon the necessary resources and determination to fight it and, with international cooperation, even totally stamp it out. . . . We must not reward the terrorists by changing our policies or questioning our own principles or wallowing in self-flagellation or self-doubt. Instead, we should understand that terrorism is aggression and like all aggression must be forcefully resisted."

Shultz urged that the U.S. should be prepared to respond "on a moment's notice," even if "we may never have the kind of evidence that can stand up in an American court of law." He argued that this approach would help guarantee U.S. safety: "Our responses should go beyond passive defense to consider means of active prevention, preemption and retaliation. Our goal must be to prevent and deter future terrorist acts; and experience has taught us over the years that one of the best deterrents to terrorism is the certainty that swift and sure measures will be taken against those who engage in it."

In effect, the use of force would demonstrate U.S. strength and help counter the image of total American vulnerability before the trend and number of attacks grew any further. One prominent U.S. specialist in terrorism explained that part of the strong language from Shultz and others in the administration, notably National Security Advisor Robert McFarlane, was also an attempt to preempt the possibility that the tactics of the suicide bombers would be adopted by other groups as a new mode of conflict. Indeed, by 1985, there were growing indications that nationalist groups were employing the strategy of the religious fanatics. The tough words were a warning not just to Iran and the Muslim fanatics.

The specialist also pointed out that the administration feared a backlash resulting from the growing frustration and outrage among the public, a reaction that dated back to the U.S. hostages in Tehran. Despite President Reagan's early pledge, his administration had not developed a policy in the intervening four years to respond to the humiliating incidents. His advisors, in an election year, also remembered the role the hostage ordeal played in the defeat of Jimmy Carter. And the wave of attacks on U.S. facilities was indeed an issue in the 1984 campaign.

The Shultz approach might have appeased a domestic audience, but the signals sparked an even angrier mood among fundamentalists. For the "Shultz doctrine" amounted to an open challenge to the crusaders: "Go ahead and try to defy us. We'll get you in the end."

But demonstrations of force are not likely to work for three reasons. First, threats against the crusaders will only fuel their resentment and passions—and commitment. American military strikes would probably only provide new reasons for revenge against the "great oppressors"—additional motivation to hijack or bomb or kidnap, as well as create an even more hostile anti-American atmosphere attracting new recruits. As the example of Israel shows, instead of eliminating the threat, "an eye for an eye" might well escalate the cycle of violence into a long-term confrontation.

Stronger cases have been made by those with more experience. On November 4, 1984, the fifth anniversary of the U.S. Embassy takeover in Iran, Moorhead Kennedy wrote a letter to *The New York Times*, in response to a column by William Safire. Kennedy, the third-ranking diplomat at the Tehran mission in 1979, wrote from deep experience with Shia fanatics:

Mr. Safire urges that the "appeasement" of terrorism invites attacks. So does martyrdom. A number of the students swarming in to take our embassy in Tehran had looks of rapture on their faces, reflecting the hope that our Marines would shoot to kill and thus gain these students instant access to a better life.

Retaliation, and especially lethal action involving the innocent, might make Americans feel a little better, but it will only bring forth more candidates willing to undertake destruction of more of our embassies. Better by far that we try to understand, as Mr. Safire plainly does not, the motivations of those willing to sacrifice themselves.

Secondly, major questions have been raised not only about the morality of a democratic nation retaliating with violence, possibly killing innocents in the process, but also about the pragmatic effects of such a policy. In effect, that tactic would be tantamount to adopting the ruthless approach of the extremists—especially when the United States appears to have little concrete information or knowledge about just who is responsible. Paul Wilkinson, a British authority on world terrorism, cautioned: "In the eyes of the local people, and of the Third World in general, you are going to be seen as deserting the rule of law approach . . . something that democracies should never be prepared to do. We must draw the line and say: We are not going to adopt the methods used by terrorists themselves. That's the slippery slope down toward the demoralization of the democratic state."

And George Ball, former Under Secretary of State, commented:

> No doubt such attacks have had some deterrent effect, but they have also, as statistics show, killed hundreds of men, women and children guilty of no offense other than living in a target area. . . . We would be tragically wrong to abandon those cherished principles of law and humanity that have given America its special standing among nations.

He added that the Shultz Doctrine also amounted to stooping to the level of terrorism. "Let us take care that we are not led, in panic and anger, to embrace counterterror and international lynch law and thus reduce America's conduct to the squalid level of terror."

Third, force is not foolproof: it carries the danger of defeat—full or partial, neither unprecedented—that could tempt intervention by others. "There are the gravest risks in following the Shultz scenario too literally," warned Robert Kupperman of the Georgetown Center for Strategic and International Studies. "Just imagine what might have happened if we had retaliated after the bombing of the Marine barracks by sending a team into Baalbeck. Suppose four or five of our team had been caught, tried and hanged. Then we'd have to raise the ante militarily, the Soviets would match it, and the situation would escalate very quickly." Or as Ball reminded: "The U.S. cannot use military force against an offending government without committing an act of war."

One obvious alternative is the use of surrogates or allies to carry out counterterrorist operations. After the 1984 directive was signed by President Reagan, this tactic was in fact attempted. "American intelligence agents and military personnel began financing, training, sharing information and in other ways supporting groups in friendly countries to combat terrorists," according to one subsequent account.

But the dangers of using surrogates became evident in the 1985 bombing near the home of Lebanon's Sheikh Fadlallah, in which eighty died. The bombers had been hired and the scheme commissioned by a counterterrorist team trained by the CIA. The questionable reliability and capability of surrogates was such that the incident reportedly led the U.S. to cancel its counterterrorist training program in the country where it had taken the highest casualties. The impracticality of using either U.S. or foreign operatives leaves no alternative for carrying out a response through force.

That force is not foolproof is further illustrated in Afghanistan, where Russian troops have had little success in eliminating the terrorist attacks against their political and military presence. And the Soviet Union has none of the constraints of a democracy.

New York Times columnist Flora Lewis summed up the overall problem:

> Shultz has advocated what sounds like an enraged bull response— charge full-tilt at the terrorists and wipe them out. It misreads the problem. Terrorism is adopted as the arm of the weak against the strong, deliberately chosen to goad and madden the bull so that he acts to weaken himself. . . . Terrorism isn't a clear, identifiable enemy

that can be overwhelmed by military means. It's a technique, and it takes astute technique to counter it.

And as a U.S. academic observed: "We should no less remind ourselves of what we tell the Iranians, that passion is not policy."

■   ■   ■

THE CONFLICT MUST first be looked at in broader terms and in historical context. The attacks are not aimed at specific people, but at a policy in general. The mood of anti-Americanism has grown to the point that many Muslims, who do not necessarily support the terrorists' tactics, do question or oppose U.S. actions in and positions on the Middle East. "The plain fact is that the suicide bombers are just the tip of the problem," noted A. R. Norton, who did extensive field work in south Lebanon and is now one of America's few academic experts on the Shia.

Retaliation and increased security

> are merely short-term tactical responses. In the longer run, terrorism . . . is merely a diversion, albeit a deadly one, and we would only play into the terrorists' hands if we allowed ourselves to be so distracted that we lost sight of the increasingly anti-American political climate that makes such violence possible. . . . We must recognize that the real problem facing the U.S. in the Middle East is not crazed terrorists driving stolen vans but the widening gulf between America and the Arabs. We must begin to take steps to bridge that gulf by acting more like the impartial arbiter we have traditionally sought to be. The remedy is clear, even if the medicine is hard to swallow.

One factor does unite the many different groups of Islamic fanatics: They do not view their militant actions as an initiative, but as a response against an enemy whom they believe started it all in the first place. Their extremism is not for love of violence. Their revolution is against foreign domination and encroachment in every aspect of their lives—symbolized most often and most recently by the United States.

To them, the U.S. is repeatedly the villain because of its record of intervention in the affairs and territory of others. In conversations with different extremist movements of varying size and militancy from Beirut to Bahrain, the list of American transgressions was always the same: the United States aborted nationalist evolution in Iran in the 1950s by restoring power to a Pahlavi shah, then equipping the draconian SAVAK secret police. In the 1960s, it tried to manipulate coups in Syria and backed a corrupt king in Libya. In the 1980s, it supported Christian minority rule in Lebanon, American troops and warships taking the offensive for the first time since Vietnam—against Muslims. The United States's rigid loyalty to Israel has almost become a secondary issue compared with separate "offenses" against Muslim states.

Indeed, fundamentalists feel the United States has "overwhelmed" the Muslim world during its brief forty-year involvement in the region. For the U.S. after World War II, fresh from victory and young in the role of superpower, adventures in the Middle East were something new. But for many Muslims the latest intruders represented the final straw.

"Since 1500 there has scarcely been any five-year period when Moslems have not been in arms against Europe somewhere *in the Muslim world,* and usually in more than one country at the same time," explained author and journalist Godfrey Jansen. Earlier, Harvard's Wilfred Cantrell Smith commented that the Iranians

> have a sense that we in the West have seen Western [ways] and Islam as alternatives. If we're going to flourish, they have to be suppressed. If they're going to flourish, we have to be frightened. . . . There is a widespread mood throughout the Moslem world that maybe that era lasting through two centuries [of Western presence] during which their realm has been backwards, oppressed, lost initiative and so on— that era is now at last coming to an end. And yes, they do have a sense that can probably only be achieved by ousting the West.

Dr. Marvin Zonis, who delivered the insightful paper at the 1984 Department of State seminar, explained: "Islam is being used as a vehicle for striking back at the West, in the sense of people trying to reclaim a very greatly damaged sense of self-esteem. They feel that for the past 150 years the West has totally overpowered them culturally, and in the process their own institutions and way of life have become second rate."

Muslim militants also feel the United States has looked at the Middle East primarily as an area for rivalry with the Soviet Union, virtually ignoring the powerful local forces at play. In a bipolar world, the U.S. has not been sensitive to the frustrated calls for recognition of the emerging Third World. And "defeat" of the Russians has not been judged merely by which side has the edge in diplomatic relations. The symbols of successful policy in Tehran or Riyadh, Beirut and particularly Cairo after the Russians were expelled in 1972 were also the proportion of U.S. weapons used by their armies, the number of technicians or military advisors, the business volume of U.S. multinational corporations, the import quotas of American goods—from Levi jeans to oil-drilling and construction equipment— and the size of their student communities training in the United States.

With each new deal or treaty, the United States felt more secure that it was "beating" the Russians. But the Muslim nations—many having become independent only after World War II—slowly began to feel as if they were being colonized again, as if yet another foreign power were establishing control. They may have appreciated the quality of American goods and expertise, but not the attitude or the motive behind the pressure for stronger diplomatic and trade relations. Successive administrations, Republican and Democratic, have shown few signs of either understanding or respecting Islam, its rich heritage, the depth of its inherent political orientation. Again, fury over U.S. policies on the Arab–Israeli dispute aside, U.S. terms for relations seemed one-sided. The paranoia was evident in a 1984 speech by Ayatollah Khomeini: "Today, when all the propaganda trumpets are directed against Islam and Iran, it is because they mean to force Iran to compromise and surrender." Implicit to most Muslims was one word he left out: "again."

"The West—like its women," explained Malise Ruthven, a British Arabist,

> has been a simultaneous source of attraction and repulsion: admiration for its institutions and for the technical prowess that has enabled so many of its citizens to enjoy the undreamed-of freedoms and opportunities; disgust at its vulgarity, its seeming callousness and spiritual emptiness, combined with a deep sense of unease that Allah, whose Way has been shown for all mankind in the holy Koran and the Sunna,

should have permitted infidels to violate all but the innermost chambers of the House of Islam.

"My beloved listeners," Ayatollah Khomeini said, "we fear neither economic boycott nor military intervention. What we fear is cultural dependence and imperialist universities."

Warned an Arab-born U.S. academic: "Americans cannot continue to believe that the most important thing about 'Islam' is whether it is pro- or anti-American. So xenophobically reductive a view of the world would guarantee a continued confrontation between the U.S. and the rest of an intransigent mankind, a policy of expanding the cold war to include an unacceptably large portion of the globe."

The growing anti-American mood has become increasingly evident after each of the crusade's recent attacks. The reaction among traditional American allies in the Middle East to the second U.S. Embassy bomb in Beirut was stunningly similar to that of radical states. Although moderate states condemned the tactics, they supported the message. Egypt's state-controlled *Al Gomhuria* commented that increased security at American installations "will not correct the mistakes of policy. Until such a time as the U.S. aligns itself with the principles of justice and peace, the Middle East and Lebanon will lack stability, and U.S. embassies will remain a target of what Washington calls 'terrorism.' "

The Gulf Times in Qatar noted: "The daring commando operation against the U.S. Embassy in Beirut reflected Arab anger in the face of the failure of the American administration to honor U.S. commitments in the Middle East, Lebanon in particular." And *Al Ittihad* in the United Arab Emirates warned that the United States "should heed a lesson from the embassy blast and modify its Middle East policy. The Americans have been trying to justify the blast and blame everything on the overused term 'international terrorism.' The Americans should know that no real harm can befall people who defend their freedom. The real harm will befall American interests in the whole world, and in the Middle East in particular."

After the 1984 Kuwaiti hijacking during which two Americans were killed, the English-language *Saudi Gazette* said Shultz's denunciation of the ordeal was "meaningless, because Washington supports most acts of organized terrorism." An editorial accused the

United States of "discriminating between various forms of terrorism, supporting some and denouncing others. Thus it has to pay the price." And on the first anniversary of the Marine bombing, Beirut's *Daily Star,* the most pro-Western paper in Lebanon, editorialized: "The Marines were hostages to Arab hatred . . . The Marines brought together the two fundamental misconceptions of the Reagan administration's Middle Eastern policy, and brave young Americans paid tragically for these errors with their lives. . . . But the biggest failure of all derives from an unwillingness or inability to analyze the underlying reasons why the Marines died and to draw the necessary policy conclusions." And those were the comments of friends!

■   ■   ■

DETERMINING APPROPRIATE RESPONSE depends in part on analyzing the crusade's future: how far it will go and how long it will last. And that is not easy. Indeed, a major debate has erupted among academics, Middle East analysts, the intelligence community and government officials. Different approaches by experts in various fields have led to radically different conclusions.

The first approach centers on the future of the crusade and of Islamic fundamentalism in general, particularly in light of the basic conflict between Islamic ideals and the realities of imperfect human governments and societies.

On the crusade specifically, some experts predict eventual failure, through either collapse or a settling down into more conventional forms of government and protest. The Ismaili sect, of which the first Assassins were members, is today headed by the Aga Khan, a philanthropist whose grandfather was his titular predecessor and whose father was married to actress Rita Hayworth.

"Such passions and the movements they inspire last for a time, sometimes for a long time, but eventually they fade. Against them, time has to be relied upon, and fortitude in one's own values," commented writer William Pfaff. Edward Said, noted author on Islam and a professor at Columbia University, predicted: "Religion often first plays a role of resistance and is seen as a haven for the downtrodden. But when religious movements are successful, they often turn to the right and become oppressive," in turn endangering their own longevity or, at minimum, fueling the opposition.

On Islamic fundamentalism in general, the debate is more complex. "The Prophet of Islam set his followers the impossible task of realizing the ideals of Islam in a violent and wicked world, using the available sources of political power.... Thus the tension between the ideal and the real, the absolute claims of God and the exigencies of human political power, was present from the first," Malise Ruthven suggested in *Islam in the World*. "The very promise of justice conveyed in the Koranic messages seems to militate against its realization; by raising expectations of such a political character, Islam presents its rulers with an impossible challenge."

Fuad Khuri, author of books on the Gulf Shia and professor of social anthropology at the American University of Beirut, told the "joke" making the rounds among non-Shia Muslims: "If Khomeini is to succeed, he must become a Sunni. Since Shia means being in a state of perpetual rebellion, he can never adapt to a state structure. To be true to the faith, he must give up either his Shi'ism or state control. Either way, the traditional Muslim world is safe again."

Small humor, perhaps, but the logic actually applies. Iranian revolutionary rule represents the first time the Shia have accepted temporal power, previously anathema to their doctrine. The rule of ayatollahs is actually a contradiction. Some argue that in the post-Khomeini era the government might revert to a more secular form with clerics gradually weeded out of powerful posts, although an advisory council of leading mullahs would probably still "supervise" the state apparatus. One of the ongoing differences among Iranian clerics centers around tactics. Many believe that, rather than trying to export the revolution, Iran should instead make itself a model Islamic nation which would then attract other states. But so far militants have had the edge.

In his controversial *In the Path of God*, Daniel Pipes offered a more decisive forecast:

> The fundamentalist experiment was doomed even before it began. The historical record shows that every effort in modern times to apply the Sharia in its entirety—such as those in Saudi Arabia, the Sudan, Libya, Iran and Pakistan—ended up disappointing the fundamentalists, for realities eventually had to be accommodated.... Fundamentalists pose special problems to governments because they insist, adamantly and often violently, on an impractical program.

This analysis is based partially on history. All earlier fundamentalist movements, Islamic as well as Christian, had petered out—even
the first Assassins—no matter how deep the fervor or charismatic the
leader, because the momentum could not be sustained. The demands
of everyday life, the imperfection of human existence, wore down
and eventually defeated the idealistic goals of earlier generations.

Pipes has also propounded a contested theory that the power of
Iran and all militant fundamentalist groups will decline with the
price of oil. It is, to say the least, a minority viewpoint.

> Iran's moral influence is fated to end as surely as the sheikhdom's
> financial power. . . . The effort to wrench Iran back to a standard that
> no one has ever been able to live by is doomed; as the Khomeinist re-
> gime falls, non- or anti-Islamic forces seem likely to take its place.
> Having found the fundamentalist's vision impractical, harsh, and un-
> stable, Iranians will probably reject any role for Islam in politics and
> return to a program which approximates that of the Shah's . . . to de-
> velop the country along Westernizing lines.
>
> No people's modern experience will have harmed Islam so much as
> the Iranians', whose experiment with theocratic government will
> surely be consigned to what Imam Khomeini calls "the refuse bin of
> history." Diminishing surpluses and collapse of Khomeini's govern-
> ment can be expected to have jolting consequences. The Islamic al-
> ternative, once so full of promise, will lose its appeal and many
> Muslims will again regard their religion as an obstacle to progress. . . .
> In retrospect, the revival will appear as a curious aberration.

Western writers, however, tolled the same kind of death knell
about the Bolsheviks in Russia and the Chinese revolution.

■   ■   ■

OTHERS ACCEPT, as do I, that the Iranian revolution is both genuine
and lasting. It is not a mirage, and the elimination of certain radical
mullahs will not make the theocracy disappear. Most Middle East
analysts now concede that Khomeini-ism, or rule based on Islam, is
certain to survive Khomeini, although no one familiar with the ec-
centricities of the Middle East would dare speculate for how long or
in what forms.

In its first six years, the Islamic republic has defied most negative
predictions and overcome many stiff obstacles. Shaul Bakhash observes in *The Reign of the Ayatollahs:* "The Islamic republic has

proved remarkably durable. The regime has survived economic boycott, internal uprising, and foreign war; the destruction of its major
port and refinery facilities; the loss through purge and emigration of
its technocratic elite; and the decimation of its leaders by guerrillas
and assassination squads."

The chambermaid in a Tehran hotel put it more basically in 1982.
After she complained bitterly about the unofficial banning of tips and
the Islamic government's tight rationing of meat and gasoline, I
asked her if she would rather have the Shah back. She squinted, and
abruptly spat on the floor. "Never!" she said. How about the Muja-
hedeen or other leftists? No, she was a good Muslim and, despite the
difficulties of life, she felt that the Ayatollah and his colleagues knew
what was best for her, better than anyone else. The replies rarely
differed among merchants and taxi drivers in Tehran, troops at the
front, and women grieving for husbands and sons, killed in the
Iran–Iraq War, at Tehran's sprawling Behesht-e-Zahra Cemetery,
where space for fresh martyrs is rapidly running out. In light of the
number of Iranians who have fled the country—including the sister
of President Ali Khamenei—or are fighting from within, support is
clearly far from unanimous, but the principles behind the Islamic
Republic would appear to have wide backing.

After the issue of the future of the crusade and Islamic fundamentalism, the second and perhaps more significant question concerns
Iran's ultimate impact on other Muslims, an important factor in determining response by the West to the crusade.

In *Faith and Power,* Edward Mortimer suggested that:

> The Iranian revolution may perhaps succeed in exporting itself, in the
> sense that it could help to inspire revolutionary change in some other
> Muslim countries. But it is impossible to imagine other Muslim coun-
> tries adopting precisely the same laws and institutions as revolu-
> tionary Iran, for these reflect a specifically Iranian Islam, which is the
> product of Iranian history. . . . Nor is there in any country an effective
> consensus on what the authentic Islamic tradition consists of, or how
> much of it can be restored in practice, or how fast, or in what order.

The key term is "any country," for nationalism is still dominant in
varying degrees in most Middle East countries. A single Islamic
realm, which existed for only 130 years in the seventh and eighth

centuries, is almost impossible to envision today. Indeed, the vast majority of the hundreds of fundamentalists I interviewed who said they wanted to live under Islamic rule added in the strongest terms that they did *not* want to come under the umbrella of Iran or any other Middle East government. Kuwaiti Shia differed from their Lebanese brethren, and Bahrainis were at odds with Saudi Shia, over their versions of an Islamic state. Cooperation, maybe, but total unity—the all-important consensus of the umma, or community—is almost certainly beyond the reach of the Islamic bloc ever again.

■   ■   ■

IRAN'S MACHINATIONS ALONE seem unlikely to bring down other governments. Lebanese, Egyptian, Saudi and other discontent would still have been played out, if perhaps in different forms. Iran served first as a catalyst, as proof of the "gains" that could be made under the Islamic banner, and then as a base of operations, a sort of command center.

But the long-term impact of an Islamic crusade, inspired by Iran, is a different matter. It has already succeeded in creating an energetic wave of militancy—bringing with it varying degrees of instability—throughout the region, as well as outside the Middle East. Besides the cases already documented in this book, there are dozens of smaller incidents.

Islamic militancy became a major political factor in Southeast Asia in the 1980s. Government officials in Indonesia, the world's most populous Islamic nation, linked a series of 1984 and 1985 antigovernment fires, bombings and other violence to fundamentalists.

In the same period, Malaysia's Deputy Foreign Minister charged that the local Islamic Party had been taken over by "extremists" who had contacts with Iranian groups. "The activities of these groups are regarded as interference by the Iranian government itself," he reportedly told a visiting Iranian envoy. And the Malaysian Prime Minister said, "We do know that some [Malaysians] have visited Iran and it is assumed that they may have gotten ideas about revolution from Iran."

In the predominantly Catholic Philippines, pro-Khomeini students carrying "Death to America" posters demonstrated at the U.S. Embassy in 1983. A bomb, reportedly wrapped in Iranian newspapers, was defused at the embassy annex shortly before it was timed to go off. *Call to Unity,* the publication of Iranian students in Manila, boasted the same year: "We have succeeded in enlightening and effectively provoking the Filipino masses. . . . They have learned what we taught them in the art and science of revolution and can proudly say now that they have already established their underground movements patterned after the one we started in Iran." The Moro Liberation Front of the Philippines has quarters at Taleghani Center in Tehran.

In Bangladesh, a government official claimed that posters of Ayatollah Khomeini "have been turning up in [Muslim] peasants' huts throughout the Indian subcontinent." More than three thousand people were killed during 1983 riots between Hindus and Muslim militants in India. In Buddhist Thailand, the government has been unsuccessful in stamping out insurgency campaigns by minority Muslim militants. Burma and Singapore have felt sufficiently threatened that the governments have detained or deported suspected extremists. "We lock them up without trial and make no apologies," one Singapore politician said. And Sunni Islam, not Shi'ism, dominates in Southeast Asia.

Nor has the East bloc been immune. More than 45 million Muslims live in the Soviet Union, accounting for an estimated 17 percent of the population. Indeed, the U.S.S.R. has the fifth-largest Muslim population in the world, more than that in any Arab state. A U.S. State Department report claimed: "There were demonstrations in Tashkent in October of 1983, which the Soviet government traced to Soviet clerics who had been at the Islamic University in Qom." Despite an official ban on religion, the Kremlin provided land and building materials for sixty new mosques between 1977 and 1984 as part of an effort to appease its Islamic community, and has usually allowed small numbers to make the Hajj pilgrimage to Mecca each year. The clergy is banned from proselytizing through radio, television and newspapers, but Tehran Radio broadcasts several hours daily in Russian and other dialects across the common border.

Riots in 1983 in Bosnia, the stronghold of Yugoslav Muslims, were reportedly "traced by the government to, in fact, clerics who had been trained in Qom and sent back to Yugoslavia by the Islamic Republic of Iran." Thirteen fundamentalists were tried for conspiring with Iran to establish a "pure ethnic Bosnia," meaning a province free of non-Muslims. Commented one Yugoslav academic, "I can stand someone being a capitalist, or even a royalist, but this fundamentalism is pure poison." In Bulgaria, more than two hundred people are estimated to have died in clashes between security forces and Muslims between the summer of 1984, when police began a crackdown, and early 1985.

China accounts for at least 14 million Muslims, three times as many as in Saudi Arabia. Even during the tough years of the Cultural Revolution, they were quietly allowed to continue their traditions, such as refusing to eat pork, which was not served in state-run workers' halls in the northwest. Since the 1982 liberalization, pilgrims have again been permitted to make the Hajj—at government expense. Some feeling of resurgent Islam has been shown in the large numbers attending reopened mosques.

Worldwide, Islam of all kinds—Sunni and Shia, populist and traditional—has been gaining more attention, and not only because of oil wealth. Britain's House of Lords has ruled that oral pronouncements of divorce, as sanctioned by Islamic law, are valid in British courts. In Italy, President Sandro Pertini laid the cornerstone of the first mosque in Rome, covered live by Italian television and attended by Vatican officials, after Roman Catholics withdrew their opposition to a mosque in the home of the Mother Church. By 1984, major European banking centers, including Geneva and London, hosted Islamic interest-free banks.

In the long term, said Michael Fischer, "Iran will continue to be a model, in the 1980s as it has been in the 1970s, for thinking about the developing world. In the 1970s, the country was a major test case for modernization theory." The rapid influx of millions of dollars in foreign aid and investment made the Shah's Iran one of the best test cases for transforming a Third World country into a modern state. That model failed, and helped promote revolution.

In the 1980s, Iran is the test case for Third World defiance of bipolar politics dominated by the U.S. and Soviet Union. Even those Third World nations that condemn the practices of the ruthless theocracy are envious of Iran's commitment and endurance in the face of such a plethora of obstacles and external opposition. The independence and survival of this dynamic new force has excited the imagination of non-Muslims around the world.

And of Muslims, British author and journalist David Hirst observed:

> They may eventually reject the Ayatollah's uncompromising doctrines. Some already do. But they could not fail to be moved by his unswerving integrity of purpose, his fearless opposition to tyranny, nor, observing the simplicity of his life—a few rugs to sit on, lentil soup and prayers five times a day—could they fail to be reminded of the classic virtues of the early caliphs . . . It can be said of Khomeini, as a historian said of Martin Luther, that he represents "the arraignment of a degenerate civilization before the majestic bar of an uncorrupted past."

■   ■   ■

THE GROWTH OF FANATICISM, accompanied by anti-Western attitudes, is likely to mean more attacks, particularly against the U.S.—and particularly in light of the potential staying power of the crusade and the Iranian revolution. If the military option is not an effective answer, then a constructive response must be found. Two alternatives avoid the high risks of using military force.

The first is an economic squeeze, which historically has not been particularly effective, either against Iran or elsewhere.

In 1983, the Reagan administration began loudly condemning Tehran as a sponsor of terrorism. But trade that year between the United States and Iran topped $1.3 billion, more than double the previous year. And officials indicated that the figures may be underestimated, since many deals—particularly in costly spare military parts—are negotiated illegally through third parties, keeping them off the national books. Ironically, most of the trade was sales *from* Iran. Iran bought little from the United States, roughly $190 million in 1983 and $162 million in 1984. Most of the goods were machinery for motor vehicles, civilian aircraft and oil exploration. But American purchases from Iran in 1983 exceeded $1.1 billion, mainly oil and special petroleum products.

Trade is still small compared to the level during the Shah's rule. In 1978, overall U.S.–Iran trade had soared to $6.6 billion, the U.S. sales of $3.7 billion representing its greatest volume with any nation outside Western Europe and Japan. When the hostages were taken in 1979, President Jimmy Carter imposed a stiff trade embargo. The restrictions were lifted as part of the 1981 agreement for the hostages' release, although purchases were so low that year that the Commerce Department did not bother to keep figures.

Then trade slowly began to increase again. In January 1984, the Reagan administration officially tried to discourage trade by designating Iran a terrorist nation, which legally made exports more difficult. U.S. firms were then required to get Commerce Department licenses to export certain kinds of goods, such as war materiel, aircraft and helicopters, crime control equipment, and technology with military capabilities worth $7 million or more. The change had a slight impact, mainly because U.S. dealers were uncertain about the extent and enforcement of the restrictions. But trade was still healthy in 1984 at $852 million.

"The fact that we are buying oil does not indicate any kind of improved U.S.–Iran relations," a State Department official said. Indeed, he explained that there are no legal contracts between U.S. firms and Iran—*because Iran had barred them.* All Iranian oil is bought through intermediaries on the spot market.

An embargo or seizure of Iranian funds in U.S. banks would deeply hurt a regime that already has a foreign-exchange shortage. "We could go into court in New York and tie up Iranian funds in American banks," Kupperman suggested. "That would provide some counterterror theater, which is what we need in this case." And Ball added: "Acting collectively [with our allies], we would threaten— and if necessary apply—economic sanctions against countries giving aid and comfort to terrorists."

The feasibility of an economic embargo and the likelihood of multi-national cooperation are doubtful, however, in light of the needs of Europe and Japan, who still trade heavily for Iranian oil. And other unilateral economic boycotts or freezes since World War II—against North Korea in 1950, Cuba in 1962, and North Vietnam in 1970—"proved much easier to impose than remove and sometimes more an embarrassment than a positive influence on policy," wrote Robert Carswell, former Deputy Secretary of the Treasury.

But above all, sanctions would probably not impose enough of a hardship to make Iran reconsider. Rhodesia, a nation that had imported almost everything but food before declaring illegal independence from Britain, managed to survive thirteen years despite United Nations sanctions; indeed, in the process, the war-torn African state became largely self-sufficient, except for military equipment. Like the Rhodesians, the Iranians have repeatedly demonstrated their ability to endure hardships in the name of their revolution, most notably in the war with Iraq. Carswell, who worked under the Carter administration, also said of the 1979–81 embargoes, involving $12 billion worth of Iranian assets: "The best that can be said now is that the sanctions undoubtedly caused Iran difficulties but probably not insuperable ones."

■   ■   ■

IN TERMS OF FINDING an effective response, the United States also needs to step back and look at the broader picture, and not let the attitude toward terrorism monopolize U.S. policy decisions about Iran, for it is counter-productive. Terrorism is just one issue, albeit an important one, of many. Too often, terrorism is a smokescreen that masks more basic disputes. The second non-military alternative for the United States lies in an initiative not using force, while still getting at the center of the dispute.

American foreign policy in the Middle East, which emphasizes the security of Israel, is, of course, a major cause of the militants' wrath. But Iran's reaction to the United States is probably linked more to America's relations with Islam over the past forty years than to U.S. positions in the Arab–Israeli dispute. Marvin Zonis, who had briefed the State Department in 1984 on the dimensions of the Iranian revolution, said later, "An American insistence on an Israeli withdrawal from Lebanon or negotiations with the Palestinians will not change America's position as the 'Great Satan.' "

The U.S. needs to begin regarding all the nations in which the crusade is alive as something more than a bloc of countries that controls the price of oil, as something beyond being simply Israel's neighborhood, as sovereign nations ultimately seeking respect and independence on equal terms instead of being looked at as client states or as pawns in bipolar games.

As uncomfortable as it might seem, many analysts now agree that the United States must better relations with Iran, as the symbol and heart of militant Islam, to defuse growing anti-Western attitudes everywhere in the diverse Muslim world. This option amounts to rapprochement. Iran has led Islam to its first total "victory" of this century, and most serious militants follow its lead—so it is Iran with whom the United States must deal. While not a popular solution, it may be the least of available evils as a policy choice, since there is no alternative which is both effective and practical for a democracy.

William Colby, a former director of the CIA, acknowledged that "We probably cannot eliminate terrorism, but we can take steps to contain it. . . . The most successful tactic against the guerrilla or terrorist is to recruit him, not shoot him."

Without positive steps, attacks are likely to continue indefinitely, and perhaps increase. The cost in lives, property and national esteem is already staggering. The United States must act for the simple reason that time is on Iran's side.

Brian Jenkins has best explained the calculus of terrorism.

> Terrorists have not been able to achieve their long-range goals anywhere. They are able to attract publicity. They can cause alarm. They can create crises. Occasionally, they can win a tactical victory. But thus far they have been unable to translate the consequences of terrorism into concrete political gain. In that sense, terrorism has failed. Yet terrorists persist. And that is the paradox that leads to increased bloodshed. . . . Governments have become more effective in combatting terrorism, yet worldwide the problems with terrorism increase. . . . As in war, when neither side prevails, escalation becomes irresistible.

From the reverse angle, waiting for or promoting instability in Iran is also not likely to work in America's favor. Many Middle East analysts have suggested that further disintegration of Iranian society is likely to leave Tehran more exposed to meddling by the neighboring Soviet Union, which has dispatched troops in the past.

In 1921, Iran and the Soviet Union signed a treaty that granted Moscow the right to intervene against forces who tried to base operations against Russian interests on Iranian soil. The Russians did intervene, along with the British, in 1941 because of the open collaboration with Nazi Germany by Reza Shah, father of the Shah deposed in 1979. He was forced to abdicate in favor of his son, and his nation was divided into three zones. The Russians patrolled the north until after the war. Indeed, they overstayed the terms of deployment, and Iran, at American prompting, finally complained to the United Nations about Russian interference, after which the Soviet troops reluctantly left.

After the 1979 revolution, Iran denounced the treaty. But the Soviet Union did not—a fact the Carter administration was well aware of during discussions of what to do about winning freedom for the hostages. Future instability or the appearance of U.S. intervention might tempt the Soviet Union to invoke the old treaty. If nothing else, the Islamic republic has been hostile to the East Bloc. "Be fully aware that the danger represented by the communist powers is no less than that of America," Ayatollah Khomeini has warned Iranians.

A nonaligned Iran—or at least an Iran against both the U.S. and the Soviet Union—is more in U.S. interests. Any campaign by the U.S. to spur instability might only prompt Iran to reconsider its attitude toward the Russians.

Rapprochement will not be easy, or quick, especially for a nation where elections are held every four years. This approach will take years and patience, which democracies and a single president often do not have. But the sooner it is begun, the sooner the fruits of peaceful coexistence may be felt. James Bill, an Iranian specialist at the University of Texas, offered: "We should maintain a very low profile and attempt, quietly, diplomatic initiatives. This public diplomacy with a flair and a tinge of military threat has been proven time and again not to work. The only solutions are political solutions. You cannot bomb delicate social and political problems into submission."

R. K. Ramazani, a professor at the University of Virginia who is the United States's leading expert on Iranian foreign policy, said in 1985:

Although the ideological crusade against the United States, the "Great Satan," has continued unabated since the hostage crisis, the emerging thrust of Iranian foreign policy may well contain potentials for ultimate reconciliation between Washington and Tehran. The Khomeini regime is now determined to terminate Iran's pariah status in world affairs. This new commitment is considered necessary for the survival of the "Islamic Revolution." . . . No matter how virulent their rhetoric, the Iranian leaders have finally come to believe that the very survival of their revolution will be in jeopardy if they fail to cope with mounting domestic political and economic pressures by breaking down the walls of their international isolation.

Indeed, economic and commercial ties between Iran and Western Europe had by 1985 almost returned to prerevolutionary levels, since those nations had lifted sanctions after the hostage ordeal. Japan and West Germany had become among Iran's main trading partners. As one scholar noted, the Iranians "unabashedly prefer the superior technology of the West to that of the East."

Zonis suggested a specific approach:

> I believe that there is still an opportunity for the United States to communicate to Iran privately that the U.S. is not interested in overthrowing the Islamic Republic of Iran—that is to say, the U.S. has no interest in the restoration of the monarchy or the return of another kind of republican regime—and that we are quite happy with the present regime and believe it to be the regime which the Iranian people have chosen. . . .
>
> The thing that we have available to us is . . . basically mostly words. Words are terribly important in the Middle East. And words express empathy . . . which does not mean accepting responsibility. It does not mean claiming, taking the blame or anything of the sort. Empathy and blame are two very different things. But essentially those kinds of things do set in motion processes . . . which are very reparative.

Words take time and, he noted rather cynically, "they are not usually the kinds of things that we think of in terms of diplomacy when we want to do something."

Neither side need "succumb" or lose face—as important a factor to a comparatively young American nation, especially after the Vietnam war, as it is to the ancient Oriental Muslims. No one need apologize or acknowledge fault. Neither side can alter the past, or bring back the dead. But U.S. recognition that the Iranian revolution has a legitimate base, and that it has no intention of repeating the CIA-supported operation that brought the Shah back to the throne in the 1950s, would go a long way toward easing the tension. This would in part deal with what is at the core of the conflict and what the militants want from the United States: Iranians do not want to subjugate the United States, they are instead seeking an end to what they sincerely feel is *their* subjugation, politically, economically, militarily and culturally. They feel the United States is a current and future threat because the Americans have a record of meddling and intervention in the past.

Ramazani commented:

> In order to retain the option of improving relations with Iran in the future, the United States should temper its containment policy now. If we are willing to listen; if we are willing to forgive and forget; and if we are willing to harness the passions of the moment, then the evidence of potentials for reconciliation with Iran already do exist in the theory and the practice of its new open-door foreign policy.... As this more pragmatic orientation begins to overshadow past ideological excesses, the opportunities for improving relations with Iran will increase.

Precedents for rapprochement do exist: after thousands of U.S. troops, along with forces from fifteen other nations, failed to stamp out the Bolshevik movement in Russia after World War I, the United States established direct, if uneasy, relations. After twenty-three years of a cold war, broken by two "hot" wars with Asian Communists, Washington did, finally, recognize China. "The United States need not wait so long to seek to improve relations with Iran as it did with China," Ramazani said. "It has taken the Iranian Revolution a fraction of the time it took the Chinese Revolution to launch an open-door foreign policy.... Opportunities for better relations with Iran are just around the corner. We should begin to reduce tensions now with an eye to future cooperation based on mutual interests and respect."

The long process could begin with encouraging U.S. allies, such as Turkey, Germany, Japan and Pakistan, which have trade and diplomatic links, to strengthen ties with Iran and encourage the Islamic republic to reopen doors to the West, according to Duke University's Bruce Kuniholm. In early 1985, Iran signed the most important economic agreement in Iran's modern history with Turkey, the United States's NATO ally.

In the short-term, the United States needs to keep a low profile for fear of "tainting" the emerging less militant faction in Iran. In the meantime, messages setting a new tone on the part of the United

States could be relayed at the United Nations or through neutral nations, such as Algeria, which negotiated the hostage release. Rapprochement would probably take years, longer than the Reagan administration has. But any administration can make a beginning. A gradual relaxation could in turn help the U.S.'s Muslim allies. If the U.S. was seen to demonstrate greater tolerance of or respect for the Islamic identity, then militants might be less critical of the relations of such countries as Saudi Arabia and Egypt with the West.

■   ■   ■

IT IS NOT OUTRAGEOUS to think that Iran can be dealt with, especially in light of developments within Iran. "The foreign policy of revolutionary Iran has been undergoing increasingly subtle, but significant changes," Ramazani explained. "The opportunities for improving relations with Iran would ultimately depend on the outcome of these changes, which would seem to indicate that we need not wait another decade before trying to temper our present containment policy with a genuine move toward reconciliation. The danger in failing to move much earlier is twofold. First, we would miss any chance of exploring the opportunities for reconciliation that might already exist. Second, we would, in effect, make continued conflict the centerpiece of our policy toward Iran."

Iran's support for the crusade and the export of revolution has, during the first six years of the theocrats' rule, usually had an edge over pragmatic considerations, but not always. Those pragmatic considerations have included not closing the strategic oil lanes to the West through the Strait of Hormuz, restraint in responding to Iraq's aerial strikes on tankers ferrying oil from Iran, and the ongoing, if troubled, relationship with other Muslim states in OPEC. And the Iranians did not retaliate when the Saudis, aided by U.S. AWACs, shot down one of their planes in mid-1984.

Admittedly, most experts feel that, while Ayatollah Khomeini is alive, the U.S. will make no tangible progress. But that does not mean that Washington should not position itself for eventually opening the door by laying the groundwork earlier, which also might help save American lives during the period in between. In other words, gradual rapprochement should be divided into two stages, now and after Ayatollah Khomeini's death.

"The domestic and international pressures that have finally produced the beginnings of a more pragmatic Iranian foreign policy will in all probability continue regardless of the makeup of the successor regime," Ramazani predicted. "The emerging open-door foreign policy will mean even more expanded relations between Iran, West European countries, Japan and China. . . . With such an improved regional environment, the United States will be even better poised to start establishing a new relationship with Iran, beginning with non-strategic trade and technical assistance for Iran's postwar reconstruction."

In all fairness, President Carter did repeatedly pursue better relations, through direct emissaries and third parties, with moderates in the then new regime. But the strategy totally failed. Indeed, many of those the United States approached were subsequently purged or executed, or they fled the country, including Iran's first President. Contact with the United States was among their sins. But the revolution had its own dynamics, and at that stage was still playing itself out as clerics competed with other groups for absolute control over the revolution. But now the mullahs have developed a firmer grip on power. A few have even hinted at a willingness to begin contacts with the West again.

In mid-1984, Iran experimented with warmer relations with the West. Foreign Minister Ali Akbar Vellayati told the parliament, "The world is determined on the diplomatic scene. If we are not present, it will be determined without us." In mid-1984, German Foreign Minister Hans Dietrich Genscher became the first important Western diplomat to visit Tehran since the revolution. He later said that the visit showed Iran's "clear wish" to open up to the West again.

Iranian President Ali Khamenei, who was the first to label Iran's new approach to world affairs "an open-door foreign policy," also called for a greater interaction between the nation's Islamic ideology and the "ideologies and cultures" of other countries. At Friday prayers at Tehran University in late 1984, he explained the distinction Iran makes between the American people and U.S. policy, an important difference in the eyes of the militants as well as many Third World nations: "We are not enemies of the U.S. nation. We bear no hostility towards that geographic region and that land. We are hostile towards domineering policies." The speech was widely noted outside the region as a departure from earlier and angrier rhetoric.

Perhaps in part because of the slight thaw within a small circle of Iranians, who face fierce opposition from hard-liners, a few lonely voices in Washington did begin in 1984 to advocate a quiet response of patience and low expectations. One senior administration official, quoted anonymously, said he hoped that "fifteen years from now, people will look back and realize that this is how a strong nation should behave. It didn't overreact. It didn't do stupid things. It recognized its limitations and it paid the cost of maintaining its own civilization. . . . But that's philosophy and that's fifteen years from now. The real bitch is putting yourself through the agony of letting the fire burn itself out."

The stakes are too high, the alternative too deadly, for the option of rapprochement to be discarded simply because it means acknowledgment of Iran, a former client state, as a major new dynamic and independent force. The goal must be to channel the growing destructive energies behind the Islamic Republic and the many arms of the crusade into a constructive form.

In the fourteenth century, ibn Khaldun, a famous philosopher widely revered today in the Muslim world, wrote that "Man's distinguishing characteristic is the ability to think . . . and through thinking to cooperate." The Koran itself demands of the faithful: "And if they incline towards peace, incline yourself also towards it."

GLOSSARY

Western translations of Arabic words are done phonetically. The spellings of Arabic names and terms in this book do not necessarily conform to the single classic standard, but instead represent common journalists' usage. Even this usage sometimes varies from place to place; I have chosen the form of a name or label most frequently used in a given area.

Allah: God.

Ayatollah: "Sign of God" or "Mirror of God." A high title for the most learned Shi'ite clerics, particularly prevalent in Iran.

Bedouin: Nomads who usually live in the desert.

Caliph: The Prophet's successor on earth, most often used to describe the Islamic leaders after Mohammed's death through the collapse of the Ottoman Empire in the early twentieth century.

Dar al Islam: House, Haven or Realm of Islam.

Dar al Harb: Realm of the non-Muslims.

Fatwa: Religious ruling by a Muslim cleric, considered as important or binding as a legal decision.

Hadith: One of the four sources of Islam, which also include the Koran, the Ijima (consensus) and Qiyas (analogy). The hadith include the reported sayings or actions of the Prophet Mohammed compiled two centuries after his death.

Hajj: Annual pilgrimage to the holy cities of Mecca and Medina, and one of the five pillars of Islam, which also include profession of the Faith (through repetition of the statement "There is no God but God, and Mohammed is his Prophet"), prayer five times a day, payment of alms or charity tax, and fasting during the holy month of Ramadan.

Hojatoleslam: "Authority on Islam." High title given Muslim religious scholars, most common in Iran.

Ikhwan: The Brethren or Brothers, which usually refers to specific groups in different places, not necessarily connected. Among the various Ikhwan groups of the twentieth century were the original society of fundamentalist warriors who fought for Abdel Aziz ibn Saud as he consolidated the Arabian peninsula into what was to become Saudi Arabia, and the society founded by Hassan al Banna in Egypt.

Imam: A religious leader. It can be used to refer to the leader of prayers on Friday, the Muslim Sabbath, or as a title indicating high esteem. Ayatollah Khomeini is often referred to as The Imam. In recent times, it is more commonly used by the Shi'ite sect, which believes that an imam can intercede with God and continue to interpret religious laws and traditions. Sunnis believe man communes directly with God.

Islam: "Submission" or "surrender" to God's will, as revealed to Mohammed.

Jihad: An "exertion"—usually meaning holy war or crusade—in the name of Islam against unbelievers or rivals.

Koran: The Muslim holy book, containing the revelations conveyed to Mohammed from God via the archangel Gabriel in the seventh century.

Mahdi: The "rightly guided one" awaited by Muslims to restore the original order and purity of the Islamic faith. Particularly important to the Shia who await the return of the Twelfth Imam, who went into occultation or hiding. Various figures in history have claimed to be Mahdis, then faded into history.

Majlis: An assembly or audience conducted by tribal or national leaders, and more recently the parliament in some Islamic societies.

Mullah: A general name for Islamic clerics, particularly among the Shia.

Muslim: A believer in Islam, one who has submitted to God.

Ramadan: The Islamic holy month, or the ninth month in the Islamic calendar during which Muslims fast from dawn to dusk to honor the period when Mohammed received his first revelations from God.

Sayyid: Religious title for particularly learned clerics, sometimes used in reference to descendants of Mohammed.

Sharia: The sacred law of Islam which governs all aspects of a Muslim's life. Literally, "the path to a water hole," or "the path to God."

Sheikh: A title of respect, generally for elders of the community and Muslim clerics, both Sunni and Shia.

Shia: Followers or partisans of Ali, the son-in-law and cousin of the Prophet Mohammed. A sect which split from the mainstream Sunni sect within thirty years of Mohammed's death in the greatest schism ever within Islam.

Shi'ite: A follower of the Shia faith.

Sunnis: Followers of the Sunna, the tradition of Muslims based on the life and actions of Mohammed. Sunnis are the largest sect of Islam.

Taqiya: Concealment of belief due to fear of repression or danger, particularly among the Shia.

Ulama: The body of learned advisors empowered to pronounce religious rulings.

Umma: The community of believers, or Muslims.

Valayat-e Faqih: Religious Guide, the most revered title of any Shi'ite leader in Iran.

Wahhabism: A fundamentalist doctrine in Saudi Arabia, named after Mohammed ibn Abdul Wahhab, a prominent eighteenth-century cleric. The doctrine used by Abdel Aziz ibn Saud to consolidate the tribes of the Arabian peninsula in the early 20th century.

Source Notes

The vast majority of new material in this book comes from personal coverage of the events, and from interviews conducted in Lebanon, Iran, Syria, Saudi Arabia, Kuwait, Bahrain, Jordan, Israel, Libya, Morocco, Algeria, Tunisia, Washington, London and Rome. Owing to the sensitive subject matter, most sources stipulated that they would talk only on condition that their names and specific titles were never used. I have honored those requests. Whenever possible, however, I have tried to cite backup material from other publications.

CHAPTER ONE

p. **16**   Robert Ames, a former: interviews, Beirut, April 1983, January and December 1984.

p. **16**   Lieutenant Joe Golebiowski: interview, Oct. 23, 1983.

p. **17**   Blood caked on: interview, Oct. 23, 1983.

p. **17**   Ahmed Shama, a U.S.: *Monday Morning* magazine, Dec. 19, 1984.

p. **18**   In 1983, more: wire service reports, Oct. 3, 1984.

p. **18**   In 1984, the: State Department figures quoted on ABC "Nightline," May 16, 1985.

p. **18**   "Normally, wars are": *Time*, Dec. 26, 1983.

p. **19**   Indeed, since the faith: Flora Lewis, "Upsurge in Islam," *New York Times* series, Dec. 28–31, 1979.

p. **20**   Third, the crusade: Thomas W. Lippman, *Islam: Politics and Religion in the Muslim World*, as quoted in Daniel Pipes, *In the Path of God*, p. 281.

p. **21**   Ayatollah Khomeini has: V. S. Naipaul, *Among the Believers*. p. 82.

p. **21**   More specifically, he said: Ayatollah Khomeini, *Islam and Revolution: Writings and Declarations of Imam Khomeini*, tr. Hamid Algar.

p. **22**   Welch was typing: interviews, September 1984.

p. **23**   "We are not": interview, Oct. 2, 1984.

p. **23**   Two greenish-black stone: visit to State Department, May 7, 1985, and *The Washington Post Weekly*, Feb. 4, 1985.

p. **24**   In an interview: interview, Washington, Aug. 7, 1984.

p. **24**   Among the other indicators: travels with Pope John Paul II to Brazil, Philippines, Germany, Pakistan, Japan, Guam and the U.S. in 1980 and 1981.

p. **24**   Ironically, he was fighting: personal coverage in South Africa, 1975–80.

p. **24**   "Religious intensity was": Edward Said, *Covering Islam*.

CHAPTER TWO

p. **26** The pastel walls: *Sunday Times*, London, Sept. 23, 1984.

p. **26** But by the spring: visit to Iran, March–April 1982.

p. **26** On a crisp: *ibid.*

p. **26** The occasion was: interviews, Bahrain, Jordan, May 1984, and Washington, August 1984; *Middle East Reporter*, Dec. 3, 1983; *International Herald Tribune*, April 7, 1982.

p. **27** "We shall export": "Excerpts from Speeches and Messages of Imam Khomeini on the Unity of the Muslims" (undated), distributed by the Ministry of Islamic Guidance, Tehran.

p. **27** The founder and: Khomeini/Algar, *Islam and Revolution*.

p. **27** Within days of: Foreign Broadcast Information Service (FBIS), Apr. 5, 1982, I-1.

p. **27** The Ayatollah often: Khomeini/Algar, *op. cit.*

p. **27** The men at: interviews with an Iranian diplomat, Bahrain, May 21, 1984, and interviews in Jordan, May 2, 1984; *International Herald Tribune*, May 7, 1982; *Middle East Reporter*, Dec. 3, 1983.

p. **28** The conclusions of: interview with an Iranian diplomat, May 21, 1984.

p. **28** "When they came": interview, May 21, 1984.

p. **28** "The turning point": interview, Jordan, May 2, 1984.

p. **29** Hundreds of thousands: visit to the Iranian war front during Operation Fateh in March 1982.

p. **29** Meanwhile, East bloc: interviews with Soviet diplomats, Beirut, 1983–84.

p. **29** In the Arab: interviews in Saudi Arabia during the 1981 Gulf Cooperation Council summit; interviews in Kuwait, May 5, 1982; interviews in Bahrain during the 1982 GCC summit.

p. **30** "The leaders of": interview with an Iranian diplomat, May 21, 1984.

p. **30** Some Gulf officials: interview, May 19, 1984.

p. **31** Exactly two years: interviews, Washington, August 1984, and Department of State document from the Mar. 1, 1984, seminar.

p. **31** Between 1925 and 1979: John Stempel, *Inside the Iranian Revolution*.

p. **32** Nicknamed Taleghani Center: interviews with Gulf security sources, May 1984.

p. **33** The preachers of: *ibid.*

p. **33** Most of the: interviews, Bahrain, May 22, and Washington, May 7, 1984; *Middle East Reporter*, Sept. 1 and Dec. 28, 1984.

p. **33** The crusade was: interviews, Washington, August 1984 and May 1985, and the Iranian Embassy in Bahrain, May 21, 1984.

p. **33** The ministry was: British Broadcasting Corp. Summary of World Broadcasts (BBC SWB), Nov. 7, 1984 (ME/7794/A/5).

p. **33** The same month: FBIS, Mar. 3, 1982, I-2.

p. **34** The combined efforts: interviews, Bahrain, May 22, 1984.

p. **34** They were not: interview with Dawa sources, June 1984, Washington interview, Aug. 7, 1984, and interviews with Gulf security sources, May 1984.

p. **34** The young men: interviews, Bahrain and Jordan in May, Syria in June and Washington in August 1984.

p. **34** The volunteers were: interviews, Bahrain, May 22, Damascus, June 5, and Washington, Aug. 7, 1984; *Jeune Afrique*, Jan. 25, 1984.

p. **35**   In early 1984: *Jeune Afrique*, Jan. 25, 1984.

p. **35**   Once trained and: interviews, in the Gulf, May 1984, in Damascus, May and June 1984, and in Beirut, October–December 1984.

p. **35**   An American professor: interviews, April and October 1984.

p. **36**   "America is now": *New York Times*, Dec. 30, 1983.

p. **36**   "Wars come to": Koran, sura 3:134, quoted in Alfred Guillaume, *Islam*.

p. **36**   One of the: interview, Bahrain, May 14, 1984.

p. **36**   The last note: "The Devil's War Against Islamic Iran," published in 1982 by the Iranian Revolutionary Guard Corps.

p. **37**   During the Fateh: visit to Tehran and the Iranian war front in March–April 1982.

p. **37**   A Western official: interview, Persian Gulf, May 1984.

p. **37**   In A.D. 680: Malise Ruthven, *Islam in the World*, pp. 188–89, and Edward Mortimer, *Faith and Power: The Politics of Islam*.

p. **38**   "The Imam Hussein": Mortimer, *op. cit.*, pp. 335–36.

p. **38**   "Hussein sacrificed his": *New York Times*, Oct. 8, 1984.

p. **38**   The word "assassin": Bernard Lewis, *The Assassins: A Radical Sect in Islam*, p. 12.

p. **39**   The first Assassins: Enno Franzius, *History of the Order of Assassins*, p. 34.

p. **39**   In his fiery: *ibid.*, pp. 35–36.

p. **39**   Retreating after a: Bernard Lewis, *op. cit.*

p. **39**   Marco Polo was: *ibid.*, pp. 7–8.

p. **40**   By the thirteenth: *ibid.*, p. 5.

p. **40**   The antagonism and: *ibid.*, p. 1.

p. **41**   Ayatollah Khomeini described: Khomeini/Algar, *op. cit.*

p. **42**   "The Islamic revolutionaries": Mortimer, *op. cit.*, p. 357.

p. **42**   Imam Khomeini's "vision": John Kifner, *New York Times*, April 13, 1982.

p. **42**   His specific power: David Hirst in *The Guardian*, London, March 17, 1979.

p. **42**   Boundaries should not: excerpts from Khomeini speeches.

p. **42**   "Not only does": Khomeini/Algar, *op. cit.*

p. **42**   "Islam wants all": excerpts from Khomeini speeches.

p. **43**   "The western media": *Tehran Times*, July 19, 1982, as quoted in James Bill and Carl Leiden, *Politics in the Middle East*, p. 399.

p. **43**   But for the average: Godfrey H. Jansen, *Militant Islam*, p. 15.

p. **44**   As the Iranian: *Middle East Reporter*, Feb. 16, 1985.

p. **44**   "We have arrived": *Jeune Afrique*, Feb. 16, 1985.

p. **44**   A Gulf cabinet: interview, Bahrain, May 21, 1984.

p. **45**   "You know and have seen": excerpts from Khomeini speeches.

p. **45**   As the Iranian: BBC SWB, Aug. 11, 1984 (ME 7719/A/3).

CHAPTER THREE

Most of the material for this chapter is based on interviews with Hamza akl Hamieh in July and December 1984, as well as my coverage of the last two of his six hijackings in 1981 and 1982, an attack led by Hamza on the Marines in Beirut in January 1984, and the aftermath of an operation he led to free Frank Regier, a kidnapped American professor, in the spring of 1984. I conducted interviews with

Les Bradley on May 14, 1984, in Kuwait, and by telephone on July 15, 1984, and several interviews with Nabih Berri and Colonel Akef Haidar, officials of the Shi'ite movement Amal in Lebanon, between 1981 and 1984. Only supplemental information or quotes from all of these sources are noted.

p. 49   At one stage: Ed Cody in *Washington Post* and John Kifner in *New York Times,* Feb. 26, 1982.
p. 50   "The leader was": Tom Baldwin, AP, Feb. 25, 1982.
p. 53   "Today at nine": NBC footage by Gary Fairman.
p. 54   As an Israeli: *New York Times,* Dec. 30, 1983.
p. 54   Earlier that month: Jack Reddon, UPI, Jan. 11, 1984.
p. 54   In the thirteen-century: Daniel Pipes, *In the Path of God,* p. 22.
p. 54   It is "an obligation": Godfrey H. Jansen, *Militant Islam,* p. 127.
p. 54   "Fighters went into": *ibid.,* pp. 127–28.
p. 55   In Arabic, *jihad: ibid.,* p. 28.
p. 55   It was a rallying cry: Pipes, *op. cit.,* p. 44.
p. 58   In early 1974: A. R. Norton doctoral thesis, "Harakat Amal and the Political Mobilization of the Shi'a of Lebanon."
p. 58   In Baalbeck a: *ibid.,* p. 81.
p. 60   More recently, exiled: Norton, "Political Violence and Shi'a Factionalism in Lebanon," *Middle East Insight,* Vol. 3, No. 2, p. 12, and interviews, Lebanon, 1984.
p. 60   After the revolution: Michael Fischer, *Iran: From Religious Dispute to Revolution,* p. 222.
p. 61   The Amal leader: David Ottaway in *Washington Post,* Dec. 12, 1983.
p. 61   In late 1983: *ibid.*
p. 62   "To be a Muslim": John Voll, *Islam: Continuity and Change in the Modern World,* p. 46.
p. 63   "Islam is not": Godfrey Jansen, *op. cit.,* p. 17.
p. 63   "It is a complete": Khurshid Ahmad, p. 37.
p. 63   The Koran, the Hadith: Godfrey Jansen, *op. cit.,* p. 17.
p. 63   "For us Sunni": *Christian Science Monitor,* July 23, 1984.
p. 63   For the Shia: *ibid.,* July 25, 1984.
p. 64   The romantic concepts: Eric Rouleau, "Khomeini's Iran," *Foreign Affairs,* Fall 1980.
p. 64   Indeed, the Shia: David Hirst in *The Guardian,* Mar. 17, 1979.
p. 64   "By the end": Edward Mortimer, *Faith and Power,* p. 87.
p. 65   For Muslims, the failure: Donald Neff, *Warriors for Jerusalem.*
p. 65   The loss of morale: Mortimer, *op. cit.;* Godfrey Jansen, *op. cit.;* Malise Ruthven, *Islam in the World.*
p. 65   "This phenomenon in Lebanon": *Washington Post,* Dec. 12, 1983.
p. 66   "The religious reaction": Mortimer, *op. cit.,* p. 286.
p. 66   The Arab offensive: Yvonne Haddad, "The Arab-Israeli Wars, Nasserism, and the Affirmation of Islamic Identity," as quoted in Pipes, *op. cit.*
p. 66   "Heightened religious fervor": Martin Kramer, *Political Islam,* as quoted in Pipes, *op. cit.,* p. 285.
p. 66   And one author: Raphael Israeli, *The New Wave of Islam,* as quoted in Pipes, *op. cit.,* p. 285.

p. **66** Mortimer explained "Above all, the morale": Mortimer, *op. cit.*, p. 289.

p. **66** "The Islamic spirit": Pipes, *op. cit.*, p. 295.

p. **67** Britain's former Foreign: interview in Saudi Arabia during visit by Lord Carrington, November 1981.

p. **67** "The expectations of": Tom Friedman in *New York Times Magazine*, Oct. 7, 1984.

p. **67** The clout and: interviews, Saudi Arabia, November 1981.

p. **67** The practice applied: interviews, Lebanon, 1981–84.

p. **68** "The seeming extremist": *New York Times*, Dec. 30, 1983.

CHAPTER FOUR

I was one of the few foreign correspondents who witnessed both the arrival and the departure of the Multi-National Force. Most of the material on the Marine bombing is based on personal coverage and interviews in Beirut, before and after the attack. I also conducted several subsequent interviews with American, French and Italian MNF officers, as well as with Lebanese, Iranians and Syrians. Most notable among the Lebanese were cadre of Hizbollah, or "the Party of God," and Sheikh Mohammed Hussein Fadlallah, with whom I had three long sessions in November 1983 and June and October 1984, and other shorter interviews.

I also covered the two bombings of the U.S. Embassy in April 1983 and the embassy annex in September 1984, the Chouf war in the fall of 1983, the Shi'ite takeover of West Beirut in February 1984, and the abductions of or attacks on American individuals between 1982 and 1984. In most cases, only supplemental interviews have been noted.

p. **71** Corporal Martucci, who: *Congressional Report*, December 1983.

p. **71** But only one: *ibid.*

p. **73** So the Israeli Air Force: interviews, Jerusalem, January 1984.

p. **74** Phil Taubman of: Phil Taubman, *New York Times Magazine*, April 14, 1985.

p. **74** The congressional report: *Congressional Report*, December 1983.

p. **74** The dissenting view: *ibid.*, minority views of David Martin (R–NY) and Bob Stump (R–Ariz).

p. **78** Colonel Fintel, the chief: interview, Oct. 7, 1983.

p. **80** Not until after: interview with a U.S. official, Jan. 16, 1984.

p. **81** "Our only goal": Robert Fisk, *The Times*, London, Nov. 3, 1983.

p. **81** He was another: interviews, August 1984.

p. **82** Musawi said of it: *Middle East Reporter*, Dec. 3, 1983.

p. **83** Shortly before the U.S.: *Monday Morning* magazine, Oct. 31, 1983.

p. **83** "The Islamic revolution": *Middle East Reporter*, Dec. 3, 1983.

p. **83** Sheikh Ibrahim al Amin: *Ash Shiraa* magazine, Nov. 29, 1983.

p. **83** Less than a week: David Ignatius, *Wall Street Journal*, Nov. 4, 1983.

p. **83** "I salute this": *ABC Close-up*, "War and Power: The Rise of Syria," June 14, 1984.

p. **83** "Iran had nothing": Beirut *Daily Star*, May 26, 1984.

p. **83** "If America kills": ABC, *op. cit.*

p. **84** An Amal official: Tom Friedman, *New York Times*, Oct. 23, 1983.

p. **84**   Colonel Ghazi Kenaan: interviews, Beirut, November and December 1983, Damascus, June 1984, and Washington, August 1984.

p. **85**   Baalbeck and the: David Ottaway, *Washington Post*, Dec. 12, 1983.

p. **85**   The 1973 constitution (footnote): interview, Damascus, June 1984.

p. **87**   One often mentioned: interviews, Bahrain, May 1984; Damascus, June 1984; Beirut, 1984; and Washington, May 7, 1985.

p. **87**   "It is a post": interview, Bahrain, May 21, 1984.

p. **87**   In the week before: interviews, Jordan and Damascus, May 1984.

p. **87**   As the Pentagon: Department of Defense Report, Dec. 20, 1983.

p. **88**   At any rate: interviews, Lebanon, October and December 1984.

p. **88**   U.S. military sources: interviews, Lebanon, June, July and October, 1984; and in Washington, August 1984. And *Washington Post* series "The Terror Factor," Feb. 1, 1984.

p. **88**   Musawi reportedly went: *Washington Post* series.

p. **88**   Iranian Chargé d'Affaires: interview, Oct. 26, 1983.

p. **89**   Roughly ten minutes: visit to Iranian Embassy in Beirut, Oct. 26, 1983; interviews, Beirut, October and November 1983, and *Wall Street Journal*, Nov. 4, 1983.

p. **90**   Intelligence agents from (and section following): interviews, Syria, May and June 1984; Washington, August 1984 and May 1985; *Jeune Afrique*, Jan. 25, 1984, and visit to Tomb of Zeinab, May 1984.

p. **92**   The chief representative: interview, June 5, 1984.

p. **93**   And he said of: UPI, May 28, 1984.

p. **93**   To a local paper: Beirut *Daily Star*, Jan. 19, 1985.

p. **94**   Hojatoleslam Rafsanjani urged: Reuters, Jan. 31, 1985.

p. **94**   "Islam is a": Beirut *Daily Star*, Aug. 18, 1984.

p. **94**   But Sheikh Fadlallah: *Monday Morning* magazine, Oct. 15, 1984.

p. **95**   And he charged: Beirut *Daily Star*, Aug. 18, 1984.

p. **95**   "Hizbollah was born": *ibid.*

p. **95**   "Hizbollah is a party": *Monday Morning* magazine, Oct. 15, 1984.

p. **95**   "Although there are": Beirut *Daily Star*, Aug. 18, 1984.

p. **95**   Of the Americans: *ibid.*, Jan. 19, 1985.

p. **96**   His line on: *Monday Morning* magazine, Oct. 15, 1984.

p. **96**   On March 8, 1985: *New York Times*, Mar. 9, 1985; *Newsweek*, Mar. 18, 1985; CBS News and ABC News, Mar. 8, 1985.

p. **97**   Two months after: Bob Woodward and Charles Babcock, *Washington Post*, May 12, 1985.

p. **97**   Without the U.S.: Stuart Taylor, *New York Times*, May 13, 1985.

p. **97**   On February 6, 1984: U.S. press pool report.

p. **98**   Just seven days: Reuters, Jan. 30, 1984.

p. **99**   "One day they": Tom Friedman, *New York Times Magazine*, Apr. 8, 1984.

p. **99**   The first public: *Middle East Reporter*, Nov. 1, 1983.

p. **99**   Shortly thereafter: *ibid.*, Nov. 23, 1983.

p. **99**   President Reagan told: *Washington Post*, Dec. 10, 1983.

p. **99**   General Joy said: interview, January 1984, and *Monday Morning* magazine, Dec. 19, 1983.

p. **101**   "I suppose it's": *Monday Morning* magazine, Jan. 23, 1984.

p. **101**   "AUB and Kerr": *Monday Morning* magazine, Aug. 18, 1984.

p. 103   Two former AUB: *New York Times*, Mar. 11, 1984.
p. 104   "Hizbollah will execute": Beirut *Daily Star*, May 30, 1984.
p. 108   "You, governor of": *Washington Post*, Sept. 21, 1984.
p. 109   During the presidential: *New York Times*, Oct. 28, 1984.

CHAPTER FIVE

Much of the material in this chapter is based on trips to Kuwait and Bahrain between 1982 and 1984, including the annual Gulf Cooperation Council summits in Bahrain (1982) and Kuwait (1984).

p. 111   The twenty-one young: interview with Mark Higson and other envoys in Kuwait, May 13, 1984.
p. 112   "They talked to": interview, Kuwait, May 16, 1984.
p. 112   They acted "like": *Time*, Apr. 8, 1984.
p. 112   "If everything had": interview, Kuwait, May 13, 1984.
p. 112   Ambassador Jean Bressot: *Time*, Dec. 26, 1983.
p. 113   Shuaiba was to: *Monday Morning* magazine, Dec. 19, 1983.
p. 113   And a Western: interview, Kuwait, May 13, 1984.
p. 113   The blasts took: *ibid.*, May 16, 1984.
p. 114   The news stunned: visits, Bahrain, 1982, 1984.
p. 115   All the ruling royal: James Bill, *Middle East Insight*, January–February 1984.
p. 115   The plan for: interviews, Bahrain, November 1982, May 1984.
p. 115   "We already had": interview with a Bahraini official, May 22, 1984.
p. 116   Most of the: interview with Gulf security source, May 1984.
p. 116   Nevertheless, on the: *Middle East Reporter*, Jan. 15, 1982.
p. 116   Officials alleged that: interview, Bahrain, May 1984.
p. 116   Dr. Tariq al Moayyed: *Newsweek*, May 31, 1982.
p. 116   A few days after: *Middle East Reporter*, Dec. 16, 1983.
p. 116   As one official: interview with Gulf security source, May 1984.
p. 116   And the trail led: interviews, Bahrain, May 1984.
p. 117   "We regarded it": interview with security sources, May 1984.
p. 117   Moudarrissi rapidly rallied: interviews, Bahrain, May 1984.
p. 117   He "preached the": interviews, Bahrain.
p. 118   The contacts between: interviews with diplomats, Bahrain, May 1984.
p. 118   The prosecution's statement: *Middle East Reporter*, Mar. 1, 1982.
p. 118   The highest government: interviews, Bahrain, May 1984.
p. 118   "The coup thing": interview, Bahrain, May 22, 1984.
p. 119   In the 1985 elections: *Middle East Reporter*, Mar. 2, 1985, and *As Safir*, March 1985.
p. 119   Other signs were: visits to Kuwait, May 1982 and May 1984.
p. 120   One professor, a Shia: interview, Kuwait, May 15, 1984.
p. 120   In late 1984: Judith Miller, *New York Times*, Dec. 17, 1984.
p. 121   In 1979, the U.S.: interviews, Kuwait, May 1982 and May 1984.
p. 121   The only early: *Monday Morning* magazine, Dec. 19, 1983.
p. 121   There had been not: interview, Kuwait, May 13, 1984.

p. **121** The bombings turned: visit to Kuwait, and *Monday Morning* magazine, Dec. 19, 1983.

p. **122** And discussion began: interviews, Beirut, autumn 1984, and Washington, August 1984.

p. **122** But more alarming: *Manassas Journal Messenger,* Nov. 29, 1983, and interviews, Washington, August 1984.

p. **123** At a conference: *Time,* Dec. 26, 1983.

p. **123** Dennis Hays, president: *Monday Morning* magazine, Dec. 19, 1983.

p. **123** Six months after: visit to Kuwait, May 1984.

p. **124** "There's been a little": interview, Kuwait, May 15, 1984.

p. **124** When I asked: interview, Kuwait, May 15, 1984.

p. **124** The twenty-one men responsible: interviews, Kuwait, May 1984.

p. **124** In 1982, the Iraqi: interviews, Kuwait, May 1984, and Damascus, June 5, 1984.

p. **125** Abdel Aziz Hussein: *New York Times,* Dec. 12, 1983.

p. **125** Sheikh Jaber al Ahmed: Reuters, Feb. 9, 1984.

p. **125** But in the end: interview, Kuwait, May 13, 1984.

p. **125** Benaid al Qarr: visits, Kuwait, May–June 1982 and May 1984.

p. **126** In the Gulf: interview, May 22, 1984.

p. **126** As Ayatollah Khomeini: Khomeini/Algar, *Islam and Revolution.*

p. **127** Kuwait also expelled: interview, Kuwait, May 14, 1984.

p. **127** Both clerics headed: interview, Kuwait, May 13, 1984.

p. **127** "If there is": interview, Kuwait, May 14, 1984.

p. **127** Sheikh Shirazi was: interview with Gulf security sources, May 1984.

p. **127** "The bombers were": interview, Kuwait, May 13, 1984.

p. **128** "I see the Islamic": interview, Bahrain, May 22, 1984.

p. **128** And it is virtually: interview with Abdullah, Kuwait, May 13, 1984.

p. **129** But the Shia pay: Eric Rouleau, "Khomeini's Iran," *Foreign Affairs,* 1980, p. 5.

p. **129** Six months after: interview, Kuwait, May 1984.

p. **129** Abdel, for instance: interview with Abdel, June 1982.

p. **130** "One of the problems": interview, May 1984.

p. **130** "The Kuwaitis told": interview, Kuwait, May 13, 1984.

p. **131** "We are going": interview, Kuwait, May 11, 1984.

p. **131** "Before the coup plot": interview, May 1984.

p. **131** Indeed they were: interview with a Gulf security source, May 1984.

p. **131** The Interior Minister: British Broadcasting Corp. Summary of World Broadcasts (BBC SWB), June 8, 1984, p. 5.

p. **131** Two months after: *Gulf Daily News,* May 27, 1984.

p. **132** Diplomats put the figure: interviews during 1982 and 1984, annual Gulf Cooperation Council summits in Bahrain and Kuwait.

p. **132** Interestingly, most of: interviews, Kuwait, May 1984.

p. **132** The Lebanese connection: interviews with diplomatic sources in Kuwait, May 1984, and Beirut, October and December 1984.

p. **133** Shortly before midnight: *Sunday Times,* London, Dec. 9, 1984.

p. **133** Kuwait Airways Flight 221 (and the section following): *Middle East Reporter,* AP, UPI and Reuters news reports, Dec. 4–14, 1984; *Time* and *Newsweek,* Dec. 17 and 24, 1984.

p. **136** Other times he was: AP, reprinted in the Beirut *Daily Star*, Dec. 11, 1984.

p. **136** The hijackers' moods: UPI, Dec. 10, 1984.

p. **136** British flight engineer: BBC World Service, Dec. 24, 1984.

p. **136** But the torture: *Time*, Dec. 24, 1984.

p. **137** But then it warned: Reuters, Feb. 7, 1985.

p. **137** In a separate: *Middle East Reporter*, Dec. 10, 1984.

p. **138** In New York, the Political: AP, Dec. 7, 1984.

p. **139** "When they arrived": UPI, reprinted in the Beirut *Daily Star*, Dec. 10, 1984.

p. **139** Costa, his eyes: Reuters, Dec. 9, 1984.

p. **139** Greeting the returning: *Middle East Reporter*, Dec. 11, 1984.

p. **139** And, once the two: *Time*, Dec. 24, 1984.

p. **139** Others charged that: *New York Times*, Dec. 23, 1984.

p. **140** Additional accusations added: *ibid.*, Dec. 18, 1984.

p. **140** Another Pakistani said: Beirut *Daily Star*, Dec. 12, 1984.

p. **140** Western sources in Beirut: interview, Dec. 10, 1984.

p. **140** *The New York Times* quoted: Reprinted in the *International Herald Tribune*, Dec. 8, 1984.

p. **140** And another U.S.: *Time*, Dec. 24, 1984.

p. **141** The Kuwaiti ambassador: UPI, reprinted in the Beirut *Daily Star*, Dec. 15, 1984.

p. **141** And the son: John Kifner, *New York Times*, Dec. 18, 1984.

p. **141** However, most of: AP, reprinted in the Beirut *Daily Star*, Dec. 11, 1984.

p. **141** Captain Clark commented: *Middle East Reporter*, Dec. 13, 1984.

p. **141** Iran defused the: *ibid.*, Dec. 11, 1984.

p. **141** And Prime Minister: AP, reprinted in the *International Herald Tribune*, Dec. 14, 1984.

p. **141** And he rejected: *Los Angeles Times*, reprinted in *The Ann Arbor News*, Dec. 14, 1984, and *Time*, Dec. 24, 1984.

p. **142** In fact, U.S. military: interview, Beirut, Dec. 10, 1984.

p. **142** Beirut was considered: interviews, Beirut, December 1984.

p. **143** "There was preparedness": *New York Times*, Dec. 23, 1984.

p. **143** Indeed, many Americans: residence in Beirut in December 1984.

p. **143** The mixture of: CBS News, quoted in an AP report, Dec. 9, 1984.

p. **143** "There was simply": Op Ed page, *New York Times*, Dec. 16, 1984.

p. **144** But the reality: Charles Wallace, *Los Angeles Times*, Dec. 13, 1984.

p. **144** The two ceremonies: *New York Times*, Dec. 18, 1984.

p. **145** In early 1985: Beirut *Daily Star*, Mar. 25, 1985.

p. **145** Then on May 16: UPI, May 16, 1985.

p. **145** Several high: interviews, Washington, May 1985.

p. **145** Nine days after: *New York Times*, May 26, 1985.

CHAPTER SIX

p. **147**   At 5:20 A.M.: David Holden and Richard Johns, *The House of Saud*, pp. 512–13.

p. **147**   The answers slowly: *Keesing's Contemporary Archives*, May 16, 1980, p. 30247.

p. **148**   Saudi Arabian officials: Holden/Johns, *op. cit.*

p. **148**   In the end: *Keesing's*, May 16, 1980.

p. **148**   At least two thousand: interview with a U.S. military source, January 1985.

p. **148**   At least 255: *Keesing's*, May 16, 1980.

p. **149**   But in this: Holden/Johns, *op. cit.*, p. 525.

p. **150**   Unimpeded by religious: Bill/Leiden, *Politics in the Middle East*, p. 404.

p. **150**   The subsequent clashes: Foreign Broadcast Information Service (FBIS), Dec. 3, and *Facts on File*, Dec. 7, 1979.

p. **150**   American columnist Carl Rowan: article reprinted in *Reader's Digest*, April 1980.

p. **150**   But former CIA: *ibid.*

p. **151**   Although relations had: interviews, November 1981, and Holden/Johns, *op. cit.*, p. 498.

p. **152**   The Grand Mosque takeover: *New York Times*, Feb. 25, 1980.

p. **152**   The chief original: Mortimer, *Faith and Power;* Holden/Johns, *op. cit.*, p. 182.

p. **152**   Sheikh Baz's (footnote): visit to Saudi Arabia, 1983.

p. **152**   Indeed, he had: Holden/Johns, *op. cit.*, p. 515.

p. **152**   And he began advocating: William B. Quandt, *Saudi Arabia in the 1980s*, p. 94, and Holden/Johns, *op. cit.*, p. 515.

p. **152**   The Saud "worship": Ruthven, *Islam in the World*, p. 30.

p. **152**   And he wrote: *New York Times*, Feb. 25, 1980.

p. **153**   Juhaiman's following grew: "The House of Saud," chapter by James Buchan in Holden/Johns, *op. cit.*, pp. 514–18.

p. **153**   "It's like the": quoted by Joseph Kraft in *The New Yorker*, July 4, 1983.

p. **153**   A long history: Ruthven, *op. cit.*, p. 31.

p. **153**   The Wahhabist Sunnis: Mortimer, *op. cit.*, pp. 63, 166.

p. **154**   Yet even after: interviews in Dhahran, Saudi Arabia, November 1981.

p. **154**   "Underlying those disturbances": Holden/Johns, *op. cit.*, p. 531.

p. **154**   Indeed, just a few: *Keesing's*, May 16, 1980.

p. **155**   In his capacity (footnote): Mortimer, *op. cit.*, p. 182.

p. **155**   Police cracked down: *Washington Post*, May 23, 1980.

p. **155**   The royal family: *Facts on File*, Mar. 14, and *Washington Post*, May 23, 1980.

p. **155**   And smaller steps: Steve Hindy, AP, May 23, 1980.

p. **155**   While Saudis were: Mortimer, *op. cit.*, p. 183.

p. **156**   A Saudi ambassador: *New York Times*, Feb. 25, 1980.

p. **156**   High-ranking officials: interviews, Dhahran, November 1981, and Quandt, *op. cit.*, p. 97.

p. **156**   By the end of: interviews, Washington, August 1984.

p. **157**   The United States became: interviews, Washington, August 1984.

p. **157**   Shi'ism contains a: interview with Fuad Khuri, Beirut, December 1984.
p. **157**   "The simple-minded Sunni": Muhibbudeen al Khateeb, *Broad Aspects of the Shi'ite Religion*, Al Khutoot al-Areedah.
p. **157**   "There are plenty": interview, Damascus, June 5, 1984.
p. **157**   And an American: interview, Washington, Aug. 7, 1984.
p. **157**   One foreign envoy: interview, Washington, Aug. 7, 1984.
p. **158**   The small acts: interviews, Dhahran, November 1981.
p. **158**   A State Department: interview, Washington, Aug. 7, 1984.
p. **158**   The BBC monitoring: BBC, as quoted in Quandt, *op. cit.*, pp. 39–40.
p. **159**   The governor of Mecca: *Facts on File*, Oct. 16, 1981.
p. **159**   In Medina, hundreds: *Keesing's*, June 4, 1982.
p. **159**   Tehran Radio actually: *Facts on File*, Nov. 27, 1981.
p. **159**   Ayatollah Khomeini wrote: *Keesing's*, June 4, 1982.
p. **159**   The Hajj trouble: *Middle East Reporter*, Dec. 5, 1981.
p. **160**   "The Saudis went crazy": interview, Washington, Aug. 7, 1984.
p. **160**   Before dashing off: *Middle East* magazine, February 1982.
p. **160**   "There was a travel": interviews, Washington, August 1984.
p. **160**   The Saudis "hardly": Ruthven, *op. cit.*, p. 32.
p. **161**   A British specialist: Mortimer, *op. cit.*, p. 64.
p. **161**   One U.S. academic: Pipes, *In the Path of God*, p. 66.
p. **161**   He wanted to: Philip Hitti, as quoted in Bill/Leiden, *op. cit.*, p. 56.
p. **161**   In 1902, with: Mortimer, *op. cit.*, p. 168.
p. **161**   Explained one Arab: Ruthven, *op. cit.*, p. 27.
p. **162**   "From 1745 to": Pipes, *op. cit.*, p. 231.
p. **162**   "Islam reverted to": Ruthven, *op. cit.*, p. 28.
p. **162**   "The Saudi state": Mortimer, *op. cit.*, p. 168.
p. **162**   By 1955, Harry: *ibid.*, p. 169.
p. **162**   Abdullah Naseef, secretary: Ali Mahmoud, Associated Press, as reprinted in the Beirut *Daily Star*, Nov. 19, 1984.
p. **163**   Nonetheless, throughout the: Quandt, *op. cit.*, p. 3.
p. **163**   In 1966 King Faisal: Mortimer, *op. cit.*, p. 159.
p. **163**   "Without the aura": Quandt, *op. cit.*, p. 36.
p. **163**   Or as the Saudi: *New York Times*, Dec. 31, 1979.
p. **163**   Unlike the splinter: Ruthven, *op. cit.*, p. 181.
p. **163**   As the Ayatollah: Shaul Bakhash, *The Reign of the Ayatollahs*, p. 32.
p. **163**   But the approaches: Mortimer, *op. cit.*, pp. 171–74.
p. **164**   His son King Faisal: Ruthven, *op. cit.*, p. 200.
p. **164**   The Islamic prohibition: Mortimer, *op. cit.*, p. 175.
p. **164**   One Western ambassador: interview, November 1984.
p. **164**   A standard feature: visit to Saudi Arabia, November 1981.
p. **165**   "Militarily, politically, economically": Ruthven, *op. cit.*, p. 292.
p. **165**   Third, Western nations: Quandt, *op. cit.*, p. 139.
p. **165**   As one noted: Bill/Leiden, *op. cit.*, pp. 378–79.
p. **166**   The grateful words: Rowan, *op. cit.*
p. **167**   In 1981, outsiders: Joseph Fitchett, *International Herald Tribune*, Feb. 11, 1981.
p. **167**   The 1982 Hajj: Ruthven, *op. cit.*, p. 34, and interviews, Riyadh, 1983.
p. **167**   The Hajj trouble: Foreign Broadcast Information Service (FBIS), Apr. 6, 1982, I-1.

p. **167**   Saudi state radio: *Facts on File*, Nov. 5, 1982.

p. **167**   He was Hojatoleslam: *Keesing's*, Nov. 12, 1982.

p. **168**   According to one: Ruthven, *op. cit.*, pp. 33–40, and BBC Monitoring Service.

p. **168**   With an average: Ruthven, *op. cit.*, p. 29.

p. **168**   To the Shia: *ibid.*, p. 187.

p. **168**   More importantly, the: *ibid.*, p. 34.

p. **168**   Before the 1984: British Broadcasting Corp. Summary of World Broadcasts (BBC SWB/ME), July 11, 1982.

p. **168**   At a separate: *ibid.*, Aug. 2, 1984.

p. **169**   The wary Saudis: Kraft, *op. cit.*

p. **169**   On its Arabic: BBC SWB/ME, Sept. 17, 1974.

p. **169**   The Saudis, through: *ibid.*, Oct. 2, 1984.

p. **170**   As a British: Ruthven, *op. cit.*, p. 34.

p. **170**   When the heads: personal coverage of the GCC summit in Kuwait, November 1984.

p. **170**   Collectively, the GCC: *International Herald Tribune*, Sept. 1, 1984.

p. **170**   But the exercises: interviews at the GCC summit, November 1984.

p. **171**   Shortly after the: interview, December 1984.

p. **171**   More American civilians (footnote): interview, Washington, Aug. 6, 1984.

p. **171**   The day after: interview by James Adams, Oct. 18, 1984.

p. **171**   "The internal social": Bill/Leiden, *op. cit.*, p. 380.

CHAPTER SEVEN

p. **173**   President Anwar Sadat (and section following): *Washington Post* and *New York Times* accounts of the assassination, Oct. 7–14, 1981, and *Time* and *Newsweek*, Oct. 19, 1981.

p. **174**   "At first, I": David Ottaway, *Washington Post*, Oct. 7, 1981.

p. **175**   The main targets: *Time*, Sept. 21, 1981.

p. **175**   The Egyptian leader: *Newsweek*, Sept. 21, 1981.

p. **175**   In a session: *Time*, Sept. 21, 1981.

p. **176**   Another U.S. analyst: Olson, *Middle East Insight*, Mar. 9, 1984.

p. **176**   Sadat's unwavering loyalty: *Newsweek*, Oct. 19, 1981.

p. **177**   Yet within hours: *Middle East Reporter*, Oct. 17, 1981.

p. **178**   Modern fundamentalism in: Mortimer, *Faith and Power*, pp. 252–54.

p. **178**   It was "the first": Richard P. Mitchell, *The Society of Muslim Brothers*.

p. **179**   From 1928 through: Mortimer, *op. cit.*, pp. 252–56.

p. **179**   The movement evolved: *ibid.*, pp. 254–56.

p. **179**   A former Egyptian: *Middle East Reporter*, Oct. 17, 1981.

p. **179**   Taking over after: Ruthven, *Islam in the World*, and Mortimer, *op. cit.*

p. **180**   Sadat began incurring: Ruthven, *op. cit.*, pp. 314–15.

p. **180**   More importantly, Sadat: Robert Fisk, *The Times*, London, Oct. 14, 1981.

p. **180**   "Throughout the 1970s": Ruthven, *op. cit.*, p. 318.

p. **180**   As a result: *ibid.*, p. 315.

p. **181**   One State Department: *Newsweek*, Oct. 19, 1981.

p. **181**   Despite the government: *Middle East* magazine, January 1982.

p. **181** The Islamic Liberation: *Middle East Reporter*, Oct. 17, 1981.
p. **181** Among a host: *ibid.*
p. **181** A subsequent disclosure: Loren Jenkins, *Washington Post*, Oct. 16, 1981.
p. **182** "I am guilty": *New York Times*, Dec. 1, 1981.
p. **182** A fifty-four-page: *Middle East Reporter*, Dec. 16, 1981.
p. **183** Perhaps the most: *ibid.*, June 5, 1982.
p. **184** When the court session: *ibid.*, Mar. 13, 1982.
p. **184** Just ten days: interview, David Ottaway, May 1985.
p. **185** The depth of: *Middle East Reporter*, Dec. 21, 1981.
p. **186** Once again, the: *Newsweek*, Dec. 20, 1982.
p. **186** The scope of: *Christian Science Monitor*, May 19, 1982.
p. **187** The prisoners ended: *Newsweek*, Dec. 2, 1982.
p. **187** Most notable among: Reuters, Oct. 1, 1984.
p. **187** The crackdown did: *Washington Post*, Jan. 26, 1984.
p. **188** On January 18, 1985: *ibid.*
p. **188** By April 1985: *Middle East Reporter*, Apr. 6, 1985.
p. **189** The National Assembly: Judith Miller, *New York Times*, May 5, 1985.
p. **189** The government also: AP, May 9, 1985.
p. **189** The series of: *Middle East Reporter*, May 29, 1982.
p. **189** Crackling flames leapt (and the section following): based on wire service reports and on interviews with diplomats, January, October and November 1984.
p. **191** The wily monarch: AP as reprinted in Beirut *Daily Star*, Jan. 26, 1984.
p. **191** But the casualty: UPI as reprinted in Beirut *Daily Star*, Feb. 2, 1984.
p. **191** After Morocco had: *Monday Morning* magazine, Jan. 30, 1984.
p. **192** In Tunisia, authorities: *ibid.*, Jan. 9, 1984.
p. **192** Richard B. Parker: article by former Ambassador Parker, Op Ed page, *New York Times*, Feb. 3, 1984.
p. **193** With its high-rise: based on visits in 1974, 1981 and 1982.
p. **193** Nevertheless, fundamentalism became: *Middle East Reporter*, Nov. 7, 1984.
p. **193** The Islamic Tendency: *New York Times*, Jan. 9, 1984.
p. **194** A resident British: interview, Nov. 21, 1984.
p. **194** In late 1984: *Monday Morning* magazine, Nov. 26, 1984.
p. **195** Poorer but more: visit to Morocco, November 1981.
p. **195** Among the early signs: Mortimer, *op. cit.*
p. **195** In 1982 and 1983: *Monday Morning* magazine, Jan. 30, 1984.
p. **195** At the trial: BBC SWB, Aug. 2, 1984.
p. **196** Ambassador Parker wrote: Parker, *op. cit.*
p. **196** The tremors were: UPI, Jan. 25, 1984.
p. **197** This first generation: interview, Nov. 21, 1984.
p. **197** In Morocco, food: *New York Times* as reprinted in *International Herald Tribune*, May 4, 1954.
p. **197** Extensive corruption and: E. J. Kahn in *The New Yorker*, July 9, 1984.
p. **198** But the movement: interviews, Damascus, June 1984.
p. **198** The French became: interview, Damascus, June 4, 1984.
p. **198** Indeed, one Iranian: interview, May 21, 1984.
p. **199** Tunisian officials may: Reuters, May 15, 1984.

p. **199**   Three were sentenced: *ibid.*, May 23, 1984.

p. **199**   The opposition Movement: Reuters as reprinted in Beirut *Daily Star*, June 13, 1984.

p. **199**   But on the first: Reuters, Jan. 5, 1985.

p. **199**   An ITM spokesman: *New York Times*, Jan. 9, 1984.

p. **200**   In Morocco, King: Reuters, Feb. 24, 1984.

p. **200**   Ambassador Parker concluded: Parker, *op. cit.*

p. **200**   Prisoners rotated in: *Washington Post*, Apr. 22, 1985.

p. **201**   Dr. Hassan Turabi: *Wall Street Journal*, Apr. 17, 1984.

p. **202**   Strapped to a chair: AP, May 12, 1984.

p. **202**   Prison orderlies often: eyewitness description from John Borrell.

p. **202**   Liquor, like Western-style: *ibid.* and AP, June 20, 1984.

p. **202**   The sequence of events: *Middle East Reporter*, Mar. 23, 1985.

p. **203**   In a 1984: *Wall Street Journal*, June 11, 1984.

p. **203**   "Until last year": interview by John Borrell, 1984.

p. **203**   Police statistics did: *Monday Morning* magazine, Oct. 15, 1984.

p. **203**   Yet the criteria (and section following): *New York Times*, Jan. 19 and 26, 1985, and AP as reprinted in Beirut *Daily Star*, Jan. 17 and 22, 1985.

p. **205**   In December 1984: *Middle East Reporter*, Jan. 5, 1985.

p. **206**   By April 1984: *Washington Post*, Aug. 30, 1984, and Reuters as reprinted in Beirut *Daily Star*, Jan. 22, 1985.

p. **206**   More important perhaps: *Washington Post*, Sept. 12, 1984.

p. **206**   Minister of Information: interview by John Borrell, 1984.

p. **207**   Of Iran, he added: Wilhelm Dietl, *Holy War.*

p. **207**   Now the Sudanese: *Middle East Reporter*, Jan. 5, 1985.

p. **208**   Washington began to: interview, Washington, Aug. 8, 1984.

p. **209**   Calling them "brothers": *Middle East Reporter*, Mar. 23, and UPI, Mar. 11, 1985.

p. **209**   More than 120: UPI in *New York Times*, Mar. 12, 1985.

p. **209**   The strikers then: AP as reprinted in Beirut *Daily Star*, Apr. 4, and *Washington Post*, Apr. 5, 1985.

p. **210**   One demonstrator: *Washington Post*, Apr. 1, 1985.

p. **210**   Indeed, one longtime: *ibid.*, Apr. 7, 1985.

p. **210**   Among the first: *ibid.*, Apr. 22, 1985.

p. **210**   As Turabi: *ibid.*

p. **211**   In May 1984: Reuters, May 26, 1984.

p. **211**   At the same time: interviews, Jordan, May and November 1984.

p. **212**   Algeria: based also on a visit and interviews, February 1983.

p. **212**   In April 1984: *Middle East Reporter*, Jan. 1, 1982.

p. **213**   About the same time: Reuters as reprinted in Beirut *Daily Star*, May 14, 1984.

p. **213**   A French ambassador: interview, June 1984.

p. **213**   Although U.S. officials: AP, June 7, and UPI, June 5, 1984.

p. **214**   The Palestinians: based also on interviews in Damascus, June 1984, and Jordan, May and November 1984.

p. **214**   Even the Palestine: BBC SWB, Oct. 24, 1984.

p. **214**   "Fundamentalism is a": interview with Dr. Nasr, May 1984, and *The Guardian*, Mar. 17, 1982.

CHAPTER EIGHT

Much of the material in this chapter is based on personal reporting from the beginning of the Israeli invasion of Lebanon in 1982, as well as trips to the south. Timur Goksel, spokesman for the United Nations Interim Force in Lebanon, also played a major role in providing information and perspective on almost a weekly basis between 1982 and 1985.

p. **215** Allon Tsur never: telephone interview with Ran Barnur in Israel, Mar. 31, 1985.

p. **216** "No one here": AP as reprinted in Beirut *Daily Star*, Oct. 22, 1984.

p. **216** The same week: Reuters as reprinted in Beirut *Daily Star*, Oct. 15, 1984.

p. **217** And the number: figures based on *Information Please Almanac, 1985* censuses. For the U.S. population, the 1970 census was used.

p. **217** Less than three: *Time*, Feb. 28, 1985.

p. **217** One of the: based on personal coverage of the two earlier series of talks between the Lebanese and the Israelis.

p. **218** Between 6 and 7 A.M.: telephone interview with Timur Goksel, Mar. 10, 1985.

p. **218** The Israeli Army: Tom Friedman, *New York Times*, Feb. 18, 1985.

p. **218** The last Israeli convoy: Ed Walsh in *Washington Post*, and *Sunday Times*, London, both Feb. 17, 1985.

p. **219** As his troops: *New York Times*, Feb. 27, 1985.

p. **219** And a captain: *Washington Post*, Jan. 26, 1985.

p. **219** At the time: *New York Times*, Jan. 20, 1985.

p. **219** And shortly after: UPI as reprinted in Beirut *Daily Star*, Feb. 4, 1985.

p. **220** An editorial in: *Maclean's Magazine*, Jan. 28, 1985.

p. **220** Maarakeh (and section following): based on a visit to the village and the south, July 1984.

p. **220** "For seven or": *New York Times*, July 22, 1984.

p. **221** In the Shi'ites': based on interviews with diplomats, international relief agency workers and residents in the south, 1983–84, including articles written for *The Sunday Times*, London, and *The Christian Science Monitor*.

p. **222** Coexistence with the: Augustus Richard Norton in *Middle East Insight*, Mar.–Apr. 1983.

p. **222** The second turning: *Middle East Reporter*, Dec. 17, 1983.

p. **223** "The terrorist looked": *Newsweek*, Nov. 14, 1983.

p. **223** As one of: *Monday Morning* magazine, Apr. 22, 1984.

p. **223** A Tyre merchant: *Washington Post*, Feb. 21, 1985.

p. **223** The clattering roar: based on subsequent interviews with UNIFIL officials and Maarakeh residents, July 1984.

p. **223** It was not: Beirut *Daily Star*, Feb. 1, 1984.

p. **223** "The old and": interview, July 1984.

p. **224** "It was the": interview, July 1984.

p. **224** The IDF also virtually: personal coverage during trips to the south in 1984.

p. **224** Sheikh Ragheb Harb: *The Times*, London, Feb. 23, 1984.

p. **225** But the Shia: interviews with Hamza akl Hamieh and Amal officials, and *Monday Morning* magazine, June 24, 1984.

p. **225** With each new (and section following): visit to Maarakeh, July 1984.
p. **226** "Israel thinks Maarakeh": interview with Khalil Jaradi, July 3, 1984.
p. **226** Seven months later: Beirut *Daily Star*, Feb. 1, 1985.
p. **227** Jaradi and other: *The Times*, London, Mar. 2, 1985, and Beirut *Daily Star*, Feb. 1, 1985.
p. **227** Indeed, he had: Beirut *Daily Star*, Oct. 31, 1984.
p. **227** One of his: *ibid.*, Feb. 1, 1985.
p. **228** Jaradi expected the: AP as reprinted in Beirut *Daily Star*, Feb. 26, 1985.
p. **228** The reaction among: *Washington Post* and *New York Times*, Feb. 19, 1985.
p. **228** The forty-eight-page manifesto: *Middle East Reporter*, Feb. 23, 1985.
p. **229** As the Party: *Washington Post*, Feb. 20, 1985.
p. **229** Only about 10 percent: *New York Times*, Feb. 17, 1985.
p. **229** Indeed, on the day: *Washington Post*, Feb. 17, 1985.
p. **229** Ten days after: Beirut *Daily Star*, Feb. 27, 1985.
p. **230** An Israeli officer: *ibid.*, Feb. 22, 1985.
p. **230** On the same day: *ibid.*
p. **230** As dawn broke: United Nations sources.
p. **230** "It is working": *New York Times*, Mar. 3, 1985.
p. **230** And Defense Minister: Reuters as reprinted in Beirut *Daily Star*, Feb. 27, 1985.
p. **230** The Maarakeh husseiniyeh: Beirut *Daily Star*, Mar. 6, 1985.
p. **230** Several copies of: *New York Times* and *Washington Post*, Mar. 3, 1985.
p. **231** On March 4: telephone interview with U.N. sources, Mar. 10, and *New York Times* and *Washington Post*, Mar. 5, 1985.
p. **231** The Lebanese government: Beirut *Daily Star*, Mar. 6, 1985.
p. **231** At the mass: *ibid.*
p. **231** A British reporter: Robert Fisk in *The Times*, London, Mar. 6, 1985.
p. **232** Six days after: interview with U.N. sources, Mar. 10, and *New York Times* and *Washington Post*, Mar. 11, 1985.
p. **232** As the cleric: Beirut *Daily Star*, July 3, 1984.
p. **232** "While the Iranian": A. R. Norton in *Middle East Insight*, March–April 1983.
p. **232** Explained Sheikh Fadlallah: *Newsweek*, Mar. 18, 1985.
p. **232** The nightmare for: Tom Friedman in *The New York Times Magazine*, Jan. 20, 1985.
p. **233** In the first: *Middle East Reporter*, Mar. 2, 1985.
p. **233** As Timur Goksel: *Maclean's Magazine*, Feb. 25, 1985.
p. **233** Israeli Defense Minister: *Time*, Feb. 11, 1985.
p. **234** "Qiryat Shemona became": interview with Hirsh Goodman, Mar. 18, 1985.
p. **234** "When a door": Reuters as reprinted in Beirut *Daily Star* and *New York Times*, Feb. 18, 1985.
p. **234** As Eli Geva: *Al Fajr*, Oct. 5, 1984.
p. **234** Geva gained fame: *Washington Post*, Apr. 20, 1985.
p. **234** By February 1985: wire reports in Beirut *Daily Star*, Jan. 1, 1985.
p. **234** "I really don't": *New York Times* and Reuters as reprinted in Beirut *Daily Star*, Feb. 18, 1985.

p. **235**   Shortly after Peres': *Washington Post*, Feb. 18, 1985.
p. **235**   Said the town's: *Maclean's Magazine*, Feb. 25, 1985.
p. **235**   "If Israel withdraws": AP, Feb. 24, 1985.
p. **235**   Said an Amal: AP as reprinted in Beirut *Daily Star*, Feb. 26, 1985.
p. **235**   Added a young: *New York Times*, Mar. 13, 1985.
p. **235**   Nabih Berri, the: *ibid.*, Mar. 3, 1985.
p. **236**   Berri has never: based on several personal interviews between 1981 and 1984.
p. **237**   The day after: *Middle East Reporter*, Feb. 23, 1985.
p. **237**   A massive painting: based on three visits and interviews with Hizbollah officials in the fall of 1984.
p. **237**   General Orr admitted: wire services as reprinted in Beirut *Daily Star*, Feb. 20, 1985.
p. **237**   Another defense official: AP as reprinted in Beirut *Daily Star*, Jan. 21, 1985.
p. **237**   On a visit: *Middle East Reporter*, Feb. 23, 1985.
p. **238**   Moshe Maoz, chairman: Reuters, reprinted in Beirut *Daily Star*, Feb. 18, 1985.
p. **238**   Boasted a key: *Washington Post*, Feb. 21, 1985.
p. **238**   "One of the important": telephone interview, Mar. 18, 1985.
p. **238**   Rabin pledged: *Time*, Feb. 11, 1985.
p. **238**   As one member: Reuters pickup on *Newsweek* story, Jan. 22, 1985.
p. **239**   A headline in: Beirut *Daily Star*, Feb. 18, 1985.
p. **239**   Among the biggest: interview with Hirsh Goodman, Mar. 18, 1985.
p. **239**   The feelings among: *CBS Evening News*, Apr. 24, 1985.
p. **239**   Dov Tamari, author: Ed Walsh in *The Washington Post*, Apr. 20, 1985.
p. **239**   In March 1985: *The Times*, London, Mar. 15, 1985.
p. **240**   Ze'ev Schiff, military: Beirut *Daily Star*, Feb. 22, 1985.
p. **240**   Former Israeli Foreign: Reuters, reprinted in Beirut *Daily Star*, Feb. 18, 1985.
p. **241**   Esther Koenigsberg Bengigi: Tom Friedman in *New York Times Magazine*, Jan. 20, 1985.
p. **241**   As Goodman said: Goodman, *op. cit.*
p. **241**   The euphoric mood: telephone interview, April 14, 1985, and *New York Times Magazine*, Jan. 20, 1985.
p. **241**   Ran Barnur, the: telephone interview, Mar. 31, 1985.

CHAPTER NINE
p. **243**   Just inside the: UPI, December 2, 1984.
p. **244**   The gravity of: *Time*, Jan. 7, 1985.
p. **244**   After the second: AP, Oct. 20, 1984.
p. **244**   But even those: *Washington Post*, Mar. 2, 1985.
p. **244**   As a State: *New York Times*, Dec. 3, 1984.
p. **244**   In early 1985, the United States: interview, Consular Affairs, Department of State, Mar. 6, 1985.
p. **244**   The United States also: interview, Public Affairs, Department of State, Mar. 6, 1985.

p. 245   Brian Jenkins, the: Jenkins, *New Modes of Conflict.*

p. 246   Tom Friedman, who: *New York Times Magazine*, Oct. 7, 1984.

p. 247   And throughout 1984, Secretary: excerpts from Shultz speeches Apr. 3, Oct. 25 and Dec. 9, 1984, as reprinted in *U.S. News & World Report*, Dec. 24, 1984.

p. 248   On April 3, 1984: Leslie Gelb, *New York Times*, May 14, 1985.

p. 248   One prominent U.S.: interview, May 25, 1985.

p. 248   Stronger cases have: Op Ed page, *New York Times*, Nov. 4, 1984.

p. 249   Paul Wilkinson, a: *Christian Science Monitor*, Jan. 31, 1985.

p. 249   And George Ball: Ball, *New York Times*, reprinted in the *International Herald Tribune*, Dec. 18, 1984.

p. 250   "There are the": *New York Times*, Dec. 2, 1984.

p. 250   Or as Ball: George Ball, *op. cit.*

p. 250   After the 1984: Leslie Gelb, *op. cit.*

p. 250   *New York Times* columnist: Flora Lewis, *New York Times*, Dec. 28, 1984.

p. 251   And as a: R. K. Ramazani, "Temper the Containment of Iran."

p. 251   "The plain fact": Augustus Richard Norton, Op Ed page in *New York Times*, Sept. 26, 1984.

p. 252   The United States aborted: Ray Cline, *Secrets, Spies and Scholars.*

p. 252   In the 1960s: Wilbur Crane Eveland, *The Ropes of Sand.*

p. 252   "Since 1500 there": Godfrey Jansen, *New York Times Magazine*, Jan. 6, 1980.

p. 252   Earlier, Harvard's Wilfred: *New York Times*, Dec. 11, 1979.

p. 252   Dr. Marvin Zonis: *Time*, Apr. 16, 1979.

p. 253   The paranoia was: British Broadcasting Corp. Summary of World Broadcasts (BBC SWB/ME), Sept. 11, 1984.

p. 253   "The West—like": Ruthven, *Islam in the World*, p. 289.

p. 254   "My beloved listeners": Khomeini/Algar, *Islam and Revolution*, p. 298.

p. 254   Warned an Arab-born: Said, *Covering Islam*, p. 100.

p. 254   Egypt's state-controlled: Robert Reid, AP, reprinted in Beirut *Daily Star*, Sept. 26, 1984.

p. 254   After the 1984: *Middle East Reporter*, Dec. 12, 1984.

p. 255   And on the: Beirut *Daily Star*, Oct. 23, 1984.

p. 255   "Such passions and": *International Herald Tribune*, Oct. 19, 1984.

p. 255   Edward Said, noted: *U.S. News & World Report*, June 25, 1984.

p. 256   "The Prophet of": Ruthven, *op. cit.*, p. 345.

p. 256   "The very promise": Ruthven, *op. cit.*, p. 227.

p. 256   Fuad Khuri, author: interview, Beirut, Nov. 19, 1984.

p. 256   Iranian Revolutionary rule: Nikkie Keddie, *New York Times*, Dec. 11, 1979.

p. 256   Many believe that: Dr. Marvin Zonis, Department of State seminar, Mar. 1, 1984.

p. 256   In his controversial: Pipes, *In the Path of God*, pp. 135–38.

p. 257   Pipes has also: *ibid.*, pp. 332–33.

p. 257   Shaul Bakhash observes: Bakhash, *The Reign of the Ayatollahs*, p. 240.

p. 258   The chambermaid in: visit to Iran, March–April, 1982.

p. 258   In *Faith and Power:* Mortimer, *Faith and Power*, p. 405.

p. **259** Government officials in Indonesia: *Washington Post*, Feb. 25, 1985.

p. **259** In the same: *New York Times*, Sept. 28, 1984.

p. **259** And the Malaysian: *Newsweek*, Sept. 28, 1984.

p. **259** In the predominantly: *Washington Post*, reprinted in *Ann Arbor News*, Apr. 8, 1984.

p. **260** The Moro Liberation: interview with Gulf security sources, May 22, 1984.

p. **260** In Bangladesh, a: *New York Times*, Sept. 28, 1984; *Washington Post*, Feb. 25, 1984.

p. **260** Nor has the: paper delivered by Dr. Marvin Zonis, Department of State, Mar. 1, 1984.

p. **260** Despite an official: *Newsweek*, Mar. 12, 1984.

p. **260** Riots in 1983: Zonis, *op. cit.*

p. **261** Thirteen fundamentalists were: *Newsweek*, Mar. 12, 1984.

p. **261** In Bulgaria, more: *Christian Science Monitor*, Feb. 25, 1985.

p. **261** China accounts for: AP, May 26, 1984, and personal visit in August 1978.

p. **261** In Italy, President: *Arab News*, Dec. 12, 1984.

p. **261** In the long term, said Michael: Michael Fischer, *Iran: From Religious Dispute to Revolution*, p. ix.

p. **262** And of Muslims: David Hirst, *The Guardian*, Mar. 17, 1979.

p. **262** In 1983, the Reagan: interview, Department of State, Mar. 6, 1985.

p. **263** "The fact that": AP, Jan. 31, 1984, and Reuters, Jan. 25, 1984.

p. **263** "We could go": *New York Times*, Dec. 16, 1984.

p. **263** And Ball added: Ball, *op. cit.*

p. **263** And other unilateral: Robert Carswell, *Foreign Affairs*, winter 1981–82.

p. **263** Rhodesia, a nation: personal coverage of Rhodesia 1975–1980.

p. **264** Marvin Zonis, who: *New York Times*, Oct. 8, 1984.

p. **265** William Colby, a former: *New York Times*, July 13, 1984.

p. **265** Brian Jenkins has: *Los Angeles Times*, reprinted in *Ann Arbor News*, Oct. 30, 1984.

p. **265** Many Middle East analysts: Shireen Hunter, *New York Times*, Aug. 23, 1984.

p. **265** In 1921, Iran: Fischer, *Iran: From Religious Dispute to Revolution*, pp. 87–88.

p. **265** The Russians did: Fischer, *op. cit.*, p. 113.

p. **266** If nothing else: Khomeini/Algar, *op. cit.*

p. **266** James Bill, an: *American-Statesman*, Nov. 14, 1984.

p. **266** R. K. Ramazani: Ramazani, *op. cit.*

p. **267** Zonis suggested a: Zonis, *op. cit.*

p. **268** Ramazani commented: Ramazani, *op. cit.*

p. **268** The long process: interview, Bruce Kuniholm, Mar. 8, 1985.

p. **269** "The foreign policy": Ramazani, *op. cit.*

p. **270** Foreign Minister Ali: Reuters, reprinted in Beirut *Daily Star*, Aug. 15, 1984.

p. **270** In mid-1984, Iran: AP, July 22, 1984.

p. **270** At Friday prayers: BBC SWB/ME, Nov. 5, 1984.

p. **271** One senior administration: Newhouse News Service, reprinted in *Ann Arbor News*, Dec. 21, 1984, and interviews in Washington, May 1985.

Selected Bibliography

Ajami, Fouad. *The Arab Predicament: Arab Political Thought and Practice since 1967*. New York: Cambridge University Press, 1982.

Ansari, Hamied. "Mubarak's Egypt," *Current History*, January 1985, pages 21–24, 39–40.

Arjomand, Said Amir. *The Shadow of God and the Hidden Imam: Religion, Political Order and Societal Change in Shi'ite Iran from the Beginning to 1890*. Chicago and London: University of Chicago Press, 1984.

Ayoob, Mohammed. "The Revolutionary Thrust of Islamic Political Tradition," *Third World Quarterly*, April 1981, pages 269-76.

Bakhash, Shaul. *The Reign of the Ayatollahs: Iran and the Islamic Revolution*. New York: Basic Books, 1984.

Ball, George W. *Error and Betrayal in Lebanon*. Washington: Foundation for Middle East Peace, 1984.

Batatu, Hanna. "Iraq's Underground Shi'a Movements: Characteristics, Causes, and Prospects," *Middle East Journal*, Vol. 35 (1981), pages 578–94.

———. *The Old Social Classes and the Revolutionary Movements of Iraq*. Princeton: Princeton University Press, 1979.

Bill, James A. "Islam, Politics, and Shi'ism in the Gulf," *Middle East Insight*, January–February 1984.

———. "Resurgent Islam in the Persian Gulf." *Foreign Affairs*, Fall 1984, pages 108–27.

——— and Leiden, Carl. *Politics in the Middle East*. Boston and Toronto: Little, Brown and Company, 1984.

Binder, Leonard. "United States Policy in the Middle East," *Current History*, January 1985, pages 1–4, 35-36.

Brinton, Crane. *The Anatomy of Revolution*. New York: Vintage Books, 1965.

Bulloch, John. *The Final Conflict: The War in Lebanon*. London: Weidenfeld and Nicolson, 1977.

———. *The Gulf: A Portrait of Kuwait, Qatar, Bahrain and the UAE*. London: Century Publishing, 1984.

Carswell, Robert. "Economic Sanctions and the Iran Experience," *Foreign Affairs*, Winter 1981/82, pages 247–65.

Cline, Ray S. *Secrets, Spies and Scholars*. Washington: Acropolis Books, 1976.

Cottrell, Alvin J., and Moodie, Michael L. *The United States and the Persian Gulf: Past Mistakes, Present Needs*. New York: National Strategy Information Center, 1984.

Cuthell, David C., Stoddard, Philip, and Sullivan, Margaret, editors. *Change and the Muslim World*. Syracuse: Syracuse University Press, 1981.

Deeb, Marius. *The Lebanese Civil War*. New York: Praeger, 1980.

———. "Lebanon's Continuing Conflict," *Current History*, January 1985, pages 13–15, 34.

Dietl, Wilhelm. *Holy War*, translated by Martha Humphreys. New York: Macmillan, 1984.

El Azhary, M. S. *The Iran Iraq War: An Historical, Economic and Political Analysis.* London and Canberra: Croom Helm, 1984.

Esposito, John L. *Islam and Politics.* Syracuse: Syracuse University Press, 1984.

Eveland, Wilbur Crane. *Ropes of Sand.* London and New York: W. W. Norton, 1980.

Fadlallah, Sheikh Mohammed Hussein. *Islam and the Logic of Force.* Beirut: Al Dar al Islamiya, 1981.

Findly, E., Haddad, Y., and Haines, B., editors. *The Islamic Impact.* Syracuse: Syracuse University Press, 1984.

Fischer, Michael M. J. *Iran: From Religious Dispute to Revolution.* Harvard Studies in Cultural Anthropology. Cambridge, Mass., and London: Harvard University Press, 1980.

Franzius, Enno. *History of the Order of Assassins.* New York: Funk and Wagnalls, 1969.

Gibb, H. A. R. *Islam: A Historical Survey.* Oxford, New York, Toronto, Melbourne: Oxford University Press, 1949.

Gilmour, David. *Lebanon: The Fractured Country.* New York: St. Martin's Press, 1984.

Gordon, David C. *Lebanon: The Fragmented Nation.* Stanford, Calif.: Hoover Institution on War, Revolution and Peace. London: Croom Helm, 1980.

Green, Jerrold D. *Revolution in Iran: The Politics of Countermobilization.* New York: Praeger, 1982.

Guillaume, Alfred. *Islam.* New York and Middlesex: Penguin Books, 1954.

Halliday, Fred. *Iran: Dictatorship and Development.* London: Penguin, 1979.

Hameed, Mazher. "The U.S. and the Middle East: Analyzing Terrorism." Unpublished paper, 1984.

Heikal, Mohammed. *Autumn of Fury.* New York: Random House, 1983.

Helms, Christine Moss. *The Cohesion of Saudi Arabia: Evolution of Political Identity.* London: Croom Helm, 1980.

Hirst, David. *The Gun and the Olive Branch.* London: Futura Publications, 1983.

Hodgson, Marshall G. S. *The Order of the Assassins.* The Hague: Mouton, 1955.

Holden, David, and Johns, Richard. *The House of Saud: The Rise and Rule of the Most Powerful Dynasty in the Arab World.* New York: Holt and Rinehart, 1981.

Holt, P. M., Lambton, Ann K. S., and Lewis, Bernard, editors. *The Cambridge History of Islam: The Central Islamic Lands Since 1918*, Vol. 1B. Cambridge and New York: Cambridge University Press, 1970.

International Institute for Strategic Studies. *The Military Balance 1984–85.* London, 1984.

Irfani, Suroosh. *Revolutionary Islam in Iran: Popular Liberation or Religious Dictatorship?* Third World Series. London: Zed Books, 1983.

"Islamic Renewal: Iran's Continuing Revolution," *Harvard International Review*, May/June 1984. Articles by Shaul Bakhash, Shapour Bakhtiar, Abolhassan Bani Sadr, Sheryl Bernard, James A. Bill, John L. Esposito. Mansour Farhang, Zalmay Khalilzad, Ardeshir Mohassess, Said Rajai Khorassani.

Jansen, Godfrey H. *Militant Islam.* London: Pan Books, 1979.

Jansen, Michael. *The Battle of Beirut.* London: Zed Press, 1982.

Jenkins, Brian M. *New Modes of Conflict.* Santa Monica: Rand Corporation, 1983.

————, editor. *Review of Trends in International Terrorism, 1982–83.* Santa Monica: Rand Corporation, 1984.

Kapuscinski, Ryszard. *Shah of Shahs.* San Diego: A Helen and Kurt Wolff Book/Harcourt Brace Jovanovich, 1985.

Keddie, Nikki R., editor. *Religion and Politics in Iran: Shi'ism from Quietism to Revolution.* New Haven and London: Yale University Press, 1983.

————, editor. *Scholars, Saints and Sufis: Muslim Religious Institutions Since 1500.* Berkeley and Los Angeles: University of California Press, 1972.

————, with a section by Yann Richard. *Roots of Revolution: An Interpretive History of Modern Iran.* New Haven and London: Yale University Press, 1981.

Khalidi, Walid. *Conflict and Violence in Lebanon.* Cambridge, Mass.: Harvard University Center for International Affairs, 1979.

Khateeb, Muhibbudeen al. *Broad Aspects of the Shi'ite Religion: An Exposition and Refutation.* Burnaby, Canada: Majliss of Al Haq Publication Society, 1983.

Khomeini, Ayatollah Ruhollah. "Excerpts from Speeches and Messages of Imam Khomeini on the Unity of the Muslims." Tehran: Distributed by the Ministry of Islamic Guidance. (Undated.)

————. *Islam and Revolution: Writings and Declarations of Imam Khomeini,* translated and annotated by Hamid Algar. Berkeley: Mizam Press, 1981.

Khuri, Fuad. *From Village to Suburb: Order and Change in Greater Beirut.* Chicago: University of Chicago Press, 1975.

————. *Tribe and State in Bahrain: The Transformation of Social and Political Authority in an Arab State.* Chicago: University of Chicago Press, 1980.

Kuniholm, Bruce R. *Persian Gulf & U.S. Policy: A Guide to Issues and References.* Regina Guides to Contemporary Issues. Claremont, Calif.: Regina Books, 1984.

Lacey, Robert. *The Kingdom: Arabia and the House of Saud.* New York: Harcourt Brace Jovanovich, 1981.

Laqueur, Walter. *Terrorism: A Study of National and International Political Violence.* Boston and Toronto: Little, Brown and Company, 1977.

Lewis, Bernard. *The Assassins: A Radical Sect in Islam.* London: Weidenfeld and Nicolson, 1967.

————. *Islam in History.* New York: The Library Press, 1973.

Lewis, Flora. "Upsurge in Islam," four-part series in *The New York Times,* December 28–31, 1979.

Livingstone, Neil C. *The War Against Terrorism.* Lexington, Mass., and Toronto: Lexington Books, 1982.

Long, Admiral Robert L. J. (ret.). *Report of the Department of Defense Commission on Beirut International Airport Terrorist Act.* Washington: Department of Defense, 1983.

Mansfield, Peter. *The New Arabians.* Chicago: J. G. Ferguson Publishing, 1981.

McDowall, David. *Lebanon: A Conflict of Minorities.* London: Minority Rights Group, 1983.

Mitchell, Richard P. *The Society of Muslim Brothers.* London: Oxford University Press, 1969.

Mortimer, Edward. *Faith and Power: The Politics of Islam.* New York: Vintage Books, 1982.

Muir, Jim. "Lebanon: Arena of Conflict, Crucible of Peace," *Middle East Journal,* Spring 1984. pages 204–19.

———. "Slotting the Shi'ites into the Lebanese Puzzle," *Middle East Insight,* May 18, 1984, pages 3–5.

Naipaul, V. S. *Among the Believers: An Islamic Journey.* New York: Vintage Books, 1981.

Neff, Donald. *Warriors for Jerusalem: The Six Days That Changed the Middle East.* New York: Simon & Schuster, 1984.

Norton, Augustus Richard. *External Intervention and the Politics of Lebanon.* Washington, D.C.: Washington Institute for Values in Public Policy, 1984.

———. "Harakat Amal and the Political Mobilization of the Shi'a of Lebanon." Unpublished thesis, University of Chicago, 1984. To be published, Austin: University of Texas Press, 1985.

———. "Occupational Risks and Planned Retirement: The Israeli Withdrawal from South Lebanon." *Middle East Insight,* March–April 1985, pages 14–18.

———. "Political Violence and Shi'a Factionalism in Lebanon," *Middle East Insight,* Vol. 3 (1983), No. 2, pages 3–12.

———. "Shi'ism and Social Protest in Lebanon," chapter in *Shi'ism and Social Protest,* edited by Nikki Keddie and Juan Cole. New Haven: Yale University Press, 1985.

Pipes, Daniel. *In the Path of God: Islam and Political Power.* New York: Basic Books, 1983.

Polk, William R. *The Arab World.* Cambridge, Mass., and London: Harvard University Press, 1980.

Quandt, William B. *Saudi Arabia in the 1980s.* Washington, D.C.: The Brookings Institute, 1981.

Rabin, Jonathan. *Arabia: A Journey Through the Labyrinth.* New York: Simon & Schuster, 1979.

Randal, Jonathan. *Going All the Way: Christian Warlords, Israeli Adventurers and the War in Lebanon.* New York: Viking Press, 1983.

Ramazani, Rouhollah K. "Iran's Islamic Revolution and the Persian Gulf," *Current History,* January 1985, pages 5–6, 40–41.

———. *The Persian Gulf: Iran's Role.* Charlottesville: University of Virginia Press, 1972.

———. "Temper the Containment of Iran." Article manuscript made available to the author, 1985.

———. "Iran's Foreign Policy 1941-1973." Charlottesville: University of Virginia Press, 1975.

———. "The United States and Iran: the Patterns of Influence." New York: Prager, 1982.

Rouleau, Eric. "Khomeini's Iran," *Foreign Affairs,* Fall 1980, pages 1–19.

Ruthven, Malise. *Islam in the World.* New York and Middlesex: Penguin Books, 1984.

Said, Edward. *Covering Islam: How the Media and the Experts Determine How We See the Rest of the World.* New York: Pantheon Books, 1981.

Salibi, Kamal S. *Crossroads to Civil War: Lebanon 1958–76.* New York: Caravan Books, 1976.

Schiff, Ze'ev, and Ya'ari, Ehud. *Israel's Lebanon War.* New York: Simon & Schuster, 1984.

Sciolino, Elaine. "Iran's Durable Revolution," *Foreign Affairs,* Spring 1983, pages 893–920.

Stempel, John D. *Inside the Iranian Revolution.* Bloomington: University of Indiana Press, 1981.

Terrorism Violence Insurgency Journal. Interview with Ambassador Robert M. Sayre on Antiterrorist Policy. Winter 1985, pages 1–4.

Timmerman, Jacobo. *The Longest War.* New York: Alfred A. Knopf, 1982.

van Dam, Nikolaos. "Middle East Political Clichés: Takriti and Sunni Rule in Iraq; Alawi Rule in Syria: A Critical Appraisal." Lecture delivered at the Center of Middle Eastern and Islamic Studies of the University of Durham, England, November 22, 1979.

———. *The Struggle for Power in Syria.* London: Croom Helm, 1979, 1981.

Voll, John O. *Islam: Continuity and Change in the Modern World.* Boulder, Col.: Westview Press, 1982.

Zonis, Marvin. "The Psychological Roots of Shi'ite Muslim Terrorism." Paper delivered at Department of State seminar, March 1, 1984.

——— and Brumberg, Daniel. "An Ideological Justification of Terrorism and Violence: Ayatollah Khomeini Interprets Shi'ism." Paper delivered at the Conference on Shi'ism, Resistance and Revolution, Israel, December 12–21, 1984.

Index

ABOUT THE AUTHOR

Robin Wright has been a foreign correspondent for *The Sunday Times* of London, CBS News, *The Washington Post*, and *The Christian Science Monitor*, covering more than sixty countries in the Middle East, Africa, Europe, Asia and Latin America. She was the winner of the 1976 Overseas Press Club Bob Considine Award for "the best reporting in any medium requiring exceptional courage and initiative." She was also the recipient in 1978 of the University of Michigan's Athena Award for "professional distinction and humanitarianism" in the field of African affairs, and in 1983 she served as the first Alumna in Residence at the University of Michigan, where she earlier received both her B.A. and M.A. In 1985, Wright was Senior Journalist in Residence at Duke University's Institute of Policy Sciences and Public Affairs.